Dariden
2005

STUDIES IN MEDIEVAL HISTORY AND CULTURE

Edited by

Francis G. Gentry

Pennsylvania State University

A ROUTLEDGE SERIES

STUDIES IN MEDIEVAL HISTORY AND CULTURE

FRANCIS G. GENTRY, General Editor

THE CONTESTED THEOLOGICAL AUTHORITY
OF THOMAS AQUINAS
*The Controversies between Hervaeus Natalis
and Durandis of St. Pourçain*
Elizabeth Lowe

BODY AND SACRED PLACE IN MEDIEVAL
EUROPE, 1100-1389
Dawn Marie Hayes

WOMEN OF THE HUMILIATI
A Lay Religious Order in Medieval Civic Life
Sally Mayall Brasher

CONSUMING PASSIONS
*The Uses of Cannibalism in Late Medieval
and Early Modern Europe*
Merrall Llewelyn Price

LITERARY HYBRIDS
*Crossdressing, Shapeshifting, and
Indeterminacy in Medieval and Modern
French Narrative*
Erika E. Hess

THE KING'S TWO MAPS
*Cartography and Culture in Thirteenth-
Century England*
Daniel Birkholz

PESTILENCE IN MEDIEVAL AND EARLY
MODERN ENGLISH LITERATURE
Bryon Lee Grigsby

RACE AND ETHNICITY IN ANGLO-SAXON
LITERATURE
Stephen J. Harris

ASPECTS OF LOVE IN JOHN GOWER'S
CONFESSIO AMANTIS
Ellen Shaw Bakalian

THE MEDIEVAL TRADITION OF THEBES
*History and Narrative in the OF Roman de
Thèbes, Boccaccio, Chaucer, and Lydgate*
Dominique Battles

WORLDS MADE FLESH
Reading Medieval Manuscript Culture
Lauryn S. Mayer

EMPOWERING COLLABORATIONS
*Writing Partnerships between Religious Women
and Scribes in the Middle Ages*
Kimberly M. Benedict

THE EPISTEMOLOGY OF THE MONSTROUS IN
THE MIDDLE AGES
Lisa Verner

THE WATER SUPPLY SYSTEM OF SIENA, ITALY
*The Medieval Roots of the Modern Networked
City*
Michael P. Kucher

DESIRING TRUTH
*The Process of Judgment in Fourteenth-
Century Art and Literature*
Jeremy Lowe

THE PREACHING FOX
*Festive Subversion in the Plays of the Wakefield
Master*
Warren Edminster

THE PREACHING FOX

Festive Subversion in the Plays of

the Wakefield Master

Warren Edminster

Routledge
New York & London

Published in 2005 by
Routledge
270 Madison Avenue
New York, NY 10016
www.routledge-ny.com

Published in Great Britain by
Routledge
2 Park Square
Milton Park, Abingdon
Oxon OX14 4RN
www.routledge.co.uk

10   9   8   7   6   5   4   3   2   1

Library of Congress Cataloging-in-Publication Data

Edminster, Warren, 1966–
    The preaching fox : festive subversion in the plays of the Wakefield
Master / Warren Edminster.
        p. cm.—(Studies in medieval history and culture ; 32)
    Includes bibliographical references and index.
    ISBN 0-415-97242-6 (alk. paper)
    1. Towneley plays. 2. Mysteries and miracle plays, English—History and criticism.
3. Literature and society—England—History—To 1500. 4. Political plays, English—
History and criticism. 5. English drama (Comedy)—History and criticism.
6. Festivals—England—History—To 1500. 7. Satire, English—History and criticism.
8. Anti-clericalism in literature. 9. Kings and rulers in literature. 10. Social norms in
literature. 11. Clergy in literature. 12. Church in literature. I. Title. II. Series.

    PR644.W3E34 2005
    822.'051609358—dc22

                                                                                      2005018255

For the wonderful women in my life,
Laurie, Ashlee, Lauren, and Hannah

Preaching Fox; ink on paper drawing by Chris Schweizer. Used by permission of the artist.

Contents

Series Editor's Foreword   ix

Preface   xi

Chapter One
Subversion and the Festive Instinct   1

Chapter Two
Typical Festive Elements in the Plays   27

Chapter Three
The Overthrow of Religious Obligation   49

Chapter Four
The Shrewish Bride of Christ   73

Chapter Five
Foolish Shepherds and Priestly Folly   99

Chapter Six
Stripping Away the Wolf-Skin of False Shepherds   119

Chapter Seven
Raging Kings and Clergy   149

Chapter Eight
Christ as a Comic Figure   173

Conclusion
A Festive Flavor   197

Notes   201

Bibliography   213

Index   221

Series Editor's Foreword

Far from providing just a musty whiff of yesteryear, research in Medieval Studies enters the new century as fresh and vigorous as never before. Scholars representing all disciplines and generations are consistently producing works of research of the highest caliber, utilizing new approaches and methodologies. Volumes in the Medieval History and Culture series include studies on individual works and authors of Latin and vernacular literatures, historical personalities and events, theological and philosophical issues, and new critical approaches to medieval literature and culture.

Momentous changes have occurred in Medieval Studies in the past thirty years, in teaching as well as in scholarship. The Medieval History and Culture series enhances research in the field by providing an outlet for monographs by scholars in the early stages of their careers on all topics related to the broad scope of Medieval Studies, while at the same time pointing to and highlighting new directions that will shape and define scholarly discourse in the future.

Francis G. Gentry

Preface

New readers of the Wakefield Master's work are invariably struck by the festive nature of the plays. Characters threaten the audience with comic bravado, engage in mocking tomfoolery, and parody any number of sacred forms; it is behavior unexpected by modern students of the drama, especially from what we assume was a serious and religious medieval past, and it is unlike what we find in the other mystery cycles. The comic elements have drawn a variety of reactions, from denunciation to acclaim, but critics have been unable to reach a consensus as to how they actually function in the plays. Beyond the odd stage direction and what we can occasionally glean from the dialogue, we have no idea how the plays were staged or how the medieval audience might have interacted with them, and lacking such contextual clues, we are left to speculate on the significance of the festive forms. In this text, I present a study of how festive elements allow a variety of subversive readings, while not, of course, asserting that these are the only possible readings of the plays. Whether or not readers accept these interpretations, they must, if they are truly to appreciate the plays, come to some understanding of the role festive forms play in the drama.

Of course, any study of the Wakefield Master must necessarily work with a number of assumptions. The name itself assumes that the plays can be attributed to a single person, and that this person, presumably a male educated in the Church, was from Wakefield. The former assumption is entirely unprovable. Given the nature of composition, the bulk of the plays is likely the work of a single person, but evidence of semi-professional troupes of actors uncovered by recent REED (Records of Early English Drama) research suggests at least the possibility that some of the text was the result of collaboration. Moreover, much of the assumed unity of the plays is based upon stanzaic evidence, despite the fact that one of the plays most commonly attributed to the master (*Mactacio Abel*) has only one of the characteristic thirteener stanzas. Nonetheless, as scholarly consensus continues to recognize the unity of these plays, I treat them as a body of work by a single author. The latter assumption has been called into doubt by a number of scholars, most notably Barbara Palmer ("Recycling the 'Wakefield Cycle': The Records"), who has presented compelling evidence that the plays in the Towneley manuscript may be a compilation of plays from a variety of towns in West Riding and Yorkshire. Palmer demonstrates conclusively that much of the evidence previously used to establish Wakefield's Corpus Christi cycle was fraudulently generated and that many of our assumptions about the provenance of the plays are based upon this fraudulent scholarship. This ongoing debate shows little sign of being resolved quickly. In this study, I do not assume a Wakefield provenance for the entire manuscript, nor do I assume that the plays in the manuscript represent a cycle. After much soul-searching, however, I continue the tradition of calling our author the Wakefield Master for two reasons. First, the evidence in the manuscript that ties the plays to Wakefield largely comes from the plays attributed to this author; therefore, even if the manuscript is a *compilatio* from several locations, the probability that the Master's plays are from Wakefield remains high. Second, there is, as yet, no acceptable replacement name for the Wakefield Master, and the appellation remains a convenient reference which I therefore use.

The study of festive forms has in the past two decades been stimulated by the translation into English of Mikhail Bakhtin's *Rabelais and His World,* and I too utilize Bakhtin's ideas on the carnivalesque. Regrettably, it must be admitted that Bakhtin's ideas are not always appropriate to the study of English drama. Bakhtin's focus ranged between the Classical Age and the Enlightenment, and he was concerned with French culture rather than English. Moreover, Bakhtin occasionally over generalizes or overstates his case, finding universal trends to support his overriding theories rather than qualifying his work with exceptions or contradictions. None of this can discount the essential truth about festive culture revealed by Bakhtin, however; nor was he the first or last to reveal it. E. K. Chambers' massive *The Mediaeval Stage* , published over a century ago, documents the culture in detail, with a specific eye to its relationship to the drama, and his work has been supplemented by the scholarship of C. L. Barber and Robert Weimann, among others. In this study, I am sensitive to the problems of interpreting English drama according to Bakhtin's scholarship on Rabelais, and I try to be more reliant on sources specifically relevant to English medieval society, but I continue to find him immeasurably helpful in defining medieval festive culture.

This preface would be incomplete without acknowledging those without whose support this book would never have been written. This study began long ago under the tutelage of Peter Beidler and continued under the direction of D. Thomas Hanks, and this work owes a great deal to their suggestions and insights. I also owe thanks to Jill Havens for her direction on Lollard thinking. I am indebted to several publishers. Passages from *The Towneley Plays* (ed. Martin Stevens and A. C. Cawley), *The English Works of Wycliff* (ed, F. D. Matthew), *Lollard Sermons* (ed. Gloria Cigman), and *Two Wycliffite Texts* (ed. Anne Hudson) are reprinted by permission of the Council of the Early English Text Society. Material from *Medieval English Political Writings* (ed. James M. Dean) and *Six Ecclesiastical Satires* (ed. James M. Dean) has been reproduced by permission of the publisher, Medieval Institute Publications. Passages from *Norwich Heresy Trials 1428–31* (ed. Norman P. Tanner) are reprinted by permission of the Royal Historical Society. Excerpts from *Selections from English Wycliffite Writings* (ed. Anne Hudson) are reprinted with the permission of Cambridge University Press. I am also grateful for permission to reprint two revisions of previously published articles: a revision of "Foolish Shepherds and Priestly Folly: Festive Influence in *Prima Pastorum*" is printed by the permission of the Southeastern Medieval Association and *Medieval Perspectives;* a revision of "Punning and Political Parody in *The Second Shepherds' Play*" is printed by permission of *English Language Notes* and the University of Colorado.

Finally, I owe sincere appreciation to my parents, Herb and Wanda Edminster, my wife, Laurie Malpass Edminster, and my daughters, Ashlee, Lauren, and Hannah, for their support, love, and patience through this project.

Chapter One
Subversion and the Festive Instinct

"[L]et furth youre geyse; the fox will preche" (l. 86).[1] These words, in the Towneley *Mactacio Abel,* are Cain's response to Abel's anachronistic call to Christian obligation, to cleanse himself, to worship, and to tithe. The comment is dismissive and scornful towards a preachy and sanctimonious Abel, but it is also a slap at the Catholic Church. Cain employs a well-known metaphor, one found in many manuscript illustrations of the period. A fox or a wolf is shown in clerical habit, typically in a pulpit, preaching to a congregation of chickens or geese. The fox is salivating, preparing for a feast, while the fowl attend piously to his words, unaware of his true intentions. The image captures the popular sense of suspicion towards late medieval churchmen, commonly portrayed as predators, hypocrites, and frauds. Yet the image could apply just as well to the Wakefield Master himself; like the preaching fox, he is not always what he seems. The Master presents a series of ostensibly religious dramas, chronicling biblical history and celebrating Christian destiny, yet his plays are riddled with subversive images and subtexts. The story of Cain holds double currency for the medieval audience; "Caym's Castel" is a term commonly applied by medieval writers to the worldliness, arrogance, and violence of the medieval Church. Nor is the subject matter of the *Mactacio Abel* unique among the Master's subjects in this regard. Noah's flood evokes the apocalyptic, and is frequently used in discussions of God's coming judgment upon a corrupt Church. The shepherds of the nativity tap the ubiquitous pastoral metaphor, used by writers to criticize medieval clergy for sins ranging from neglect to predation. Herod's raging evokes contemporary criticism of tyranny and abuse of worldly power. The story of Annas and Caiaphas is frequently applied to the inquisitorial persecution of many groups who fall foul of Church orthodoxy. The Wakefield Master's plays are double edged; they play out the traditional stories upon which conventional Christian values are based, and yet they simultaneously evoke widespread ideas of popular subversion.

That ideas of popular subversion were widespread in the medieval world is a relatively recent realization by scholars, but evidence of popular discontent with the social order has been growing for some time. The traditional vision of a serene medieval population anchored by tradition, religion, and social hierarchy and disturbed only occasionally by enthusiastic and unbalanced rabble rousers is one perpetuated by sparse and typically slanted historical record. In recent decades, this picture has given way to a more tumultuous one as scholars dig deeper into the documentary record and take greater notice of the perspective and possible bias of medieval recorders. Rodney Hilton's *Bond Men Made Free*, for example, places the famous "Peasant Revolt" of 1381 within the context of long-term working class agitation against the ruling classes and makes the argument that we should see the revolt "not in isolation but as the most striking manifestation of discontent in a century which saw a mass of sporadic local actions by peasants against landowners" (231). There were, in fact, a number of localized rebellions before and after the 1381 revolt, including Jack Cade's 1450 rebellion, and these are only the most violent of the many concerted working-class movements (mass petitions, peasant litigation, organized avoidance of feudal obligation, etc.) in late medieval England. Hilton argues that peasant movements both in England and on the continent were typically well organized, had reasonably clear objectives, and were informed by a consistent set of values (214–32). These values may be defined in part by the confessions of the leaders of the 1381 rebellion, which were recorded in detail by several chroniclers. The principal demand of the rebels seems to have been freedom and equality, an end to nobility and serfdom (222–6). There is, however, an equal insistence on the ending of those mechanisms of administration (feudal law, the manorial system, noble advisors to the crown, etc.) which perpetuate unjust inequalities in society (226–7). Moreover, there is a deep hatred of organized ecclesiastical structures (228–9). Notably, the rich ecclesiastics are often targeted and killed, including Sudbury, Archbishop of Canterbury; this instance is paralleled by the execution of other high ecclesiastics in more local rebellions. Nor was the discontent voiced in the 1381 rebellion limited to *villains*. Hilton notes that with the exception of "the nobility, the gentry, the lawyers, and the beneficed ecclesiastics," the "composition of the rebel armies seems to have been a fair cross-section of rural society" and included parish priests, a variety of local officials, and in some cases, minor gentry (221).

Of equal interest are the many subversive religious ideas that were circulating in the late middle ages. There were, of course, a variety of heretical movements, although many of these were limited to the continent, but anti-clerical and anti-ecclesiastical ideas circulated widely even among the orthodox. The most common complaint concerned the perceived corruption of the various clerical orders. Chaucer's *Canterbury Tales* taps into this widespread disenchantment, as does Langland's *Piers Plowman* and Gower's *Vox Clamantis*. The primary issue here seems to be the failure of late medieval clergy to fulfill their proper role. Chaucer satirizes the Prioress and Monk for excessive worldliness, and the mendicant Friar, who should be devoted to a life of poverty and service, despises the needy and spends his time seeking carnal pleasures. More severe criticism of the Church can be seen in anonymous anti-ecclesiastical works such as *The Plowman's Tale* and *Piers the Plowman's Creed*. In these tales, the problem is not so much the failure of individuals in the Church but rather the entire corrupt structure of a worldly and irreligious Church. Priests, monks and canons are portrayed as neglectful shepherds; friars and pardoners, as ravening wolves; bishops and prelates, as servants of Satan; and the Pope, as antichrist. Such works share much with the principal ideas of Lollardy and indeed may have been written by Lollards. However, mainstream Lollardy was even more aggressive in its denunciation of the Church. Anne Hudson's groundbreaking *The Premature Reformation* and John A. F. Thomson's *The Later Lollards* have done much to demonstrate that, contrary to earlier opinions, Lollardy was a widespread and long-lasting phenomenon, reaching far into the north and causing persecution well into the Sixteenth Century. The Lollards believed that the official ecclesiastical structure of the Catholic Church was inherently corrupt and idolatrous. They received much attention for their rejection of the doctrine of transubstantiation, but perhaps their greatest offense was their argument that the Church should be disendowed of its massive estates. This argument was itself declared heretical, and it became one of the principal points upon which suspected Lollards were examined (Aston 107), but it was an idea that existed long before Wycliffe and lasted long after the Lollards had been hounded from the public eye. Indeed, the mendicant orders had been founded centuries before upon the idea of clerical poverty, although their fervor for it had largely cooled by the late Middle Ages. In addition to preaching disendowment, the Lollards too attacked the wealth and corruption of the medieval clergy, denying that tithes should be rendered to corrupt clerics. A fuller examination of these various movements lies beyond the scope of this study, but it will suffice to state that resentment towards the established social order and the ecclesiastical structure of the Church was both wide and deep in the English population, that open expression of this discontent was likely to be harshly repressed, and that covert expression of these ideas was therefore commonplace.

Many of these subversive ideas crop up in the plays. Herod's offer to reward the advisor who advocates the slaughter of the innocents by making him a pope, for example, connects this dramatic archetype of abusive worldly power with the medieval papacy. The portrayal of Annas and Cayphas as medieval bishops aligns

Too broad or symbolic argument ?

Christ himself with all manner of heretics persecuted by the Church. Yet these apparently shocking subtexts are excusable by their context within festive moments. Herod is a clown, as are his advisors, and the reference to the papacy is part of a larger pattern of extreme bravado which is not to be taken at face value. Annas and Cayphas also play the part of festive lords; their Laurel-and-Hardy-like examination of Christ culminates in an overtly carnivalesque game, hot cockles, which renders the entire episode comic and unserious. The festive nature of the plays allows extreme license; comic reversals and burlesques of the dominant order are expected in such forms. Within the protected space of the festive moment, characters can say and do things that would not normally be tolerated. Nonetheless, these ideas remain profoundly subversive, a subversiveness specifically enabled and protected by the conventions of festive disorder.

This festive component, and in particular its relationship to subversive ideas in the plays, is a unique characteristic of the Wakefield Master's work. The *Prima Pastorum* presents the nativity much like other shepherds' plays, but the Master adds a decidedly festive component in which the shepherds, archetypes of the priesthood, engage in hilarious buffoonery while ignoring their flocks. The *Magnus Herodes* is faithful to the biblical account of the slaughter of the innocents, but the Master turns Herod's court into a court of misrule, one that claims the appurtenances of medieval kings, knights, and ecclesiastics. In both plays, festive components refrain from undermining the traditional interpretation; however, the subversive ideas they present combine with this message to give new significance to the events played out upon the stage. It is this reinterpretation of conventional biblical history through the agency of festive forms that most distinguishes the Master as a dramatist, and yet it is this which has been least recognized in his work.

Critics have long noticed the festive nature of the plays; in particular, they have noted the grotesque and burlesque elements. At one moment the plays indulge in raucous debauchery; in the next they solemnly examine religious mysteries. In one scene the plays bow to the sacred; in the next, they revel in the profane. Yet most critics are either dismayed by the inconsistencies or disposed to ignore them altogether. In his book *The Dialogic Imagination*, Mikhail Bakhtin analyzes the tendency of critics to seek a single viewpoint in "heteroglossic" works:

> Philosophy of language, linguistics and stylistics [i.e., such as they have come down to us] [Bakhtin's brackets]have all postulated a simple and unmediated relation of the speaker to his unitary and singular 'own' language, and have postulated as well a simple realization of this language in the monologic utterance of the individual. (*Dialogic* 269)

It is this very need to find unity, in both structure and form, which motivates Eleanor Prosser to write of the festive forms in the Towneley plays, "If a comic scene breaks the mode, negates the theme or destroys audience participation, sympathy, or necessary emotional response—if, in short, comedy works against the requisite effect of the play—is it not 'bad drama,' judged solely on esthetic grounds?" (187). This logic, which holds that good art must be single-minded, has led many critics of the Wakefield Master's plays to emphasize one set of forms and suppress or negate any material which is contradictory. Thus, some critics have concluded that the plays strive to present Christian ideas but spice them up with popular forms. Jeffrey Helterman, for instance, recognizes that "Several of [the Wakefield Master's] plays end with the evil characters still in power"; nonetheless he dismisses outright any possible alteration of the conventional message. Instead, he argues that the burlesque elements are self-parodying and that "only by the apprehension of the parody can their audience understand their punishment" (18). In a similar fashion, Peter Meredith dismisses the subversive social satire of Tutivillius and his demons in *Iudicium* as unnecessary distractions from the play's thematic coherence (151–2). Such critical readings disfigure the very essence of the plays, the central dynamic which sets the Master's plays apart from other mystery drama. The plays of the Wakefield Master are unusual, and hold our attention so persistently, precisely because they are not monologic. The plays present a striking interplay between two very different worldviews: a popular, festive worldview, and one that is official, static, and orthodox. It is the dialogue between these two opposed perspectives that drives meaning in the plays. This "dialogue conflict," as Aron Gurevich describes it (xx), must be considered before the thematic significance of the plays can be fully appreciated.

Thematic studies of the plays of the Wakefield Master have often focused exclusively upon the sacred elements. Indeed, Christian interpretations, or interpretations which read orthodox Christian ideas into the plays, have dominated Towneley scholarship.[2] Such studies hold that the plays are primarily Christian art, evangelism for the untutored masses, the monologic expression of the dominant Roman Catholic culture. Thus Karl Holzknecht writes of the mystery cycles, "The themes were always biblical, and the purpose, achieved with varying degrees of skill and piety, was always to vivify the entire Bible story from the creation to the Last Judgement" (66). Hardin Craig qualifies this argument. Craig acknowledges that cycle plays contain much material not relevant to biblical themes, but he agrees with Holzknecht's main thesis: "The medieval religious drama existed primarily to give religious instruction, establish faith, and encourage piety" (15). Those extra elements "of human interest" which often occupy critical attention "were in their drama produced more or less unconsciously" (3). Despite critical interest in what he calls the "excrescences and aberrations" of some plays, such as "the shrewishness of Noah's wife" or "the sheep-stealing episode of the Towneley Second Shepherds' Play," Craig maintains that "the medieval religious drama existed for itself and for the discharge of a religious purpose" (6). Indeed, Craig insists that the "aim and end [of the drama] was not dramatic but religious" (2).

Alan H. Nelson agrees with Craig, arguing that the events of the Towneley plays are not significant in themselves. Nelson applies Erich Auerbach's observations about scriptural narrative in general to the mystery cycles in particular. The drama of each event in the cycles, Nelson argues, derives not from universal significance (as we might find in Homer), but from its relationship to the overall biblical narrative. For example, the Towneley depiction of Noah "has significance only as it stands in a specific place in a series of events which begin with creation and end with salvation" (*Medieval* 395). Catherine Dunn agrees with Nelson; she writes that only "when the cycle is regarded in this light does its totality become meaningful, so that its individual scenes have an organic relationship to a unifying theme" (80). The purpose of the playwright, Nelson argues, was not to engage in creative analysis of the human condition, but to "make the full significance of the event clear to [the] audience" (*Medieval* 396).

Lauren Lepow takes the argument even further. In *Enacting the Sacrament*, she makes a case for viewing the Towneley plays as a dramatic defense of Catholic Orthodoxy against the heresies of Wyclif's Lollards. She points out that Northern England was a bastion of orthodoxy during the Lollard movement. Lepow cites several examples of extreme actions against Lollardy by northern clerics, including aggressive prosecution and even execution of wandering Lollard preachers by the established clerical hierarchy (23). Further, she notes the widely accepted theory that cycle plays were, in fact, written by clerics:

> Still more to the point is the virtual certainty that the Corpus Christi plays are products of clerical authorship: the theological sophistication evident in the plays has been identified by many scholars as a voice of the Orthodox Church. (28)3

Lepow combines these premises to argue her concludes that Corpus Christi plays are a "religious drama designed to fortify veneration of the sacrament" (25). She writes, "It is possible that the Corpus Christi plays were not only a characteristically northern expression of orthodoxy, but in fact—and perhaps intentionally—a bastion for the time against the encroaching heresy" (23).

The consensus of Holzknecht, Craig, Nelson, Dunn, Lepow, and similar scholars is that the plays are only meaningful within an orthodox Christian context. Any elements contradictory to a Christian theme, especially the grotesque or burlesque forms so often employed by the Wakefield Master, are irrelevant to the play, and are therefore bad drama, useless distractions, or "excrescences and aberrations."

The logic behind these assumptions is obvious. The mystery plays share much subject matter with, and certainly echo, the liturgical drama. Traditional scholarship traced a direct line of descent from the "Quem Quaeritis" trope during the Easter mass, through a gradual process of development and secularization, and finally to the Corpus Christi cycles and beyond.[4] Current scholarship usually discounts such a direct line, opting for cross-pollination between secular and religious sources.[5] Nonetheless, the influence of liturgical drama upon the cycle plays remains an assumption which most scholars are willing to make. Further, the cycle plays concerned Christian subject matter and were usually performed on feast days. The plays enact religious history, usually beginning with the creation of the earth and proceeding through biblical content to the future final judgment. The Corpus Christi cycle plays were typically acted on or about the feast of Corpus Christi, but they share styles and forms with plays acted upon other holy days both in England and upon the Continent. Few such plays have ever been associated with days which are not specifically Christian feast days.

The obvious influence of the Church notwithstanding, however, it hardly seems possible for such an immense and varied body of work to have only one thematic principle. Can a piebald patchwork of images and forms such as we see in the Wakefield Master's plays ever be purely monologic? Indeed, it is important to note that while orthodox Christian ideas and theories are the driving principle of many of the cycle plays, their unilateral application to the plays of the Wakefield Master is problematic for several reasons.

First, while the occasion and titular subject matter is Christian, most of the dominant themes and images in the plays are not. In the *Secunda Pastorum,* for example, only the 168 final lines of the 1088 line play deal with the biblical story of the shepherds. The first 920 lines flesh out a rough, bawdy story which doubtless means to parody the miraculous birth but which never mentions it by name. Critics have repeatedly and creatively argued that the main body of the play serves as a comic foil for the short ending and that the ending is the heart of the play; but surely they protest too much. The first 920 lines are filled with conflict and resolution, villains and justice, and interest and climax. The ending, by contrast, contains only formal elements from a traditional narrative. Robert Weimann writes that "such an astonishing preponderance of secular sources . . . cannot be viewed as a simple contrast to the Christian story of the final part, as, again, just so much comic relief or 'broad fun'" (90). If anything, the Christian element seems only a formality, the expected Christian aspect of an otherwise comic play. Similarly, the *Prima Pastorum* frolics well past the midpoint of the play, developing separate and complete plots, before the angels appear to introduce the subject of Christ. Even in plays such as the *Mactacio Abel* and the *Processus Noe,* which deal specifically with episodes mentioned in the scriptures, traditional biblical characters are superseded by extra-biblical ones, and the author introduces non-traditional themes, plots, and images which shift the emphasis of the story substantially. It is thus illogical to interpret these plays purely on an orthodox Christian level.

Second, much of the content in these plays seems hostile and subversive towards the medieval guardian of orthodoxy, namely the Roman Catholic Church. In the *Coliphizacio,* as has been mentioned, Cayphas and Annas, the worst villains of the story, are portrayed as bishops. The play creates enormous irony as these two members of the high clergy insult, condemn, abuse, and threaten the Christ. Similarly, much of the condemnation in the *Judicium* is directed at corrupt clergy. Such hostile references to the Church cast serious doubt on strictly orthodox Christian readings of the plays, at least orthodoxy as interpreted by the medieval Church, and have occasioned dissenting views from several critics. John Speirs argues,

> As for the view that the Christian drama was invented and devised by ecclesiastics to instruct an ignorant and illiterate populace in the facts of their religion, that it was intended as visual education for those who for the most part could not read, the Vulgate made visible as a sequence of tableaux for instructional purposes—the plays themselves do not seem to bear out such a view. (310–11)

Speirs' statement is perhaps too absolute; Corpus Christi drama is plainly a Christian enterprise. The plays certainly do show, as do all miracle plays, the choice of Christian topics, the influence of Christian design, and the use of Christian imagery. However, the traditional interpretation of the Wakefield Master's work within the strict boundaries of Roman Catholic doctrine goes too far. By forcing the plays into *a priori* orthodox readings, and by rejecting as "excrescences and aberrations" those elements of the drama which cannot be made to match those *a priori* expectations, many critics have failed to recognize the profoundly important influence of the medieval festival.

A handful of scholars have noted that while the plays contain many standard Christian themes and narratives, they are also deeply influenced by festive ideas and values.[6] A. C. Cawley writes, "it is likely that some of the comic elements in the Corpus Christi pageants show the influence of medieval folk-drama or festival. Thus the parody of the nativity in the *Secunda Pastorum* is comparable to the burlesque ceremonies enacted on the feast of fools" (xxiv). A. P. Rossiter notes the bawdy humor, grotesque forms, and folk laughter of the plays (67–75) and writes of this irreverence that "It derives from that opposite and antithetic world of the diabolical, in which the shadows of primitive paganism survived" (73). Many scholars examine these festive elements as "secular" play development, but because the designation "secular" implies an amoral or non-religious set of concerns, it is inaccurate. In fact, the festive or carnivalesque elements which so distinguish the Master's plays reflect a highly value-laden sub-culture with views and beliefs often at odds with ecclesiastical Christian culture. John Speirs argues that the plays are genetically linked to pre-Christian rituals (319), saying about the *Processus Noe,* for example, that while the play "is based on the biblical narrative, what has re-animated and re-created it in this version . . . is clearly the seasonal theme of the Nature rituals, the festivals of the Year" (325). More recently, Martin Stevens and Anthony Gash have used the Bakhtinian model of carnival to look at how festive elements disrupt the orthodox message of the plays.[7]

Since many scholars, among them the influential V. A. Kolve, have discounted the possibility of festive culture's influence upon medieval religious drama, it is necessary to review the breadth of this culture in more detail to show how deeply its conventions were ingrained within the medieval psyche. Scholars have long documented the existence of an ancient festive sub-culture in medieval Europe, one attached neither to the dominant social hierarchy nor to official Christian doctrine. According to Bakhtin,

> The scope and the importance of this culture were immense in the Renaissance and the Middle Ages. A boundless world of humorous forms and manifestations opposed the official and serious tone of medieval ecclesiastical and feudal culture. In spite of their variety, folk festivities of the carnival type, the comic rites and cults, the clowns and fools, giants, dwarfs, and jugglers, the vast and manifold literature of parody—all these forms have one style in common: they belong to one culture of folk carnival humor. (*Rabelais* 4)

Throughout medieval Europe, folk festivals, drama, and processions expressed themselves in colorful but distinct forms. Typical, for example, was the selection of a festival king and/or queen, who would later be deposed and/or ritually beaten and abused. Reversal, parody, and inversion were characteristic, as were bawdy, explicit language, grotesque excesses of form or behavior, exaggerated abuse, and heavy feasting (Bakhtin, *Rabelais* 7–21). This

culture seems to have reflected the fertility and regeneration rituals of an ancient, cyclical world view, and it was genetically related to the saturnalia of the
classical world, even though these roots had generally been forgotten. Such
rituals were inherently dramatic. John Wesley Harris writes,

> The seasonal events celebrated were all basic to an agricultural society,
> and the festivals marking them were extremely ancient and seem to have
> involved traditional ceremonies or rituals—usually short plays or
> mimetic dances which symbolically enacted the death and resurrection
> of the 'spirit' of the corn, or the triumph of spring sunlight over the dark-
> ness of winter, or the wooing of the spirit of the new year by the son of
> the old, or the casting out of characters representing the sins and short-
> comings of the community—all ceremonies stressing the sheer continu-
> ity of life and the well-being and preservation of the society. (58)

At the heart of festive expression is a powerful sense of and appreciation
for seasonal, or cyclical time. Elaborate communal feasts marked transitions
from one part of the yearly cycle to another. The revelry and indulgence of the
feasts—eating, drinking, dancing, playing games, and engaging in ritual—
celebrated the continuity and renewal of life inherent in cyclical regeneration.
Any feast or even any annual occasion, whether it was the ancient winter feast
when animals were slaughtered for the winter or a new Saint's day, became an
opportunity for celebration, and we find even the most solemn Christian
feasts invaded by festive revelry. Such behavior was, therefore, common at social occasions and seasonal celebrations. C. L. Barber writes,

> Such pastimes were a regular part of the celebration of a marriage, of the vil-
> lage wassail or wake, of Candlemas, Shrove Tuesday, Hocktide, May Day,
> Whitsuntide, Midsummer Eve, Harvest-home, Halloween, and the twelve
> days of Christmas season ending with Twelfth Night. Custom prescribed,
> more or less definitely, some ways of making merry at each occasion. (5).

According to C. R. Baskerville, festive celebration might occur during

> a simple gathering on the village green of a summer afternoon or in the
> hall on a winter night. It might be a marriage feast, a harvest supper, or
> a local wake or fair. More likely it was one of the great festivals celebrated
> pretty generally throughout Western Europe, as those of Easter, May,
> Whitsuntide, Midsummer, or the Christmas season. (6)

The event itself varied, but the festive spirit remained largely the same, with practices and customs leaping from occasion to occasion. Some festive observances

were rather mild, such as the traditional May Day celebrations, while others, such as a Christmas Lord of Misrule, might become raucous and outrageous.

The May Day festivals, almost universally observed in England, celebrated the changing seasons and the regeneration of spring. People abandoned traditional roles and duties for a day to participate in the festivities. A common practice was the "gathering in" of flowers and foliage (most commonly hawthorn) to decorate the village. Another comprised selecting, cutting, bringing back, raising, and decorating the maypole. Villagers engaged in indulgent feasting and drinking; restrictions were replaced with a certain amount of license, and participants often chose a king and queen of the feast (Barber18–24). The feast was pleasant and generally inoffensive (except to ecclesiastics), and its traditional observance existed long after other festive events had long been suppressed.

Choosing and following a Lord of Misrule was a more disruptive practice, although it was equally popular with the folk. Barber writes that

> In the customs which center on a Lord of Misrule, the rougher pleasures of defiance and mockery are uppermost . . . ; Abuse predominates over Invocation, though both gestures are equally present, in varying degree, when a holiday group asserts its liberty and promotes its solidarity. The formal Lord of Misrule presided over the eating and drinking within-doors in the cold season. But the title was also applied to the captain of a summer Sunday drinking and dancing by the young men of a parish, a leader whose role was not necessarily distinct from the Robin or King of the Maying. (24)

Lords of Misrule presided over ritualized bouts of drinking, and both verbal and physical abuse was common, especially towards any kill-joy who refused to join in the celebration. The Lord of Misrule claimed to replace the proper authorities, and, in several recorded cases, homage and even monetary tribute were demanded by his followers. The practice radically undermined authority. Barber writes, "The village saturnalia of the Lord of Misrule's men was in its way a sort of rising; setting up a mock lord and demanding homage for him are playfully rebellious gestures" (29).

There were several specific dramatic forms that served exclusively as festive expressions. Chambers notes,

> The festival customs include a number of dramatic rites which appear to have been originally symbolical expressions of the facts of seasonal recurrence lying at the root of the festivals themselves. The antithesis of winter and summer, the *renouveau* of spring, are mimed in three or four distinct fashions. (183)

These specific and well known 'dramas' often moved from occasion to occasion. For example, Robin Hood plays, Mummer's plays, sword dances, processions, or morris dances were almost always performed singly or in combination at a festive gathering. Barber notes,

> Mirth took form in morris dances, sword dances, wassailings, mock ceremonies of summer kings and queens and of lords of misrule, mummings, disguisings, masques—and a bewildering variety of sports, games, shows, and pageants improvised on traditional models. (5)

Robin Hood, originally perhaps a May Day figure, is irrevocably tied to Spring and rebirth. Many May Kings and Queens were titled Robin and Marian, which fact suggests a common ritual source. The series of stories which grow up around them, such as the fight with little John, usually concern a struggle, Robin's defeat and/or death, and his subsequent victory or resurrection (Chambers 174–8).[8] Mummer's plays focus on similar themes, albeit with different characters. The drama is usually about a hero's struggle with and death at the hands of a fearsome antagonist. The legend of St. George and the dragon, for example, was a popular topic. Usually a "doctor" was then brought in to find that the character was not really dead and to revive or resurrect him (207, 213). Sword dances were frequently more stylized. They involved a series of elaborate moves and jumps by multiple characters, all wielding swords. The object, writes Chambers, "was to suggest not a fight but a mock or symbolical sacrifice" (203). The dance culminated with several dancers ringing a certain character with their swords and pretending to kill him. As with the Mummer's play, a 'doctor' was frequently then used to revive this unfortunate dancer. Morris dances, unlike the narrative-driven performances, were merely a series of characteristically grotesque yet regular steps performed by groups of dancers whose limbs were normally decorated by bells and/or handkerchiefs. Barber writes that

> group dancing was the chief thing. The jerking about of handkerchiefs and the stiff-kneed step of the morris conveyed a super-abundance of vitality. Each foot was brought 'forward alternately with a sharp swing (almost a jerk)'; frequently every alternate or fourth step was a hop; a dancer made capers by exaggerating the regular step with a vigorous jump by the supporting foot; he made jumps by springing as high as possible with both legs straight. (29)

Festive processions were similar to and often included morris dances, but the object was for celebrants to proceed throughout the village or town in part, no doubt, to announce their celebrations. Processions usually included a mock authority figure, and participants frequently demanded that passers-by pay forms of homage to him. The same types of rituals, enactments, and celebrations also dominated the church-sanctioned carnivals and the marketplace festivals, both because these offered periods of temporary liberation and because the carnivals were almost always positioned in the calendar by the church to coincide with previous pagan festivals. However, folk festive culture was not limited to specific calendar dates; it found its way into every folk celebration, whether spontaneous or planned.

The festive spirit also crept into parts of the Church itself. Chambers documents in detail the amazing number of festive celebrations in the Church, most notably in the reversed or parodied masses of the feast of Fools, the feast of Innocents, and the feast of the Ass. The feast of Fools introduced a radical inversion of ecclesiastical order and behavior. For a day, the higher clergy were deposed and replaced by a member of the lower clergy who then wielded authority until the end of the feast. Chambers describes the feast thus:

> It seemed to be indifferently called *festum stultorum* and *festum fatuorum*. It takes place in cathedrals and collegiate churches, on Innocents' day, on St. Stephen's, on the Circumcision, or on other dates. 'Bishops' or 'archbishops' of Fools are chosen, who wear mitres and pastoral staffs, and have crosses borne before them, as if they were on a visitation. They take the Office, and give Benedictions to the readers of the lessons at Matins, and to the congregations. (295)

Despite the appearance of authority and convention, however, the feast was anything but orderly. Chambers writes, "It was largely an ebullition of the natural lout beneath the cassock. The vicars hooted and sang improper ditties, and played dice upon the altar, in a reaction from the wonted restraints of choir discipline" (325). Related to the feast of Fools was the feast of the Ass, which often took place in conjunction with or before or after *festum fatuorum*. The feast of the Ass was often vaguely connected with the travels of Mary and Joseph or with Balaam's Ass, but the relationship is, at best, a creative one. Like the Fool, the Ass replaces or mocks that which is sacred. Chambers recounts a Benedictine account of one such ceremony:

> A pretty girl, with a child in her arms, was set upon an ass, to represent the Flight into Egypt. There was a procession from the cathedral to the church of St. Stephen. The ass and its riders were stationed on the gospel side of the altar. A solemn mass was sung, in which *Introit, Kyrie, Gloria* and *Credo* ended with a bray. To crown it all, the rubrics direct that the celebrant, instead of saying *Ite, missa est,* shall bray three times (*ter hinhannabit*) and that the people shall respond in similar fashion. (287)

The celebration of the feast of the Innocents, or the Boy Bishop, parallels the
feast of Fools in many significant points, most notably in its suspension of hierarchical order for a specified period, in the election of a mock ecclesiastical
ruler from lower ranks (in this case choir boys), and in the festive celebrations
which accompanied the feast. Celebrations of the feast of Innocents were generally milder, probably because the younger boys were less likely than the ma-
ture sub-deacons to defy authority (Chambers 368). Nonetheless, the
celebrations were extensive and, in most cases, highly formalized. Chambers
gives the ceremonial guidelines of one such celebration at Bayeux:

> Precise directions are given as to the functions of the 'bishop.' He is to wear
> a silk tunic and a cope, and to have a mitre and pastoral staff, but not a
> ring. The boys are to do him the same reverence that is done to the real
> bishop. There are also to be a boy cantor and a boy 'chaplain.' The 'bishop'
> is to perform the duties of a priest, so long as the feast lasts, except in the
> Mass. He is to give the benediction after *Benedicamus* at first Vespers. Then
> the boys are to take the higher stalls, and to keep them throughout the fol-
> lowing day, the 'bishop' sitting in the dean's chair. (345–6)

Despite the formality of the feast, however, many of the excesses that marked
the feast of Fools were also manifested in the celebrations surrounding the
feast of Innocents. Contemporary accounts complain of disgraceful actions,
damage to church property, and violence among the celebrants. While the
feast was popular and widespread in Europe from the eleventh through the
fourteenth centuries, it met with increasing disapproval from church authorities and was gradually and thoroughly suppressed (Chambers 349–54). So
too were the feast of the Ass and the feast of Fools. Chambers notes that from
the Twelfth through the Fifteenth Centuries, "the abuses which clung about
the feast of Fools rendered them everywhere a mark for the eloquence of ecclesiastical reformers" (292). Serious churchmen disliked the chaos, the sacri-
lege, and the damage, and they periodically sought to ban such forms.

In addition to festive masses, the numerous accounts of seasonal processions and of peasants dancing in churchyards attest to many spontaneous, unau-
thorized, and probably unrecorded celebrations. Barber notes that "the
churchyard was certainly a center for merrymaking, partly because the church
had taken the place of the pagan fane which dances once honoured, partly because
the churchyard was in any case the parish meeting place, partly perhaps because
to go there was excitingly impudent" (29–30). In fact, such celebrations seem
only to be recorded when they are condemned. Chambers tells us that

the *ludi* of the folk come into prominence with the attacks made upon them by the reforming ecclesiastics of the thirteenth century and in particular by Robert Grosseteste. Between 1236 and 1244 Grosseteste issued a series of disciplinary pronouncements, in which he condemned many customs prevalent in his diocese. Amongst these are included miracle plays, 'scotales' or drinking-bouts, 'ram-raisings' and other contests of athletic prowess, together with ceremonies known respectively as the *festum stultorum* and the *Inductio Maii sive Autumni.* (90–91)

Grosseteste's pronouncements clearly record a prominent culture of revelry and play in medieval England, but they also indicate the popularity of specifically festive elements such as the feast of Fools. They also record the emphasis upon time and cyclic, seasonal transition in the *Inductio Maii sive Autumni.* Chambers also mentions like reformers:

> Very similar are the prohibitions contained in the Constitutions (1240) of Walter de Chanteloup, bishop of Worcester. These particularly specify the ludus de Rege et Regina, a term which may be taken as generally applicable to the typical English folk festival, of which the *Inductio Maii sive Autumni,* the 'May-game' and 'mell-supper,' mentioned by Grosseteste, are varieties. . . . Walter de Chanteloup also lays stress upon an aggravation of the *ludi inhonesti* by the performance of them in churchyards and other holy places, and on Sundays or the vigils and days of saints. (91–92)

To these records may be added the decrees of the University of Oxford in 1250, which apparently "found it necessary to forbid the routs of masked and garlanded students in the churches and open places of the city" during the celebration of annual feasts (Chambers 92). Again, the records of such activities are solely in the form of strong condemnation by Church reformers. This fact suggests two conclusions: first, that the celebrations, even where widespread, were not generally recorded, and, second, that the festive elements were likely "part of the parochial organization, and were conducted through the parochial machinery" (93). At any rate, festive culture was clearly widespread and influential, and its influences persist to this day.

Functioning within the context of a lower-class existence that was often brutal, humiliating, and short, these folk celebrations were times of release from the strictures and hardships of life. Carnivals and festivals were marked by license and riot; morality was suspended, law blurred, and social rank put aside. Carnival, says Bakhtin, "is the people's second life, organized on the basis of laughter" (*Rabelais* 8). It is an impulse inherently hostile to authority, rank, or official dogma. Bakhtin writes that

> carnival celebrated temporary liberation from the prevailing truth and from the established order; it marked the suspension of all hierarchical rank, privileges, norms, and prohibitions. Carnival was the true feast of time, the feast of becoming, change, and renewal. It was hostile to all that was immortalized and completed. (*Rabelais* 10)

That which was completed or immortal was static and without life. Life depended upon death and decay; regeneration was begotten by degeneration. Folk culture "demanded ever changing, playful, undefined forms" (11).

Such festive expressions were pagan in origin and not indigenous to orthodox Christian culture. Many of the festive celebrations, such as Easter and Yule, were incorporated into the Church calendar, just as pagan fanes and shrines were adopted as the sites of Christian worship. However, the forms and behaviors of these celebrations, while tolerated with the limits of the festival, were discouraged by the ecclesiastical hierarchy of the Church, just as the pre-existing pagan practices which continued in churchyards, such as dancing and processions, were consistently denounced by the Church (Axton 27–8, Bradbury 158–63). We have specific evidence of the Church denouncing such behavior during the performance of mystery plays in the York cycle. Hans-Jürgen Diller writes of records in the York *Memorandum Book* that demonstrate clerical action against festive behavior:

> In 1431 the masons of that city asked to be relieved of their pageant because it caused more laughter and clamor than devotion. And in 1426 the *Memorandum Book* tells of a most famous preacher and professor of scripture, who found that on Corpus Christi Day many people not only saw the play but also participated in feastings, drunkenness, clamors, gossipings, and other wantonness, thus risking the loss of the pardon that was promised for participation in the procession. ("Laughter" 4)

Certainly individual members of the clergy participated in festive behavior, but reform-minded churchmen shrank from the "uninhibited merrymaking and heavy drinking" (Harris 58) of this culture and repeatedly condemned it as rebellious and sinful rioting. Chambers notes,

> On the one hand [the clergy] could point to the ethical lapses of which the *ludi* were undoubtedly the cause—the drunkenness, the quarrels, the wantonings, by which they were disgraced. And on the other they could—if

they were historically minded—recall the origin of the objectionable rites in some of those obscure survivals of heathenism in the rustic blood, which half a dozen centuries of Christianity had failed to purge. (93–94)

Indeed, the festive value system was at odds with many central tenets of Christianity, or at least with Christianity as it was then constructed by the official hierarchy of the Church. Medieval Catholicism was hierarchical, priests submitting to the authority of bishops, and bishops submitting to the authority of the Pope. Christians certainly expressed their forms in many original ways, but the truths of canon law and of official doctrine were absolute and rested ultimately upon the authority of the Pope. Dissent from official doctrine was typically prosecuted as heresy. For example, Lollards were prosecuted for believing that Christians should not give tithes to the Church, that the saints had no power to affect the believer's spiritual state, that a corrupt priest could not sanctify the host, that priests had no power to absolve sins, and that Sundays were no holier than other days (Tanner 3–22). The Waldensians were prosecuted for believing "that poverty is the true Christian way of life and that Holy Scripture is the infallible guide in religion, . . . [and] that every good man is competent to preach and expound Holy Writ" (Previté-Orton 661). After being arrested and examined, such heretics were given the opportunity to recant, to submit to the authority and doctrine of the Church, and to suffer public penance (e.g. public whippings). If they refused to recant their beliefs, they were usually handed over to the secular authorities to be burned (Thompson 1–16). If secular authorities protected dissenters, the Church proclaimed crusades against the entire region, compelling orthodox military authorities to attack the area, reduce resistance, and enforce orthodox beliefs. Such was the crusade against the Catharans, or Albigensians, in Southern France from 1204 through1229 (Previté-Orton 663–5). The wars against the Hussites in Bohemia from 1420 through 1436 were also anti-heretical (Waugh 223–39). Dissenters were frequently given leeway as the Church tried to return them to orthodoxy, but such tolerance went only so far. Ultimately, the Christian and the cleric had to submit to the authority of the Church. According to C. W. Previté-Orton, "Submission was the test of orthodoxy" (665).

The Church also differed from festive culture in its approach to mirth and play. In his discussion of medieval views of laughter, V. A. Kolve notes,

> The fact of death was offered [by the Church] as another teacher of how men should live (the *ars moriendi* is by implication also an *ars vivendi*), for it can teach us how to value life, and, most especially, as Everyman learns in the play called by his name, how to value Fellowship—the

mirth, gaiety, and laughter born of good company. Fellowship is the first
of Everyman's friends to desert him on his journey to the grave. (125–6)

While many individual churchmen valued mirth and festive fellowship, the orthodox position of the Church discouraged it. Laughter was often regarded as
dangerous; mockery was sinful, and playfulness could be irreverent. Kolve writes,

> . . . a powerful case was established and reiterated throughout the Middle
> Ages that laughter and frivolity, the temporary abstention from involve-
> ment in all that is serious in the human condition, was an offense against
> God, a negation of the example of Christ, and a peril to men's souls. (126)

Thus, while the general population, including great numbers of minor
and even some major clergy, valued and celebrated mirth, the official culture
of the Church typically frowned upon it. Consequently, medieval society developed a split personality concerning festivals and celebration. Festive ideology was rejected by the official culture and remained only unofficially, in the
celebrations of the lower classes or folk. Abstract festive concepts, if they were
consciously recognized, were never openly stated, but rather manifested
themselves in representative forms which enacted fertility and regeneration
with a wink and a nod. As Bahktin notes,

> All these forms of protocol and ritual based on laughter and consecrated by
> tradition existed in all the countries of medieval Europe; they were sharply
> distinct from the serious official, ecclesiastical, feudal, and political cult
> forms and ceremonials. They offered a completely different, nonofficial,
> extraecclesiastical and extrapolitical aspect of the world, of man, and of
> human relations; they built a second world and a second life outside offi-
> cialdom, a world in which all medieval people participated more or less, in
> which they lived during a given time of the year. (*Rabelais* 5–6)

Therefore, despite the hostility of the Church, these festive ideas and forms
remained a powerful influence in the popular culture. They pervaded medieval European culture in myriad forms, from irreverent masses to holiday
processions and carnival gatherings. In light of the wealth of festive forms
present in the Wakefield Master's plays, the influence of this festive culture
must surely be taken into consideration.

However, despite the documentary evidence to support this alternate
cultural influence and its frequent impact upon the Wakefield Master's plays,
most scholars have refused to accept the impact of festive forms in the Master's
dramatic art. Elements easily understood within the context of carnival values

are jammed awkwardly into modern theories, with often humorous results. For example, the violent physical beatings traded between Noah and his wife, which are strikingly similar to the ritual violence that accompanies reversals and uncrownings in seasonal festivals and folk drama, are interpreted by John Gardner within a Christian context: "as God chastises man for his bad behavior, Noah strives, mostly in vain, to chastise his wife" (39). Similarly, the raging behavior of Herod and Cain, so typical of "blocking" or "winter" figures in carnival culture, is seen by Heltermann as only frightened bravado, or "unspoken terror" of God (26). The parodic reversals of the nativity, such as the stolen sheep in the child's cradle masquerading as a miraculous birth before we behold the miraculous child in the animal's manger, are characteristic of carnivalesque imagery and ritual, but Morgan reads it as a symbolic foil, purifying and sanctifying the nativity (64). In these cases and in others, analyses tend to make the content of the plays conform to an *a priori* theoretical framework. These examples are only representative of the generations of critics who have chosen to ignore the effects of festive influence (and the radical implications of this influence) when they discuss the Wakefield Master's plays. Many are aware of and even acknowledge festive elements, but they refuse to consider them anything more than marginal and irrelevant. Perhaps the most influential apologist for this viewpoint is V. A. Kolve.

Kolve, renowned for his excellent analysis of laughter in Corpus Christi plays, completely discounts anything more than a nominal festive influence. In his classic book, *The Play Called Corpus Christi,* Kolve addresses the work of Chambers, Rossiter, and A. C. Cawley on the influence of festive elements. Specifically, he focuses on the established similarities between the feasts of Fools and Innocents and the festive elements in the plays. Kolve summarizes the work of Chambers, Rossiter, and Cawley thus:

> The evidence in question has been printed or described in Chambers' *The Mediaeval Stage,* where nearly a hundred pages are devoted to two feasts that are considered to embody this mockery: the feast of Fools, and the feast of the Innocents, commonly known in England as the feast of the Boys or of the Boy Bishop. Rossiter's study devotes a chapter to these festivals, as proof of the "Ritual Comic Relief" which also informs the Corpus Christi cycles. And a student as cautious as A. C. Cawley continues the tradition in his recent edition of the *Wakefield Pageants* when he concludes that "it is plain that the spirit of nonsense has infected the Wakefield playwright. . . ." (135)

In dismissing Chambers, Rossiter, and Cawley, Kolve points out that the two masses, the feast of Fools and the feast of Innocents, are not equal:

The feast of Fools allowed the inferior clergy (the subdeacons) one day in the year in which they took control of ritual observances within the cathedral. The result was often a full-scale burlesque of sacred ceremony. . . . The feast of the Boys is quite different in nature and importance. It was celebrated on Innocents' day, when in honor of the young martyrs, the boys of the cathedral choir were ceremonially installed in office and authority over the senior clergy. The feast grew from an important biblical text—"He hath put down the mighty from their seat, and hath exalted the humble"—and it was conceived as a reverent celebration of this Christian truth. (135–6)

Kolve argues that while celebrations of the feast of Innocents were often recorded in England, celebrations of the feast of Fools were not:

The ceremony [of the feast of Boys] was common and well loved in England, far more common than the feast of Fools. . . . These distinctions turn out to be important: the feast of the Boys is geographically relevant to a study of medieval English culture and . . . to certain English Shepherds' plays; the feast of Fools, at least as described by French documents, is probably not. (136–7)

Thus, Kolve reasons, the English cycle plays were probably not influenced by these types of festive elements:

The Boy Bishop ceremony was probably never comic, and the feast of Fools was probably not known to the writers and audiences of most of these plays. Furthermore, the Church opposed the feast of Fools with its gravest authority, and in England only Lincoln seems to have resisted censure for a time. It is unlikely that ceremonies thus prohibited would serve either as models or as authorizations for a drama sanctioned and supported by the Church. (137)

Kolve thus discounts the festive influence in the plays as little more than scenery for the "reverently conceived" objects of the plays (139).

     However, even if we accept Kolve's key points, first that the feast of Boys was not particularly festive, and second that the feast of Fools was foreign to England, both of which points are at best unverifiable, Kolve's primary argument remains problematic. He misreads the scholarship of at least Chambers and Cawley, reducing their arguments to a proposed direct link between *festum fatuorum* and the Towneley cycle, and examining the comic mass only as a proposed ancestor of comic elements in the plays. While this might be an acceptable representation of Rossiter, it twists the perspectives of Chambers and Cawley, who suggest, rather, that the festive masses are brethren to the festive elements in the plays, jointly generated by the massive and popular festive sub-culture.

As has been documented above, festive forms pervaded medieval England. In addition to the feasts of Fools, Boys, and Asses, we find festive traditions in virtually all holiday celebrations (into which category Corpus Christi certainly falls), in popular festive *ludi,* in marriages and other social occasions, and in contemporary medieval literature. Chambers notes that as late as 1576, Archbishop Grindal's Visitation Articles seek to find out

> whether the minister and churchwardens have suffered any lords of mis-rule or summer lords or ladies, or any disguised persons, or others, in Christmas or at May-games, or any morris dancers, or at any other times, to come unreverently into the church or churchyard. . . . (181)

Clearly, the reach and influence of festive culture was extensive, and one need not, as Kolve suggests, establish a purely causal link between one manifestation and another to argue that they are nonetheless related.

Speaking of the Corpus Christi cycles in general, Kolve further argues that "neither in detail nor in spirit do the cycles display any tendency to mock, blaspheme, or make merry with the sacred characters" (137). While Kolve's point is perhaps correct in regard to most of the cycles, it is surprising if applied to the Wakefield Master. The plays identified as this author's work are filled with mockery, revelry, and general disorder. Abel is transformed into an obnoxious nag. Noah becomes a hen-pecked husband. Shepherds engage in drunken gluttony only moments before they are summoned to the Nativity. The Nativity is burlesqued; the Mass is parodied. The papacy is offered as a reward for atrocity, and bishops gleefully persecute Christ. Perhaps no outright blasphemy occurs, but considerable license is taken with that which is usually sacred. Clearly, an alternate voice asserts itself in the plays, and it does so through festive forms.

Kolve's argument is based upon his masterful analysis of normative Church texts on the appropriate uses of laughter, which largely forbad the type of unrestricted laughter typical of festive culture. However, these texts represent only the official perspective of the ecclesiastical authority and should by no means be considered the sole viewpoint of medieval culture. The notion that such popular forms as the *Secunda Pastorum, Mactacio Abel,* and *Coliphizacio* should be interpreted solely by the dictates of the Church hierarchy is akin to suggesting that the meaning of a reform school play should be analyzed purely through the stated policies of the warden. Certainly the Church has a supervisory role in dramatic productions, but the plays are the work of a variety of guilds, writers, and actors playing to the tastes of a diverse and holiday-minded audience. As noted above, large sections of the population were hostile to ecclesiastical authority, and the general populace embraced the festive culture so pilloried by the Church, even where they maintained an essential devotion to Christianity. The accounts from the York *Memorandum Book,* for example, illustrate a profound divergence between the official policies of the Church and the festive instinct of the crowd at a dramatic holiday production.

Of course Kolve's primary point, that the principal Christian message of the play remains, is absolutely correct. With the possible exception of the *Mactacio Abel,* this study does not assert that festive forms erase the traditional meaning of the plays. However, festive forms create their own meaning, a meaning that exists separate from, and independent of, the traditional message, and this meaning often warps or transforms the overall significance of the play. It is in the interplay between the traditional message and the festive forms that the subversive ideas have their greatest impact. For instance, the Pilate of the Towneley *Conspiracio* (generally accepted as the creation of the Master) follows most of the traditional expectations: he is evil incarnate, the grandson of "Mahowne," unwilling to accept the innocence of Christ because of his stubborn hatred of good. Yet this Pilate is also the dramatic manifestation of a Lord of Misrule, engaging in excessive and comic boasting, demanding tribute from the crowd, and threatening comic violence upon all who question his lordship. As a comic lord, he claims the rights of contemporary European kingship, speaking in the terms of "cowrte" and of the seigneurial system. Playing to the crowd, he boasts of the abuses of his reign, abuses that just happen to have real parallels in the contemporary world. He welcomes "fals indytars," (l. 36) "Questmangers and iurers," (l. 37) and "fals outrydars," (l. 38) or tax collectors. Such references could be a direct reference to the grievances of the rebels in the 1381 rebellion; it is precisely peasant perceptions of a corrupt legal system and unreasonable taxes that spark the revolt. The conventional evil character of Pilate remains, but his significance is warped by his additional role as Lord of Misrule, and the interplay between the two meanings allows the subversive alignment of evil with the contemporary feudal structure and tax system. Such interactions take many forms, not always so shocking or so neat, but they create an ever-present tension in the Master's plays.

In analyzing plays that are both strongly Christian and deeply festive, most critics have chosen to focus on only one influence to the exclusion of the other. They choose to listen to only one voice, to interpret the plays according to only one framework, one system of ideas, and one set of values. In this way, they ignore the very quality of the plays which makes them profoundly original and deeply entertaining. The *Secunda Pastorum* is not remarkable for its raucously comic scenes alone; neither is it unusual in its solemnly religious ending. It is, rather, the unique interaction between these two sections, or the very proximity of the jocular and the reverent, which makes the play superior drama. In all of

the Wakefield Master's plays, the relationship between the religious and the festive creates a lively and inspiring dynamic unlike what is typical of the cycle dramas. It is what Mikhail Bakhtin calls the "dialogic," or the interactive relationship
between the official and the unofficial cultures of the Middle Ages:

> Nearly every Church feast had its comic folk aspect, which was also tra-
> ditionally recognized. Such, for instance, were the parish feasts, usually
> marked by fairs and varied open air amusements, with the participation
> of giants, dwarfs, monsters, and trained animals. A carnival atmosphere
> reigned on days when mysteries and *soties* were produced. (*Rabelais* 5)

In other words, the official and the unofficial cultures coexisted, even if they
were hostile to one another. The reverence of Lent was preceded by the excesses of *carnival,* or "farewell to flesh." Lent was then followed by *paschal rire,*
or the laughter of Easter. On religious holidays such as Christmas, Easter, and
Corpus Christi, festive celebration shared the stage with religious impulses.
Therefore, the two influences together, rather than individually, must provide
the basis for an analysis of these plays.

To date, too little criticism has done so. As Kolve's analysis exemplifies,
most criticism has been drawn to one or the other influence, usually towards
the influence of official Christianity as defined by the ecclesiastical hierarchy.
It is perhaps a trend that illustrates the critic's need to project monologic interpretation onto dialogic cultural forms. Bakhtin writes that literary criticism
has traditionally been

> . . . completely deaf to dialogue. A literary work has been conceived by
> stylistics as if it were a hermetic and self-sufficient whole, one whose el-
> ements constitute a closed system presuming nothing beyond them-
> selves, no other utterances. . . . Stylistics locks every stylistic
> phenomenon into the monologic context of a given self-sufficient and
> hermetic utterance, imprisoning it, as it were, in the dungeon of a single
> context. (*Dialogic* 273, 274)

Traditional literary criticism is essentially constructed so as to find in each
work a single viewpoint, a unifying principle, whether it be that of the author,
of the author's culture, or of a particular form or style, with which to define
that work fully. Those elements seen as irrelevant to the unifying principle become, as Hardin Craig so succinctly expresses it, "excrescences and aberrations" (6). Such criticism, however, is essentially flawed if the thematic
development in the text is driven by multiple perspectives or principles.
Bakhtin writes that language itself is "ideologically saturated," that the forms

used to present concepts are themselves conceptually significant (*Dialogic* 270). Linguistic and artistic forms, such as the nonsensical speech of Pikeharnes in *Mactacio Abel,* or the conflicts between Noah and his wife in *Processus Noe,* contain by their very existence meaning which is quite separate from the meaning of the words themselves. Bakhtin writes:

> At the time when poetry was accomplishing the task of cultural, national and political centralization of the verbal-ideological world in the higher official socio-ideological levels, on the lower levels, on the stages of local fairs and at buffoon spectacles, the heteroglossia of the clown sounded forth, ridiculing all "languages" and dialects; there developed the literature of the fabliaux and Schwanke of street songs, folksayings, anecdotes . . . , where there was to be found a lively play with the "languages" of poets, scholars, monks, knights and others . . . (*Dialogic* 273).

Bakhtin refers here to the language, or values and forms, of the festive culture. Forced into a marginal existence beneath the shadow of official Christian culture, festive culture became a counter-culture, a culture in constant dialogue-conflict with official views and values. It was, says Bakhtin, a "heteroglossia that had been dialogized" (*Dialogic* 273).

Nowhere is this festive culture and its "dialogue-conflict" with the official secular and Christian culture better exemplified than in the plays of the Wakefield Master. There is in the plays a dialogue between two voices, that of the established, official religious and secular order and that of the unofficial, festive folk instinct. The former promotes forms and images of order, justice, sanctity, and immortality, while the latter parodies and undermines these values, even appropriating and reinventing official forms to express its own values. The two exist side by side within the same plays, but they are, nonetheless, profoundly opposed to one another. This oppositional or dialogic nature forms an axis in the plays, and any accurate analysis of the plays must be formulated along this axis. While the plays officially present orthodox biblical history and Christian theology, the structural, thematic, and symbolic vocabulary of festive culture intrudes into and subverts official truth in order to present its own viewpoint. The orthodox voice preaches order, holiness, and respect, while the festive voice manifests itself in unruliness, violence, and regeneration. A graphic example of this interplay can be seen in the final dialogue between Cain and Garcio Pikharnes in *Mactacio Abel.* After his condemnation by Deus, Cain warps the prohibition against killing him into a form of royal protection, and he attempts to assert this authority to the audience. Yet as he does so, Pikeharnes keeps up a running festive commentary of silly and sarcastic statements:

Caym: I commaund you in the kyngys nayme
Garcio: And in my masteres, fals Cayme.
Caym.: That no man at thame fynd fawt ne blame,
Garcio: Yey, cold rost is at my masteres hame.
Caym.: Nowther with hym nor with his knafe,
Garcio: What! I hope my master rafe
Caym: For thay ar trew full manyfold.
Garcio: My master suppys no coyle bot cold.
Caym: The kyng wrytys you vntill,
Garcio: Yit ete I neuer half my fill.
Caym: The king will that thay be safe.
Garcio: Yey, a draght of drynke fayne wolde I hayfe.
Caym: At thare awne will let tham wafe;
Garcio: My stomak is redy to receyfe.
Caym.: Loke no man say to theym, on nor other—
Garcio: This same is he that slo his brother.
Caym: Byd euery man thaym luf and lowt.
Garcio: Yey, ill-spon weft ay comes foule out.
Caym: Long or thou get thi hoyse and thou go thus aboute! Byd euery man
theym pleasse to pay.
Garcio: Yey, gif Don, thyne hors, a wisp of hay. (ll. 421–41)

It is a comic scene, made more so by Cain's assumed pomposity; one can imagine him booming out the pronouncements in a bass voice, one hand behind his
back, the other gesturing broadly to the crowd, while Pikeharnes plays to the
crowd with winks, nudges, and perhaps an occasional falsetto. Cain's speech attempts to manifest the voice of established authority, but Garcio's festive commentary carries its own meaning. The interplay between the two changes the
overall significance of the speech, and Cain's authority is characterized as a
sham. Just so, festive forms intrude into the orthodox framework of the
Wakefield Master's plays, challenging the verities of religious and secular authority and changing the context by which the overall message is interpreted.

In neglecting to consider this duality, many critics have failed to grasp
the profoundly subversive nature of the Towneley plays. Interaction between
the traditional elements of the plays and the festive forms introduced by the
Master is what makes these plays so interesting. It also destabilizes the significance of the plays. The otherwise predictable moral conclusion of the tales in
the plays is rendered unpredictable, necessitating a fundamental re-examination of the purpose, function, and meaning of the Wakefield Master's plays.
The following chapters initiate just such a re-examination, focusing on subversive elements specifically enabled by festive forms. Chapter Two classifies
forms and symbols popular among festive celebrations, such as ritual invocation of chaos, usurpation of authority, ritual violence, and emphasis upon the

material body. These are the vocabulary of festive culture, the semantic structures which propel a message separate from and frequently counter to official Christian truth. Each category of a specific festive form is followed by multiple examples of such forms or symbols in the Wakefield Master's plays in order to prove that they are a considerable force in the entire group. With the groundwork laid as to what constitutes festive forms and how plentiful they are throughout all the plays, the following chapters examine six specific plays to show how these forms develop semantic dialogues with the dominant Christian elements in the same plays. Chapter Three shows how festive elements in the *Mactacio Abel* lead to a dramatic overthrow and rejection of orthodox Christian obligation. Chapter Four examines how festive elements in the *Processus Noe* reinterpret orthodox significance and transform the Noah story into a festive satire of the relationship between Christ and his bride, the ecclesiastical Church. Chapter Five examines the blending of festive folly and scriptural folly in *Prima Pastorum,* where foolish shepherds parody foolish priests. Chapter Six examines *Secunda Pastorum,* showing how the predatory tactics of the anti-shepherd, Mak, satirize the predatory nature of certain corrupt clerics. Chapter Seven shows how festive elements in the *Magnus Herodes* change the Herod story from a didactic lesson into a reformer's attack upon aristocratic abuse and Church complicity in that abuse. Chapter Eight demonstrates how festive elements in the *Coliphizacio* create a double reversal in which representatives of secular and religious law reject Christ as the King of Fools, thus demonstrating their own folly. The concluding chapter of the study discusses why the Wakefield Master chose the plays he revised or rewrote, how each is related or resonant to folk festive traditions, how his choices allow for fundamentally subversive interpretations, and how this festive reinterpretation is the most distinguishing feature of his work. Throughout the study, I hope to demonstrate that beneath the Master's ostensibly orthodox subject matter lurks a thinly veiled subversion of a variety of social ills, the sharp-toothed satire of a preaching fox.

Chapter Two
Typical Festive Elements in the Plays

To follow any dialogue, a reader must understand the linguistic markers, or the vocabulary and sentence structures which convey meaning. Similarly, before we can study cultural forms as an influence upon the Wakefield Master's plays, we must first define the "vocabulary," or forms of festive culture, which are commonly used. Festive manifestations typically took specific, easily recognizable forms; however, we must be careful not to expect a precise, consistent, and coherent pattern in every expression of festive culture. Festive celebration was by its very nature marginalized in the Middle Ages, and its patterns were handed down in an oral and traditional manner rather than in the precise, written manner of the orthodox culture. Therefore, while general patterns are almost always consistent, specific elements of festive culture often merge, divide, and migrate within the larger scheme.

On an abstract level, for example, regeneration was acted out through the ritual invocation of, indulgence in, and dethroning of chaos. As Harris tells us, "chaos, or disorder, was recreated for a brief period so that it could clearly be seen to be overcome and order restored" (62). Thus the pattern is usually simple. In the first stage, invocation invites everyone to enter festive time and space; traditional order is put aside, and rulers of the festivities are often selected. In the second stage, participants in the festivities engage in festive celebration, including games, feasting, dancing, processions, bawdy storytelling, etc. In the third and final stage, celebrations are brought to a close; festive rulers are abusively overthrown, and traditional order is re-accepted.

These types of cyclical patterns, where order is replaced by chaos and then restored, are common throughout the Wakefield group. In *Processus Noe,* for instance, Noe opens the play with a serene account of the creation and fall. He is followed by Deus, who speaks in an equally dignified and authoritative manner of the deviation of mankind from his commands. Even the language here is formal and dignified, "more Latinate and less colloquial" than the middle section

of the text (Helterman 49). The play makes note of the stars in their fixed order
(Gardner 42) as a symbol of the proper order and hierarchy of the world. After
Deus commands the building of the ark, however, the play descends into chaos.
Noe meets hs wife, Uxor, who immediately rejects his authority and engages
him in a series of hit-and-run domestic battles that last through the flood. The
language becomes more common (Helterman 49) and more profane. As they
enter the ark, the narrative becomes more confusing, and the three sons have to
step in between Noe and his wife to restore a semblance of order. John Gardner
notes that this is "a comic reversal of the family chain of authority," perhaps
symbolic of the world's rejection of God's authority (47). Similarly, Noe observes that the stars are now out of their place, and the universe seems disjointed
(47). Certainly in real terms the human race is in the process of near extinction,
and Noe and his family (unlike in other accounts of the flood) are terrified.
Finally, as the flood wanes, the play returns to order. The language again becomes dignified, the stars return to their proper place (47), domestic peace is restored, and the earth becomes a place of hope and tranquility. The cycle is
particularly obvious in the *Processus Noe,* but we may also see similar patterns in
the other Towneley plays. These basic patterns of cyclical regeneration, so typical of medieval festival culture, serve to provide the skeleton around which other
festive elements combine.

However, this pattern often blurs or merges with other elements in festive
culture. For example, the pattern involves two points of reversal or overthrow.
In the first stage, order is overthrown in favor of chaos, and in the final stage,
chaos is overthrown in favor of order. Each point of reversal has its own unique
characteristics and aims: the first stage is marked by verbal invocation while the
last stage is more characteristically violent (perhaps due to ancient traditions of
sacrifice). This clear delineation is quickly lost, however, in the chaotic, spontaneous, and changeable world of festive celebration. The elements of reversal, of
dethroning, and of inversion, which are themselves specific parts of a larger pattern, become independent forms and take on lives of their own. In the *Processus
Noe,* for example, the domestic violence between Noe and Uxor extends
throughout the middle section of the play; it is not confined to the final period
of violent overthrow. Similarly, the soldiers in *Magnus Herodes* are comically
chased off by the enraged mothers in the middle of the play, not at the end.
Multiple reversals and uncrownings are celebrated throughout the festive celebrations, and specifically what object or concept is being overthrown is not always clear. Patterns of order/chaos/order are found within each other, often in
multiple layers, and they serve a symbolic purpose, as representative of the general festive cycle, as well as a structural one. Additionally, elements of ritual violence, typical of the final festive overthrow, nonetheless find their way into

invocation and actually become dispersed throughout the larger festive pattern. Some festive forms are particularly popular with the audience and are thus emphasized or repeated; comic violence tends to migrate throughout festive space, for example, as do abusive speeches. Therefore, while we can identify larger patterns, it is best to focus on more general characteristic elements and their typical roles rather than on exact, prescriptive formulas.[1]

INVOCATION

Festive celebration in its myriad forms almost always begins with an invocation. The invocation is on one level a simple announcement of demarcation: at this point begins the festive celebration. Weimann writes of characters who present invocations,

> these characters [stand] between the hero-combat or the cure and the festive occasion at which these were performed. Their processional function [entails] the opening of the play, a request for room and attention, the summoning of the doctor and the general hubbub of a final song or request for gratuities. (30–31)

Yet the invocation is also an invitation, an invitation for participants to abandon traditional order, and an invitation for the forces of chaos and misrule to descend upon the participants. For this second reason, invocations are highly stylized and are directed to audiences or to potential participants. A typical dramatic invocation, for example, calls for listeners to quit whatever pursuits they are currently engaged in. The invocation is frequently abusive, showering the listeners with profanities, for example, or threatening violence. The invocation then establishes an order, asking for attention to the players, for example, or for space for the drama to be played. Even in this dramatic form, then, the audience itself is incorporated as part of the environment, part of the makeup of the festive world. Like carnival invocations which serve to elect carnival lords, dramatic invocations often introduce primary figures who are later to be overthrown.

Such invocations are obvious in many of the Towneley plays. The *Mactacio Abel* begins with an invocation by Garcio Pikeharnes which is filled with festive reference and abuse:

> All hayll, all hayll, both blithe and glad,
> For here com I, a mery lad!
> Be peasse youre dyn, my master bad,
> Or els the dwill you spede. (ll. 1–4)

Pikeharnes uses extreme profanity as he calls for silence:

> Bot who that ianglis any more,
> He must blaw my blak hoill bore,
> Both behynd and before,
> Till his tethe bleed.
> Felows, here I you forbede
> To make nother nose ne cry;
> Whoso is so hardy to do that dede,
> The dwill hang hym vp to dry! (ll. 6–13)

He threatens violence as he introduces Cain, the primary figure and the Lord of Misrule in the play:

> Wote ye not I com before?
> . . .
> Gedlyngys, I am a full grete wat.
> A good yoman my master hat:
> Full well ye all hym ken.
> Begyn he with you for to stryfe,
> Certys, then mon ye neuer thryfe. . . . (ll. 5, 14–18)

Another Lord of Misrule, Herod, is similarly introduced by Nuncius at the beginning of *Magnus Herodes*. Nuncius begins with references to festive celebration:

> Most myghty Mahowne
> Meng you with myrth!
> Both of burgh and of towne,
> By felles and by fyrth. (ll.1–4)

Nuncius then threatens violence and broken bones if the audience is not quiet and respectful for the entrance of Herod:

> Take tenderly intent
> What sondys are sent,
> Els harmes shall ye hent,
> And lothes you to lap.
> . . .
> Begyn he to brall,
> Many men cach skorne;
> Obey must we all,
> Or els ye be lorne
> Att onys.
> Down dyng of youre knees
> All that hym seys;
> Dysplesed he beys,
> And byrkyn many bonys. (ll. 10–13, 83–91)

Interestingly, the two formal examples of invocation listed here come at the beginning of the two plays dominated by raging, lord-of-misrule characters. Perhaps this indicates some connection in the mind of the Wakefield Master between this type of formal invocation and a disruptive festive ruler. In the other fragments of the master's work with similar Lord of Misrule characters, such as Pilate in *Conspiracio, Processus Crucis,* and *Processus Talorum,* we are treated to similarly abusive dramatic invocations, all following the same festive formula.

The other plays lack such formal invocations; nonetheless, they do begin with elements of festive invocation. *Prima Pastorum* and *Secunda Pastorum,* for example, begin with speeches that evoke festive themes. The *Prima Pastorum* opens with a monologue by Gyb, who asserts the uncertain and variable nature of life, especially in the barren, winter landscape of the play. This theme is strikingly festive, as Bakhtin tells us. While official church feasts "asserted all that was stable, unchanging, perennial" (Bakhtin, *Rabelais* 9), festive folk celebrations "were linked to moments of crisis, of breaking points in the cycle of nature or in the life of society and man" (9), and festive forms were "filled with this pathos of change and renewal" (11). Thus, Gyb's speech in the *Prima Pastorum* projects a festive world view from the beginning of the play.

Notably, Gyb proceeds in this play to act as a fool, not in the formal sense (although he is called one by Iak Garcio), but by introducing multiple elements of topsy-turvydom and burlesque. He brings an imaginary herd of sheep onto stage, and he and Iohn Horne, the second shepherd, engage in a verbal tug-of-war over them, furiously directing this imaginary herd back and forth:

> *2 Pastor:* Not oone shepe-tayll
> Shall thou bryng hedyr.
> *1 Pastor:* I shall bryng, no fayll,
> A hundred togedyr.
> *2 Pastor:* What, art thou in ayll?
> Longys thou oght-whedir?
> *1 Pastor:* They shall go, saunce fayll.
> Go now, bell-weder!
> *2 Pastor:* I say, tyr!
> *1 Pastor:* I say, tyr, now agane!
> I say skyp ouer the plane.
> *2 Pastor:* Wold thou neuer so fane,
> Tup, I say, whyr! (ll. 157–69)

Later in the play, Gyb proceeds to lead the shepherds in an extravagant and imaginary feast. As a fool figure, therefore, his speech at the beginning of the play performs many of the traditional roles of a festive invocation.

The *Secunda Pastorum* opens with monologues by Coll and Gyb which also introduce festive themes. Both note the extreme winter weather. Coll says,

> Lord, what these weders are cold!
> And I am yll happyd.
> I am nerehande dold,
> So long have I nappyd;
> My legys thay fold,
> My fyngers ar chappyd. (ll. 1–6)

Gyb says,

> Lord, thyse weders ar spytus
> And the wyndys full kene,
> And the frostys so hydus
> That water myn eeyne. (ll. 83–6)

outside?

These references to Winter conditions, as they do in the *Prima Pastorum,* provide the necessary environment for a festive winter game, which is precisely what the story of Mak, and by connection the nativity, becomes.

Yet comments on the weather are only prefatory. During most of the opening lines of the poem, Coll and the other shepherds complain about authority. Coll complains specifically about the oppressive policies of the aristocracy and the abusive tactics of their agents:

> We ar so hamyd,
> Fortaxed and ramyd,
> We ar mayde handtamyd
> With these gentlery-men. . . . (ll. 23–6)

When Daw, the servant of Coll and Gyb, arrives, he complains about the treatment he receives from his masters:

> Sich seruandys as I,
> That swettys and swynkys,
> Etys oure brede full dry,
> And that me forthynkys.
> We ar oft weytt and wery
> When master-men wynkys,
> Yit comys full lately
> Both dyners and drynkys;
> Bot nately
> Both oure dame and oure syre,
> When we have ryn in the myre,

> Thay can nyp at oure hyre,
> And pay vs full lately. (ll. 222–34)

Again, this theme parallels festive value systems, which were consistently hostile to authority and sought to remove hierarchical barriers. Bakhtin writes that

> All were considered equal during carnival. Here, in the town square, a special form of free and familiar contact reigned among people who were usually divided by the barriers of caste, property, profession, and age. The hierarchical background and the extreme corporative and caste divisions of the medieval social order were exceptionally strong. Therefore such free, familiar contacts were deeply felt and formed an essential element of the carnival spirit. (*Rabelais* 10)

Thus, even those plays which do not open with a formal festive invocation begin with festive characters and themes which serve to invoke festive values.

MOCK KINGS

A primary manifestation of the cyclical pattern in medieval festive culture was the election of mock rulers and the ritual usurpation of authority. The two forms typically relate to one another. Mock rulers are a form of usurpation, and mock rulers are themselves often usurped at the end of the festive celebration. The two forms occasionally develop expressions independent of one another, however. Therefore, I will treat them separately here.

During festive celebrations, a Lord of Misrule, Boy Bishop, May King, Abbot of Misrule or other mock authority figure was typically elected from the lower classes to replace the regular civil and ecclesiastical authorities. E. K. Chambers writes that

> one ceremony . . . has proved remarkably enduring. This is the election of the temporary king. . . . The English 'May-king,' or 'summer-king,' or 'harvest-lord,' or 'mock-mayor,' is a very familiar personage, and can be even more abundantly paralleled from continental festivals. (143–4)

Mock kings were also common in Christmas customs, as we see in the "Epiphany king or 'king of the bean'" (Chambers 260). In addition to the festive rulers in burlesque Christmas masses, Chambers lists several English folk examples:

> Tenby . . . elects its Christmas mock mayor. At York, the proclaiming of Yule by 'Yule' and 'Yule's wife' on St. Thomas's day was once a notable pageant. At Norwich, the riding of a 'kyng of Crestemesse' was

the occasion of a serious riot in 1443. These may be regarded as 'folk' versions of the mock king. (261–2)

Baskerville tells us that "the general tendency, especially on the great festival occasions, was to organize the celebration under leaders, usually a lord and a lady or a king and a queen, with attendants who paralleled the functionaries of a castle or a royal court" (7).

The plays provide several mock king figures. Herod is perhaps the most obvious. Nuncius introduces him as a king, but as the ruler of the audience as well as the king of Judah:

> Herode, the heynd kyng—
> By grace of Mahowne—
> Of Iury, sourmontyng
> Sternly with crowne
> On lyfe that ar lyfyng
> In towre and in towne,
> Gracyus you gretyng,
> Commaundys you be bowne
> At his bydyng. (ll. 14–22)

When Herod enters, he commands their silence with threats of violence typical of mock-ruler ranting:

> Stynt, brodels, youre dyn—
> Yei, euerychon!
> I red that ye harkyn
> To I be gone;
> For if I begyn,
> I breke ilka bone,
> And pull fro the skyn
> The carcas anone—(ll. 118–25)

Robert Weimann writes that Herod's character is the result of "New testament and apocryphal sources combined with the postritual tradition of the Lord of Misrule, the *festum stultorum* or similar forms of festive release" (65). Indeed, Weimann argues, the characteristics associated with Herod, namely the ranting, the topsy turvydom, and the ritual references to violence, all stem from summer lord traditions, not from biblical sources (64–6). Cain also shares mock ruler characteristics. In *Mactacio Abel,* Pikeharnes introduces him as "master" to the audience in the invocation and pleads for their silence in his name and with threats of his violence:

Be peasse youre dyn, my master bad,
Or els the dwill you spede. (ll. 1–4)
Wote ye not I com before?
. . .

A good yoman my master hat:
Full well ye all hym ken.
Begyn he with you for to stryfe,
Certys, them mon ye neuer thryfe. . . . (ll. 3–5, 15–18)

Cain enters the play and proceeds to rage, be abusive, and introduce elements
of inversion. In *Coliphizacio,* Cayphas and Annas are introduced by the torturers with some of the same threats used by Nuncius to introduce Herod,
and Cayphas displays many of the same characteristics as Herod (raging,
threatening violence, etc.). He says of Christ, for example,

Bot I gif hym a blaw
My hart will brist.
. . .
Nay, bot I shall out-thrist
Both his een on a raw.
. . .
Nay, I myself shall hym kyll,
And murder with knokys.
. . .
I shall gyf hym a wryng
That his nek shall crak. (ll. 276–7, 279–80, 298–9, 343–4)

This is particularly ironic as they condemn Christ, the ultimate ruler whose
authority they industriously usurp. Yet oddly enough, as I shall show, Christ
himself is overtly treated as a mock king, with Cayphas declaring him "King
Copyn" (l. 241), and the torturers sitting him on a mock throne to teach him
a new Yule game (ll. 497–8).

USURPATION OF AUTHORITY

The very presence of mock or substitute rulers creates an air of usurpation.
Traditional authorities, be they political or spiritual, are deposed in mock
ruler rituals, both symbolically and often in practice. Medieval usurpation
was rarely either gentle or civilized. Festive lords were either brazen themselves
or forced into bold acts by the nature of the celebrations. Barber writes, "The
village saturnalia of the Lord of Misrule's men was in its way a sort of rising;
setting up a mock lord and demanding homage for him are playfully rebellious gestures" (29). Indeed, as Barber notes, the deposing of authority inevitably leads to at least a momentary sense of anarchy: "the instability of an

interregnum is built into the dynamics of misrule: the game at once appropriates and annihilates the manna of authority" (37–38). Therefore, the form of
overthrow or of usurpation became typical of festive celebration. Bakhtin
writes that carnivals were dominated by ritual "humiliations, profanations,
comic crownings and uncrownings" (*Rabelais* 11).

Furthermore, when the festival was over, the mock authority figures were
themselves overthrown through abuse and mock beatings in order to complete
the symbolic seasonal cycle of change, death, and renewal. The overthrow of
these festive rulers was often quite stylized. Barber relates an elaborate death sequence from an "early sixteenth century Lincolnshire Summer Lord Game" in
which last wishes are attended to and a will is read (36–51). He notes,

> Winter reigns of Lords of Misrule might end with formal mourning: for
> example, the 'Christmas Lord, or Prince of the Revels' whose rule after a
> lapse of thirty years was elaborately revived at St. John's, Oxford, in 1607,
> reigned through the winter until Shrove Tuesday, when 'after a show
> called *Ira seu Tumulus Fortunae,* the Prince was conducted to his private
> chamber in mourning procession' and there expired. (45)

While this is a late example, it is a revival of an older custom, and its general
pattern might be taken as typical of Summer Lord customs. Barber also points
out that Nashe's *Summer's Last Will and Testament* (1592, 1600) is an outright
reference to the ritual reading of a summer lord's will, proving that the practice was at least well known (52–54). In whatever form it took, the ritualized
death of the festive ruler would reverse the original reversal and restore order.

The plays are filled with usurpations and uncrownings. In *Mactacio Abel,*
for example, Abel is presented as the representative of the Church only to be

murderously overthrown. Abel's principle actions in the play consist of reminding Cain of his religious obligations to worship and to tithe. Many of his references to obligation are anachronistic and suggest the role of the medieval priest.
For instance, he urges something like confession before the sacrifice or "service":

> And first clens vs from the feynd
> Or we make sacrifice;
> Then blis withoutten end
> Get we for oure seruyce. (ll. 81–84)

Thus, when Cain murders him, he usurps a symbol of religious authority in a
classic pattern of festive overthrow. Deus phrases Cain's animosity towards Abel
in terms of rebellion against authority: "Cam, whi art thou so rebell / Agans thi
brother Abell?" (ll. 293–4). The concept of Abel's authority is otherwise a strange

one, as he is the youngest of the two brothers; the only sense of authority in the play is Abel's spiritual authority as the voice of the religious hierarchy. After Cain murders his brother, he assumes his own mantle of mock authority, issuing orders "in the kyngys nayme" (l. 421), and engaging with Pikeharnes in his own mock Mass.[2] Usurpation of authority is common in the other plays as well. In *Processus Noe,* Noe's wife repeatedly usurps Noe's assumed authority even as the order of the world is overthrown into chaos. Even as the two scuffle, Noe significantly lets slip that he is on the bottom of the pile: "Se how she can grone, / And I lig vnder" (ll. 592–3). Similarly, the tossing of Mak in a blanket at the climax of *Secunda Pastorum* follows ritual forms of festive overthrow. In *Magnus Herodes,* the authority of the *Miles* can't prevent the enraged *Muliers* from chasing them unceremoniously. As the women buffet them, the knights decide literally to hotfoot it away: "Lett vs ryn fote-hote—/ Now wold I we hyde" (ll. 575–6). At the same time, Herod's anger towards Christ is based upon his own fear of being overthrown by the infant Christ. *Coliphizacio* displays the ultimate uncrowning, the abuse of Christ himself, specifically performed as a comic game.

REVERSAL

In keeping with the general theme of reversal inherent in mock kings and usurpations, inversions of any manner of established order, whether it is the churl ruling the king , the mule riding the man, or the wife controlling the husband, become a popular image and form in festive celebration. Bakhtin tells us that folk festivals display "a characteristic logic, the peculiar logic of the 'inside out (*á l'envers*), of the 'turnabout,' of a continual shifting from top to bottom, from front to rear" (11). Weimann writes, "Repeatedly there is a topsy-turvy inversion of normal controls or standards of behavior in a brief festive moment, or a reversal of values" (19).

The plays are filled with such comic reversals or topsy-turvy images. In *Mactacio Abel,* Cain reverses his condemnation by Deus into a declaration of royal privilege and protection. Also, the servant Pikeharnes flippantly declares he has given the plough animals stones to eat while placing their food at their rear end:

> Thare prouand, syr, forthi,
> I lay behynd thare ars,
> And tyes them fast bi the nekys,
> With many stanys in thare hekys. (ll. 46–9)

Processus Noe uses several role reversals. In contrast to medieval views of the family, Noe's wife is the dominant member of the relationship, and the children have to keep peace between their parents. *Secunda Pastorum* reverses the nativity by replacing the child in the animal manger with the sheep in the child's cradle. Mak

passes the sheep off as a child, thus wringing sympathy and good will from the very shepherds he has just robbed. As I have already noted, *Magnus Herodes* presents us with soldiers beaten and chased away by the very women they originally menaced. In *Coliphizacio,* Christ is condemned and profaned by men who clearly play the role of bishops. Cayphas, who is called "A man of holy kyrk" (l. 301), nonetheless curses at Christ: "Weme! The dwillys durt in thi berd, / Vyle fals tratur" (246–7). Also, as I have noted, Cayphas displays uncontrollable rage, a surprising characteristic in a "man of holy kyrk" (l. 301).

The plays also reverse the sense of normalcy. The *Prima Pastorum,* for example, is steeped in the nonsensical: without a herd, Gyb simply creates one in his imagination, and later the shepherds battle over the non-existent sheep and strive to outdo each other as they eat an imaginary feast. Slawpase attempts to illustrate their folly by pouring out his wheat upon the ground, an even greater act of folly. Nature and reason are similarly overthrown in *Coliphizacio,* as the torturers struggle through a strange environment where short trips become arduous journeys and simple attempts to beat a prisoner end in frustrating failure. In part this nonsensical environment is characteristic of the chaos found in festive culture, as when the planets leave their orbit in *Processus Noe,* or when the plough animals refuse to plough in *Mactacio Abel,* but it is also an incarnation of the topsy-turvy world, where normalcy is reversed and you may expect the unexpected.

Furthermore, the specific reversals and usurpations generally take place within the context of cyclical patterns and at important points of the cycles. For example, Noe's wife challenges his authority most at the height of the chaotic, regenerative flood. The reversal of the child in the manger takes place at the point of greatest disruption in the *Secunda Pastorum,* as the shepherds search the house and just before Mak is tossed in the blanket. Similarly, the beating of the soldiers by the irate women in *Magnus Herodes* takes place during and after the slaughter of the innocents. Thus, the reversals and usurpations serve to magnify and enhance the sense of disorder at the center of the festive cycle.

FORMS OF BURLESQUE

Festive culture is also characterized by burlesque and parody. As I have shown, mock lords are essentially parodies of official authoritarian figures. Further, inversion or reversal of any kind is fundamentally parodic. However, the festive pattern of parodying the official and serious side of life extends far beyond points of overthrow or reversal. Burlesques are common throughout medieval festive celebration; they display a free and easy attitude toward the official and serious culture that renders this culture non-threatening and inconsequential.

Forms of especial seriousness or import outside of the festival world, such as the feudal structure, the Church Mass, and so on, are reduplicated with irreverent and degrading changes made to critical parts of the form. Thus, in the feast of the Ass, braying replaces traditional parts of the Mass. Bakhtin describes one such Mass: "Each part of the mass was accompanied by the comic braying, 'hinham!' At the end of the service, instead of the usual blessing, the priest repeated the braying three times, and the final Amen was replaced by the same cry" (*Rabelais* 78). Similarly, the feast of Fools and the feast of Innocents parodied traditional church services. Bakhtin writes, "Nearly all the rituals of the feast of fools are a grotesque degradation of various church rituals and symbols" (74). Serious civil traditions were also parodied. Bakhtin notes

> Civil and social ceremonies and rituals took on a comic aspect as clowns and fools, constant participants in these festivals, mimicked serious rituals such as the tribute rendered to the victors at tournaments, the transfer of feudal rights, or the initiation of a knight. (*Rabelais* 5)

Similar parodies surround the ritual rise and fall of mock lords, such as the frequent burlesquing of the last will and testament, a heavy and serious matter, at the end of a summer lord's rule.

We see such burlesques throughout the Wakefield Master's plays. Most well known, perhaps, is the aforementioned parody of the nativity in the *Secunda Pastorum*. The miraculous birth that saves men's souls is reduced to a sham claim of the miraculous used to steal men's sheep. Instead of a holy child in an animal's manger, we are given a stolen sheep in a child's cradle, parodying the lamb of God. In the same play, Coll and Mak burlesque Christ's death and resurrection. As they go to sleep, Mak parodies Christ's final words during the crucifixion by commending them into the hands of Pontius Pilate: "*Manus tuas commendo, / Poncio Pilato*" (ll. 384–5). When they awaken, Coll describes himself with a twisted form of Christ's resurrection: "*Resurrex a mortruus*" (l. 504).

The other plays are also filled with parody and burlesque. In *Mactacio Abel,* Cain and Pikeharnes parody the Mass even as Abel's body lies unburied, implying that Abel is the host of their Mass. Cain's declaration of pardon also burlesques contemporary Royal pardons. Bennett A. Brockman notes that Cain's commands "in the kyngys nayme" (l. 421) are consistent with at least three contemporary forms of Royal pardon, all of which were resented by the populace (701–4).

In *Prima Pastorum,* the foolish shepherds parody contemporary clergy; they utter blessings, quote scripture in Latin, display extensive technical knowledge of religious choral music, and even give mock sermons. Indeed, they accuse each other of acting like priests. Gyb tells Slawpase, "Yee speke all by clerge, / I here by youre clause" (ll346–7), and soon after Iohn Horne says to Gyb,

> What speke ye
> Here in my eeres?
> Tell vs no clerge!
> I hold you of the freres;
> Ye preche. (ll. 560–4)

The shepherds' parody of the clergy climaxes in another profane mock mass, where the phrase "boyte of oure bayle," usually used to refer to Christ, the cure for our suffering, refers instead to "Good holsom ayll" (ll. 357–8).

In *Coliphizacio,* many of the offices of the church are parodied. In particular, the serious and, at the time, frightening examination of dissenters is parodied by the actions of Cayphas and Annas as they examine Christ. Cayphas informs Christ that he is a "prelate" and that he sings mass (ll. 222, 231). When Cayphas becomes angry, Anna reminds him that he is "A man of holy kyrk" (l. 301). Cayphas and Anna proceed to examine Christ before they condemn him (ll. 339–40). Anna speaks of the examination as if it is the inquisition of a heretic:

> Bot herys:
> Wold ye sesse and abyde,
> I shuld take hym on syde,
> And inquere of his pryde
> How he oure folke lerys. (ll. 321–5)

The second torturer testifies that Christ has been preaching a new law, or heresy (94–7). When Cayphas and Anna decide to have Christ beaten, the first torturer asks Cayphas to "Sayn vs, lord, with thy ryng" (l. 492), as a medieval Bishop would have signed his flock, and Cayphas promises his blessing to whomever beats Christ most thoroughly (ll. 493–4).

These examples are by no means a comprehensive list, if indeed one could be written. The plays are filled with puns and actions that mimic the official and serious aspects of medieval life. In *Magnus Herodes,* Herod's court echoes the medieval English court, and Herod's comic soldiers parallel the socially significant role of the medieval knight. In *Secunda Pastorum,* the plight of many contemporary peasants, prevented from ploughing and forced to tend sheep, is skillfully and humorously paralleled by the plight of the "husband" (farmer and married man) or "wed-man" (wedded man and man tending to "weders") who cannot enjoy relations with his wife (ploughing) because he must tend to his many children.

THE FOOL

The fool was an essential component of festive parody and burlesque. Festive fools were common in medieval England. Martin Stevens and James Paxon note that while Bishop Grossteste prohibited the feast of Fools in 1238,

> the feast clearly lingered on as attested by still another prohibition by Archbishop Arundel in 1391 (roughly the times when the Corpus Christi performances began to take shape) with an injunction to his Provost insisting 'that he abolish the corrupt and ancient custom of the King of Fools, both within the Church and without.' And it wasn't until 1542 that fool festivals of all kinds were finally prohibited by royal proclamation. (49)

Stevens and Paxon conclude that even beyond the feast of Fools, "The fool did in fact remain a palpable presence in England throughout the Middle Ages as part of popular seasonal festivals" (49). Stevens and Paxon note that the role of the fool was particularly well known in the North:

> It is especially in the North and the North Midlands of England that the festive Yuletide fool seems to have had wide currency. The city of Beverley provides us with an especially relevant example, since it is so much in the geographical proximity of York and Wakefield. A prominent misericord carving in the Beverley Minster (at the end of the top row of the North Choir) provides us with a representation of five fools. The three in the center are clearly dancing hand-in-hand, wearing the typical peaked hoods of the fool and scalloped tunics. An additional fool in the left carving is shown with the traditional staff and bladder, while the one on the right carving plays a pipe and tabor. (54)

The fool is occasionally interchangeable with the festival ruler, and Chambers hypothesizes that his dress is irrevocably tied up with the symbols of pagan sacrifice (384).[3] However, in the medieval festival and carnival, the fool serves the primary purpose of burlesquing that which is serious. He is the epitome of topsy-turvydom, the center of nonsense in the festive celebration just as the mock ruler is the center of chaos. This is the role of the fool in the feast of Fools and later in the "Société Joyeuse" (Chambers 372–89). The fool in his recognizable spiked cowl and pied costume is an important symbol of inversion and nonsense, but the fool is also a role to be played, a set of actions performed by an actor which reverses normal reality and sets the world topsy-turvy. Often, the fool is therefore used in the role of festive invocation, or as a frame for the festive celebration. Weimann writes,

> Like Robin Hood, the fool in the May procession also functioned as organizer and presenter of the ceremonial action. In the Mummer's Play and Sword Play (especially in their respective wooing ceremonies), fools or clowns served very similar functions. (30)

later

But the fool's inversions continue throughout festive celebration; he provides constant reversal and repeated parody, as if to maintain the momentum of festive life.

Lacking explicit stage directions, we cannot know if any characters in the plays actually wear the formal dress of the fool. However, many characters play the part of the fool. Stevens and Paxon write that the Towneley plays, in marked contrast to the other cycles and morality plays, "attests to the centrality of [the fool's] role in its dramatic design" (48). I have already touched on the rich festive invocations in some of the plays. Garcio Pikeharnes in *Mactacio Abel* is particularly reminiscent of a medieval fool. Stevens and Paxon point out that Pikeharnes ushers in folly and parody and generally plays the role of the rebel fool (68). His language is comic, abusive, and degrading, and his name perhaps identifies him as a fool figure.[4] Further, his role is always to usurp, ridicule, and parody. Pikeharnes's character type serves a very similar role in *Prima Pastorum*, where he is titled "Iak Garcio" and where he serves to introduce the same burlesque language and themes. In *Prima Pastorum*, the name "Jack" clearly identifies him as a fool, as the "Jack" of playing cards, "jack in the box," and the term "Jack of all trades" still attest to modern audiences. The use of the name with festive fools in the middle ages was widespread, as we see in the festive terms "jack o' th' green," "jack o' th' harvest," and "jack of lent." The name is also common in standard festive dramatic roles, as we see in the name "Jack Finney" from the Mummer's Play. Iak Garcio's actions are consistent with those of a fool. He serves no clear purpose in the *Prima Pastorum* other than to introduce inversion, mockery, and, as I will show, folly. However, all of the shepherds seem to engage in foolery in *Prima Pastorum*. Slawpase, the third shepherd, calls the other two, Gyb and Iohn Horne, fools when he sees them arguing over the imaginary sheep (l. 203). He then proceeds to demonstrate their lack of wits by emptying his bag of meal onto the ground (ll. 237–251). This prompts Iak Garcio to call them all fools (ll. 258, 266) and to make a specific comparison to "the foles of Gotham" (l. 260). The demon Tutivilus is also reminiscent of the fool, particularly in his use of bawdy language and puns.

Interestingly, Christ himself is twice called a fool in *Coliphizacio,* even as the torturers beat him (495–520). Indeed, five of the nine references to the words "foyll" and "foyn" in the Stevens and Cawley glossary of the entire Towneley cycle come from plays attributed to the Wakefield Master (674).[5] The term "fatur" is similarly common in these plays.

IMAGES OF FEASTING

Another common element of folk festivals was the celebration of the holiday feast. As the name indicates, the feast was central to many festive celebrations, particularly the more ancient ones. Chambers writes, "The sacrificial banquet, the great chines of flesh, and the beakers of ale, cider, and mead, endured, but the central rite of the old festival, the ceremonial slaying of the animal, vanished" (140). As a descendent of the sacrificial feast, holiday feasts are marked by excess and abundance. Participants are allowed to gorge themselves upon a menu of unusual variety and exaggerated amount.[6] On an immediate level, feasting is a celebration of license and freedom. Conceptually, however, it is also illustrative of the material body and the grotesque image. Bakhtin says of festive art that " the material bodily principle, that is, images of the human body with its food, drink, defecation, and sexual life, plays a predominant role" (*Rabelais* 18). Such images stood for "fertility, growth, and a brimming-over abundance" (19). Feasting celebrates the material body and its consumption. Feasting is a triumph of life within and through the regenerative process. It is the ultimate symbol of becoming, change, and development. Bakhtin says,

> Eating and drinking are one of the most significant manifestations of the grotesque body. The distinctive character of this body is its open, unfinished nature, its interaction with the world. These traits are most fully and concretely revealed in the act of eating; the body transgresses here its own limits: it swallows, devours, rends the world apart, is enriched and grows at the world's expense. (281)

Such a feast is clearly presented in the *Prima Pastorum,* where the lowly shepherds engage in a feast which is excessive and wildly abundant. The feast is probably imaginary, but it represents the abundant hope and excessive optimism of all festive banquets. It is the Yule feast, the feast of the New Year and new beginnings, and it is significantly placed directly before the birth of Christ, or the birth of hope and of a new era. Similarly, feasting references dot the plays, as when Coll and Mak complain of their wives' excessive drinking habits in *Secunda Pastorum;* Mak, for example, says of his wife, "She drynkys well, to;" and "[She] Etys as fast as she can" (ll. 344, 348).

PATTERNS OF ABUSE—BEATINGS

Another important element of folk festivals was abuse. Abuse in both physical and verbal forms is common in virtually all festive celebrations. Physical abuse normally accompanied points of reversal or usurpation, perhaps because it is symbolically sacrificial. Chambers notes that mock killings were central to the various folk dramas that attended festival:

> The mock death or burial type of folk-drama resolves itself, then, into two varieties. In one, it is winter whose passing is represented. . . . In the other, which is not really complete without a resurrection, it is summer, whose death is mimed merely as a preliminary to its joyful renewal. (186)

Mock killings represented both the death caused by winter and the death of winter in spring, or, in general, the violence inherent in cyclical change. Fake, heavily exaggerated beatings were used to highlight significant parts of ritual ceremonies, as when the Lord of Misrule was deposed, but beatings were also general symbols of the entire process. Bakhtin tells us that in folk rituals, "thrashing and abuse are not a personal chastisement but are symbolic actions directed at something on a higher level" (197). In fact, ritualized beatings were a dramatic illustration of the larger cyclical principle. Bakhtin says, "Abuse is death, it is former youth transformed into old age, the living body turned into a corpse" (197). In keeping with their illustrative function, mock beatings were greatly exaggerated, and as the symbolic death of the material body, they were usually accompanied by specific anatomical references (197–211).

We see such beatings, violence, or threatened violence in virtually all the plays. In *Mactacio Abel,* for example, Cain beats Pikeharnes several times, and he beats Abel to death. Noe and his wife engage in repeated beatings of one another in *Processus Noe.* In *Magnus Herodus,* Herod repeatedly threatens violence and uses specific anatomical language to do so. He warns the audience that if they are not respectful, he will "breke ilka bone, / And pull fro the skyn / The carcas anone," " ryfe you in sonder," "brane hym thrugh the hede," and "clefe / You small as flesh to pott" (ll. 123–5,129,136,142–3). Speaking of the child Christ, he says, among other things, "Had I that lad in hand, / . . . I shuld with this steyll brand / Byrkyn all his bonys" (ll. 148–51), and, "It mefys my hart right noght / To breke his nek in two" (ll. 181–2). Cayphas and the torturers in *Coliphizacio* engage in similar violence. Consider the following threats by Cayphas in only 70 lines of text.

> Bot I gif hym a blaw
> My hart will brist. (ll. 276–7)

Nay, bot I shall out-thrist
Both his een on a raw. (ll. 279–80)
I pray you—and sloes him! (ll. 284)
War! Let me gyrd him of his hede! (ll. 289)
Shall I neuer ete bred
To that he be stald
In the stokys. (ll. 293–95)
Nay, I myself shall hym kyll,
And murder with knokys. (ll. 298–99)
War! Let me bett hym! (ll. 317)
Therefor shall I hym hang (ll. 330)
I shall gyf hym a wryng
That his nek shall crak. (ll. 343–4)

Generally, such beatings and violence highlight significant moments in the cycle, such as the overthrow of Mak in the *Secunda Pastorum,* the murder of Abel in the *Mactacio Abel,* or the beating of Christ in the *Coliphizacio.* The shepherds toss Mak in a blanket, for example, at the height of chaos in the cycle and before the return to order through regeneration, which will take place with Christ's nativity. Having attempted to foist a fake birth upon the shepherds, Mak is then punished by being tossed in a blanket, a practice which several critics have noted was used in the Middle Ages to induce labor (Stevens and Cawley 509). Appropriately, then, the violence visited upon him, symbolic of the death of the blocking or winter figure which leads to re-birth or spring, is actually both a real technique used to cause birth and a transitional device which leads to the birth of Christ in the play. The beatings in the Towneley group stand out for their ferocity and frequency as well. In *Processus Noe,* for instance, the Wakefield Master includes four scenes of domestic violence. By comparison, the York and Chester Noah plays each include only one off-hand reference. The beating references are particularly graphic as well, with anatomical reference to breaking bones and backs.

VERBAL ABUSE AND PROFANITY

Verbal abuse and profanity are central to festive life. On a general level, they demonstrate the freedom and license of the festival, the ability to do and say things which might ordinarily be restricted. The repeated expression of this license is important on a broad symbolic level; it constitutes verbal maintenance of the festive state, and particularly so in two specific ways. First, profanity is itself a form of parody. In *Magnus Herodes,* when Herod says "by Gottys dere nalys," (l. 168) for example, he turns the form of a sacred vow into a blasphemous oath. Second, verbal abuse directed at a person is a part of the mechanism of usurpation. When a killjoy or mock lord was overthrown in a Medieval festival, degrading comments accompanied ritual violence. In fact, verbal abuse like this is common throughout the festive celebration, maintaining a sense of overthrow even when there are no specific usurpations.

Profane language is common throughout the plays. In the *Secunda Pastorum,* for example, the shepherds repeatedly swear by and misuse holy symbols and personages. In his opening monologue, Coll calls down a curse upon the nobility in the name of Mary (l. 28). Gyb enters and uses God's name to declare the hardships of married men (l. 109–10). When Daw enters, Coll declares, "Crystys curs" (l. 213). When Daw complains, Gyb threatens to make him sorry "By the heuens kyng" (l. 255). Coll then swears "By the roode" that the nights are long (l. 263). When Mak enters, the profanity increases. Mak swears to his own hardships "by the roode" (l. 341). As he prepares to cast his spell upon the shepherds, he says "Cryst-crosse me spede!" (l. 386). When Coll awakens from the spell, he swears that his foot is asleep, "by Iesus" (l. 508). When they awaken Mak, who pretends to be sleeping, he swears, in succession, by "Crystys holy name" (l. 545), by "Sant Iame" (l. 547), and by "Sant Stevyn" (l. 553). As Gyll and Mak prepare their deception, Gyll agrees to cry out "On Mary and Iohn" (l. 641). Later, as she swears that she practices no deception by "God so mylde" (l. 773), Mak asks her to calm down "for Godys payn" (l. 777). These blasphemous parodies of sacred vows are intermixed with milder oaths which, if not blasphemous, are nonetheless inappropriate within a nativity play.

The language of overthrow and abuse is also common in the plays. In *Coliphizacio,* for example, the second torturer wishes bad luck upon Christ: "Haue he mekill myschaunsce" (l. 59). Cayphas declares him to be unluckily born: "Illa-hayll was thou borne!" (l. 196). Cayphas then wishes him shame from the devil: "The dwill gif the shame" (l. 235). Cayphas next curses Christ's teacher, wishes bad luck upon his feet, and commends his bones to the devil (ll. 245, 369–70, 637). Further, the curses are supplemented by multiple threats and promises of violence, as I have already shown.

One specific form of abusive verbal degradation was particularly important in medieval festive culture; this involved the degradation of the head and mouth through contact with what Bakhtin calls the lower bodily stratum. Bakhtin describes this as

> the zone of belly, buttocks, and genitals, or of life, death, and regenerative fertility, which zone is directly opposed, in a symbolic sense, to the upper stratum, the zone of the speaking mouth, mind, and soul, of immortalized language, ideas, and religion (*Rabelais* 21).

The upper stratum of the head and mouth is the seat of ideal images and rational thought. Abstract concepts of hierarchy and order depend upon mind and language. Festive life, by contrast, celebrated change, inversion of order, the material body, and grotesque realism; it abhorred the ideal, the rational, and the hierarchical. The opposition between the official culture and the unofficial festive culture was easily represented by the contrast between the upper and lower bodily strata. Therefore, references to the carnal were deliberately fostered and used to degrade and thus fertilize the static, completed world of the intellectual and spiritual. We see such images when Chaucer's Absolon (a cleric) puts his mouth to the arse of the Carpenter's wife in "The Miller's Tale" and when the fart is divided between the noses of Friars in "The Summoner's Tale." Also in "The Summoner's Tale," we see a nest of Friars placed beneath the tail of Satan. The fabliaux tradition also exposes the clergy to similar degradation. In such cases, the upper stratum is debased by the lower one, or the spiritual and intellectual zone of the official culture is lowered into the realm of the fertile and regenerative. Such degradation was common and important. Bakhtin says, "Degradation . . . means coming down to earth, the contact with earth as an element that swallows up and gives birth at the same time. To degrade is to bury, to sow, and to kill simultaneously, in order to bring forth something more and better" (21). Degradation, therefore, is intended, like violence, as a positive action, an invocation of the regenerative principle.

We see such degradation in many short references throughout the plays. In *Mactacio Abel,* for example, Garcio begins the play by inviting audiences to "blaw my blak hoill bore, / Both behynd and before" until their teeth bleed (ll. 7–9). Cain's first greeting to the priestly Abel is "Com kis myne ars!" and "kiss the dwillis toute! / Go grese thy shepe vnder the toute" (ll. 61, 65–66). Later, as Abel's role as representative of Christian duty is clarified, Cain repeatedly directs him to kiss the devil's "ars." This imagery extends to other plays as well. In *Secunda Pastorum,* as Mak uses a fake accent to pass himself off as a gentleman, Coll tells him to stop his false southern speech and replace it with a turd: "Now take outt that Sothren tothe, / And sett in a torde!" (ll. 311–12). Cayphas evokes the same symbolic opposition in *Coliphizacio;* speaking to Jesus, he connects Christ's speech with dung: "Speke on in a torde" (l. 215). Later, When Christ refuses to answer, Cayphas curses him by projecting the devil's excrement into Christ's beard: "the dwillis durt in thi berd" (l. 246). The plays repeatedly use such images to degrade the upper stratum with the lower.

These, then, are the patterns and images, or vocabulary and syntax, of the festive world. They are more than occasional in the Towneley plays, and even more than common. They pervade the plays, often pushing orthodox

Christian forms and images aside and wresting meaning from traditional truths. Their very presence projects the values of the festive sub-culture, advocating unruliness, violence, degradation, and regeneration. In some plays, such as the *Mactacio Abel,* the carnivalesque idiom seems like a hermit crab, hijacking traditional Christian structures and turning them to its own purposes; in other plays, such as the *Iudicium,* the two systems work well together, and the festive forms merely seem like minor parasites upon the otherwise healthy body of the host. In all the plays, however, there develops a unique dialogue between the voice of the official culture and the voice of the unofficial festive sub-culture. From these dialogues arise the profoundly subversive expressions that characterize the Wakefield Master's work. I begin my examination of these dialogues by focusing now upon the first play, *Mactacio Abel.*

Chapter Three

The Overthrow of
Religious Obligation

The first play in the manuscript to show the influence of the Wakefield Master's hand is the *Mactacio Abel.* The play is a hodge-podge of verse forms, but on stylistic grounds it is considered chiefly the work of the Master.[1] His choice of plays on which to work is telling here, since the play is one which is particularly relevant to festive culture. In any rendering, the story is certain to contain a sacrifice and a violent overthrow. Yet perhaps for this reason, the play is difficult to read and has occasioned a great deal of critical controversy. In particular, there are two factors, dramatically related as I will argue, which render the play confusing to the modern critic. First, festive forms in the play are particularly disruptive, more so than in any of the other plays. Second, the two principle characters are ambivalent ones; Cain, the supposedly evil character, is nonetheless entertaining and compelling at times, and the playwright allows him to suffer final condemnation in relative comfort, while Abel, the good character, is surprisingly unsympathetic. I propose that the one is partially the cause of the other; Cain, or "Caym," as a festive Lord of Misrule is able to project many of the repressed views of the audience, while Abel, as the typological representative of the priesthood, comes off as a bit of a festive killjoy.

One element previously unremarked upon is the significance of the "Caym" legend to the medieval audience, and this significance is worth a closer look before moving on to analyze the play. Margaret Aston writes, "The attributes of Cain in late medieval literature and art were various—and all bad. Cain was of course the prototype murderer, a fratricide at that. He also stood for possession—false possession—and indeed his name is associated with the Hebrew word meaning to acquire or get" (95–96). The connection between Cain and clerical possessioners was particularly widespread at the time, especially in the term "Caym's Castels." The author of *De Officio Pastorali* uses the term for rich

churchmen who demand alms from poor parishioners: "Also almes shulde be
fre & discreet as goddis lawe techith, for ellis it were not meedeful, and god
gave no leeue to do it; what meede shal a pore man haue that he sufferith
agenus his wille his almes be borun to cayms castel to fede a floc of anticristis?
(Matthew 420)"[2] One reason Cain's name evoked the excessive worldliness of
the medieval Church was his common association with the unpopular manda-
tory tithe. In *De Officio Pastorali,* this practice is traced back to the offering of
Cain and Abel: "The firste bok of the olde law tellith of abel & caym, hou they
brenten ther tithes to god" (Matthews 431).[3] The biblical offering of Cain and
Abel was of course not a tithe, but centuries of exegetical scholarship had established it as such in the popular medieval mind. Thus, in addition to the orthodox significance of Cain as murderer, the story of Cain would have evoked
associations of Church possessions and the onerous tithe for the Wakefield
Master's audience. Both of these subjects are, as we shall see, raised in the festive ranting of Cain.

Orthodox interpretations of the Cain and Abel story are neither festive
nor concerned with clerical wealth. Within a Christian context, the tale
demonstrates the dangers of avarice and wrath. Cain's reluctance to abandon
his produce smacks of *cupiditas,* an evil far more sinister to the medieval priest
than to many modern Christians. When Cain does sacrifice, it is with a poor
spirit, and this insincerity angers God and causes the rejection of Cain's offering. Cain's jealousy at his brother's success leads to rage, and his rage leads to
fratricide. In the Christian universe, Cain becomes the symbol of willful sin,
the progenitor of the worst evils upon the earth. The story is also significant
as a precursor of Christ's passion. Within the medieval typological tradition,
each character in the Cain and Abel story corresponds to a later character or
series of characters in Christian history. As D. Thomas Hanks Jr. writes, "The
play of the Old Testament killing of Abel, then, prefigures the New Testament
betrayal and crucifixion of Christ" (56). Abel is a type of Christ, and Cain is
a type of Christ's persecutors. Thus, in traditional Christian representation of
the Abel story, the death of the innocent Abel has symbolic meaning in connection to the sacrifice of the sinless Christ. Finally, the story illustrates the division between the City of God and the City of Man. Worldly power may
temporarily triumph in this life, as Cain's escape from earthly punishment
shows, but worldly power is fleeting, only an illusion which will inevitably
fade in the light of God's eternal power. Cain does triumph in this life, but
even as he does, his punishment hangs over him in the form of God's damnation. God's refusal to punish him in this life attests to the Christian doctrine
that God's judgment awaits in the afterlife.

Mactacio Abel certainly contains the outline of this interpretation. Abel's comments highlight Cain's grudging nature and God's damnation of Cain seems to cement his status as a cursed evil doer. Yet the bulk of the play avoids the standard interpretation; festive elements and characters intrude into the biblical story and transform it from a didactic tale into an irreverent and chaotic celebration of misrule.

The first festive addition is the play's first character, Garcio Pikeharnes. Pikeharnes opens with an address to the audience which does little to set the scene for the Cain and Abel story. Instead, the opening monologue introduces festive themes, follows festive patterns, and prepares for festive characters. Pikeharnes' address to the audience is rich with the symbols of festive invocation. He begins with festive language: "All hayll, all hayll, both blithe and glad/ For here com I, a mery lad!" (ll. 1–2). Such jocularity surely is inappropriate as a preface to the first homicide, but it is a suitable pattern for the beginning of a festive occasion. Further, it is followed by calls for silence and abuse of the audience, elements characteristic of festive invocations. Pikeharnes twice threatens to assign noisemakers to the devil if they do not quiet down:

> Be peasse youre dyn, my master bad,
> Or else the dwill you speed.
> . . .
> Felows, here I you forbede
> To make nother nose ne cry;
> Whoso is so hardy to do that dede,
> The dwill hang him vp to dry! (ll. 3–4, 10–13)

Pikeharnes also introduces obscenity as he abuses the audience: "Bot he that ianglis any more, / He must blaw my blak hoill bore," (ll. 6–7). Finally, he insults their moral character: "Bot let youre lippis cover youre ten, / Harlottys euerichon;" (ll. 21–22).

Pikeharnes' role is that of the boy / fool / servant, and he introduces most of the burlesque in the play. Mendal Frampton argues that he is patterned after the folk play ruffler ("Brewbarret" 900). R. J. E. Tiddy points out the many similarities between Pikeharnes and the servant boy Jack Finney in the Mummer's play; both are disobedient and cheeky to their masters, and both strike back when their masters beat them (111). Similar boy / fool / servants are also observable in several others of the Wakefield Master's plays. Hanks writes, "Pikeharnes . . . is the type of the impudent servant. His mirror images appear throughout the cycle. Whether he is called Pikeharnes/Garcio, Jak Garcio (in the *Prima Pastorum*) Froward (in *Coliphizacio*) . . . , he is a thorn in the side of his master" (49–50).

As noted in Chapter Two, the boy's name, Pikeharnes, is likely also the mark of the fool. Fools are invariably portrayed in pied, tattered, or ragged costume, visible signs of their folly. "Pike" or "pyke" is used twice in the Towneley cycle in the context of picking, plucking, or pecking at something (Stevens and Cawley 699). "Harnes" is used twice in the *Processus Talentorum* as a reference to "personal apparel, clothes, livery" (680). "Pikeharnes," therefore, is logically interpreted as picked or tattered costume, the special dress for a fool character. It could also refer to the peaked hood, the other piece of costume typical of fools.

The theory that his name might reflect a fool's costume is supported by Pikeharnes' actions and comments. When Cain points out that the animals have not been properly fed, Pikeharnes replies,

> Thare Prouand, syr, forthi,
> I lay behynd thare ars,
> And tyes them fast bi the nekys,
> With many stanys in thare hekys. (ll. 46–9)

In other words, Pikeharnes has placed their feed at their rumps and given them stones to eat. The significance of this nonsensical action lies in its conventional symbolic value. Martin Stevens and James Paxson note,

> The act of trying to feed stones to the animals seems at first to be [a] whimsical prank. . . . The action is neither innocent nor insignificant. In general, such a switch is the office of the fool: to substitute that which is inedible, not life-sustaining, valueless for that which is edible and life sustaining. More specifically, the large stone held up to the mouth as if it were food or offered in the place of real bread is . . . one of the basic attributes of the medieval fool. In the Mactacio Abel, stone is substituted for grass or grain, the latter being the constituent raw material for bread. (69)

Further, Pikeharnes' actions reverse the natural order in typical festive fashion. Stevens and Paxson point out that by placing the animals' food at the body's point of excrement, Garcio Pikeharnes has "in specific terms, reversed nourishing and excretion, the two most fundamental and vital functions of animal life and human activity" (70). Cain, as we will see, does much the same later in the play. Thus, Stevens and Paxson add, Pikeharnes has "invested in what we may call the category of reversal, or contrariness for its own sake. Such . . . is the customary investment of the fool" (70).

Notably Pikeharnes' role in this story is an innovation. Cain's servant is neither biblical nor traditional, and only one contemporary dramatization includes a third character.[4] More profound than the addition of a new character, however, is the impact of a festive fool introducing the Cain and Abel story. Most critics have failed to notice that as a fool, Pikeharnes creates a new dynamic and injects a new set of conventions into the drama. The festive world parodies and mocks all that is serious or solemn. The fool is the purest form of the burlesque; all the fool says or does takes on the life of a parody. Therefore, when a fool introduces the Cain and Abel story with a festive invocation, the serious and sacred content is automatically exposed to burlesque. In addition, by presenting a serious story as a festive occasion, the play allows for fundamental reinterpretations of the tale. Events or characters interpreted one way within a biblical narrative are likely to be perceived differently within a festive context. For example violence is ritual, meaningful, and regenerative in the festive world, whereas it is simply brutal within a biblical context. Therefore, how is the slaughter of Abel to be interpreted? Is it a brutal act or a regenerative one? Indeed, the principal effect of Pikeharnes' invocation is to introduce themes and images of verbal abuse and physical violence that will come to fruition in Cain and ultimately warp the significance of the murder.

After Pikeharnes' festive invocation, Cain enters the play, bringing with him chaos, violence, and abuse. Cain's chaotic entry with unruly and uncooperative plough animals directly parallels the festive indulgence in chaos:

> Io forth, Greyhorne! And war oute, Gryme!
> Drawes on, God gif you ill to tyme!
> Ye stand as ye were fallen in swyme.
> What, will ye no forther, mare?
> War! Let me se how Down will draw;
> Yit, shrew, yit, pull on a thraw! (ll. 25–30)

The plough animals are clearly not cooperating with Cain. He rages at their lack of obedience:

> What, it semys for me ye stand none aw—
> I say, Donnyng, go fare!
> Aha, God gif the soro and care!
> Lo, now hard she what I saide;
> Now yit art thou the warst mare
> In plogh that euer I haide. (ll. 31–6)

The disorder continues when Pikeharnes, Cain's servant, reenters the play. When Cain asks for help, Pikeharnes does nothing. When Cain complains that the animals have not been fed well, Pikeharnes responds with his cheeky inversion of the digestive process. Angered, Cain strikes Garcio, only to be struck back. Cain's world is in chaos. Animals rebel against their owner.

The servant rebels against his master. Natural orders have been reversed. The play has descended into a disorder typical of festive celebration.

Surrounded as he is by chaos and reversal, Cain resembles in many ways a Lord of Misrule. He is thrice introduced as "master" in the invocation, and Pikeharnes pleads for silence in his name and with threats of his violence, yet the master is master only of unruly animals, disobedient servants, and general chaos. As the epitome of chaos and disruption in the play Cain is quite literally the lord of misrule.

Cain's entrance also contains significant festive images. Diller observes that Cain's entry with plow animals parallels the popular (and festive) Plough Monday drama:

> Cain's ploughing-team may also derive from non-religious acting traditions. The fact that he ploughs with no fewer than four horses and four oxen has led to speculations on the size of the stage which are almost certainly misguided; it seems far more likely that eight boys were disguised with animals' skins as oxen and horses. . . . If this assumption is correct, we are observing a transfer from the Plough Monday Play into a mystery play. There are more similarities than this: the Plough Monday Play has a killing (which, however, is purely comical), and unlike all other Abel plays the Towneley *Mactacio* resembles the Plough Play in allowing Abel a last outcry after he has received the deadly blow. (*Middle English Mystery Play* 230)

While we cannot know whether boys or real animals were used, Diller's arguments for parallels between the two plays seem difficult to dispute. If he is correct, then the festive invocation of Pikeharnes is followed by a scene drawn from an equally festive popular drama, a drama involving participants in animal skins, ritual violence, and murderous overthrow within a comic setting. Again, the effect of such a comic opening is to transfer meaning into a festive context and, thus, fundamentally to transform the overall significance of the events of the play.

As Cain enters the play, he also expands the obscenity and threats of violence introduced by Pikeharnes. While obscenity and violence are perhaps natural in the orthodox characterization of Cain, the extent and nature of both are not. In this play, obscenity and violence are developed with such relish and enthusiasm that they transgress the function of character development and become thematically significant in their own right. Cain, for example, does not merely demonstrate that he is profane through one or two regrettable examples. He spews out profanity with energy and conviction, profanity that is creative and funny, profanity that borders upon the artistic. Hanks notes that Cain is "possessed of a seemingly inexhaustible and certainly inspired fund of earthy profanity and obscenity" (51). Such profanity is significant within a festive context for two reasons. On one level, it is an expression of the license and freedom of the festival. Festival participants are blasphemous and crude because it is allowed, because the normal restrictions have been temporarily lifted. In addition to license, however, Cain's profanity creates a specific festive theme in the play. Note, for example, that most of Cain's verbal abuse is scatological. He says to Abel, at their first meeting, "Com kis myne ars!" and "kiss the dwillis toute!" (ll. 61, 65).

Cain's profane references invariably degrade the head, lips, and mouth through contact with what Bakhtin calls the "lower bodily stratum." As Abel reminds him of his duty, for example, he says, "Hold thi tong, yit I say,/ Euen ther the good wife strokid the hay" (ll. 89–90). As noted in Chapter Two, such "nether kisses" are typical of festive expression. In such cases, the upper stratum is debased by the lower one, or the spiritual and intellectual zone of the official culture is lowered into the realm of the fertile and regenerative. The profanity of Pikeharnes, when he says, "He must blaw my blak hoill bore, / Both behynd and before, / Till his tethe blede" (ll. 7–9), introduces this pattern of degradation, and it is continued by Cain. Cain specifically connects the scolding mouth of Abel, who, as I will argue, represents the orthodoxy of the Church, with the anus of the devil, such as when he says, "Yei, kys the dwill's ars behynde" and "Com kys the dwill right in the ars" (ll. 268, 289). This particular degradation, Stevens and Paxson write,

> invokes the ritual particulars of the Black Mass, particulars such as the climactic kissing of the devil's ass in submission. Such an imagined satanic rite would be common folk-knowledge to the medieval Northerner in England, common even to those unfamiliar with such famous witch treatises as the *Maleus Maleficarum*. (69)

Cain's profanity also suggests the same unnatural inversion introduced by Pikeharnes. As he curses at Abel, Cain says, "Go grese thy shepe vnder the toute" (l. 66). The reference, as Stevens and Paxson note, is suggestive of both sodomy and bestiality (70), a perennial degradation of the role of the shepherd. Yet it also suggests reversal of natural order. Stevens and Paxson write,

> The word, as it operates here, can mean not only "to grease" or lubricate, but also "to graze" or "to grass"—that is, to feed with grass (to "gresen shepe" or "beestys" is a common Middle English expression; see MED, s.v. grassen and cf. Gresen). In accordance with this meaning, we have

another inversion, a grossly unnatural one. Cain is calling on his brother
to feed his animals from the end naturally relegated to excretion. He has
absolutely reversed the order of ingestion/excretion, the oppositional cat-
egories of fuel/waste. (70)

If Stevens' and Paxson's interpretation seems far-fetched, consider it in context with Pikharnes' earlier act of placing the animals' nourishment behind
their asses, or in the context of Cain repeatedly telling Abel to kiss the devil's
ass. These two characters provide a consistent festive pattern of reversal, inversion, and degradation through their obscenity.

Cain also makes many threats of violence, and he backs it up with actual violence towards Pikeharnes. We have noted Pikeharnes' introductory
threats; as with his profanity, they seem to be a precursor to Cain's violence.
Pikeharnes, the fool, provides an invocation filled with festive profanity and
violence. Cain then becomes the center of serious verbal and physical abuse,
serving in much the role of a Lord of Misrule. In the initial discussion with
Pikeharnes, as the servant/fool talks scornfully back to him, Cain strikes him:
"That shall bi thy fals chekys" (l.50). Pikeharnes responds in kind: "And haue
agane as right" (l. 51). After the murder, he strikes Pikeharnes again, several
times: "Take the that, boy, take the that" (389). Pikeharnes complains bitterly about this unwarranted abuse, and Cain declares that he did it just to
use his hand (l. 395). The violence seems random and causeless, but such is
typical of festive violence. With threats and confrontational boasts mixed
with profanity, the violence creates a festive atmosphere in which standard
order is overthrown. The violence in the *Mactacio Abel,* when seen through
the prism of the festive world, signifies more than brutality; it is the embodiment of festive regeneration. And it is against this background that the murder of Abel proceeds.

Following the invocation and the entrance of Cain, Abel finally appears. In contrast to Pikeharnes and Cain, Abel is unremarkable. His speech
is respectful and moderate. He doesn't take offense at the many personal insults leveled at him. For example, when Cain curses Abel, treats him like a
servant, bids him "kys the dwillis toute" (l. 65), and perhaps insinuates that
he has bestial sexual relations with his sheep (ll. 66–7), Abel calmly replies,
"Broder, ther is none hereaboute/ That wold the any grefe" (ll. 68–9). After
each insult, Abel responds quietly and serenely, gently remonstrating with
Cain to do the right thing. Yet while this is perhaps righteous, it is also weari-
some, repetitive, and, as many critics have pointed out, annoying.[5] Indeed,
for the subject of the drama, Abel is surprisingly underdeveloped. He makes
no mention of himself, his background, or his personal wants and fears. His

principal role is firmly and consistently to remind Cain of his religious obligations. Hanks calls Abel, "a flat character, a character that the playwright creates only to personify and to verbalize the virtue against which Cain revolts" (50). Abel seems little more than a straw man for Cain to knock down.

Abel introduces three ideas of obligation. The first is that of worship. Abel says, "Com furth, brothere, and let us gang / To worship God; we dwell full lang" (ll. 76–77). The biblical account of the murder of Abel does not include a temporal factor. In the *Mactacio Abel,* however, time is a driving force. As the conversation drags on, Abel emphasizes again the need for haste: "Leif brother, let us be walkand; / I wold our tend were profyrd" (ll. 108–9). As Cain continues to grumble, Abel again urges him to hurry: "Brother, com furth, in Godys name; / I am full ferd that we get blame. / Hy we fast, that we were thore" (ll. 146–8). Cain is reluctant and grudging, and much of his argument dwells upon the time needed for such worship: "Shuld I leife my plogh and all thyng, / And go with the to make offeryng? / Nay, thou fyndys me not so mad!" (ll. 93–5). This stress upon time, while misplaced in the Cain and Abel story, is nonetheless appropriate in the context of medieval Christianity. Catholic Christians were and are obliged to attend mass at least once a week. Medieval Christians were also supposed to abstain from profitable activity on Sundays and Church-designated feast days. Abel's call to worship of a neglectful Cain thus presents the idea of orthodox Christian obligation.

This hint at orthodox obligation is further reinforced by other ties between Abel's intended sacrifice and the orthodox Christian mass. For example, Abel seems to hint at the obligation of confession within the context of a religious service. He says,

> And therefor, brother, let vs weynd,
> And first clens vs from the feynd
> Or we make sacrifice;
> Then blis withoutten end
> Get we for oure seruyce (ll. 80–84)

Aside from the obvious pun upon "seruyce" as both service to God and a religious service or mass, several parts of the quotation suggest the Catholic Mass here. The first is the phrase "bliss withoutten end," which, as we will see, is an English echo of the end of the consecration of the Mass. This echo, occurring as it does after "sacrifice," hints at a connection between the sacrifice proposed by Abel and the Mass, which literally relives the sacrifice made by Christ. This connection is further reinforced by the typological connection between the slain Abel and the slain Christ, as well as by the connection between the "lamb of God" and the lambs to be sacrificed by Abel. Therefore, the "cleansing from the fiend" needed before the sacrifice parallels the confession required of medieval Christians before they could partake of the Eucharist. Only by confession to and absolution by a priest could a Christian be absolved of sin. Significantly, these obligations also carry implied financial obligation. In addition to their tithes, medieval Christians were often expected to give offerings and oblations for masses and confessions.

The third and most obvious obligation introduced by Abel is the tithe due to God. Abel says,

> All that wyrk as the wise
> Shall worship God with sacrifice.
> Oure fader us bad, oure fader vs kend,
> That oure tend shuld be brend. (ll. 72–75)

This reference to the tithe is anachronistic. The story of Cain and Abel never mentions a tenth, and the idea of rendering a tithe is a later Jewish one. In this context, however, it has more meaning to the medieval world than to the biblical one. The medieval tithe was compulsory and was usually levied directly by the Church. As an enforced tax, it often caused great resentment, especially in the face of Church luxury and clerical corruption. Of all obligations laid upon medieval Christians, the Wakefield Master has thus presented the most onerous, and those which an audience would most have resented.

Indeed, real resistance to these obligations was widespread in medieval England, and anti-clerical riots were often severe. An examination of Lollard beliefs is pertinent here because they represent an extreme version of anti-clerical views that were widespread in England. Reviewing defendant statements from the fifteenth century Norwich heresy trials, Norman P. Tanner writes that most of the "lollards" examined scorned the prohibition against work on Sundays:

> The argument that the precept was of man and not of God, and there-
> fore was invalid, . . . seems to have been the basic objection to keeping
> Sundays and feast-days holy. Thus, most defendants were charged with
> believing it was lawful to perform corporal work on these days, or that
> there was no need to 'sanctify' them or go to church on them. (15–16)

In one of the transcripts, for example, John Fynche admits to believing "that every man may lefully doo all bodely werkis, save oonly synne, on Sondays and all other festival day[s] whyche prestis commaunde to be kept holy be ordinance of the Churche" (185).

Lollards were equally dismissive of the obligation to confess sins unto a priest, the second obligation asserted by Abel. Summarizing defendant statements from Norwich, Tanner writes, "Oral confession to a priest was said to be of no value . . . because God alone could forgive and remit sins" (12). Indeed, this belief is almost universal among the heretics examined at Norwich. For example, John Eldon admits his belief "that confession oweth to be made unto no prest, but oonly to God, for no prest hath poar to assoile a man of ony synne" (134). The same John Eldon admits believing, as do most of the sixty heretics, "that man ne woman is bounde to do ony penance whiche is enjoyned to hym of ony prest in Confession" (135).

In part, these first two obligations were annoying to the population because many people believed they were used to generate tithes and offerings, the third obligation asserted by Abel. Indeed, this obligation caused the others to be suspect. Priests were suspected of using multiple religious obligations to generate income. Tanner notes in his summary that

> One other reason for not keeping the days holy was mentioned: namely, priests had established them out of greed, so as to collect tithes and oblations from the people. Regarding the payment of tithes and oblations, which was also, of course, an issue much discussed outside Lollard circles, most defendants were accused of holding that a man had a right not to pay them to a church or its curate. A few were accused of believing it was better or more meritorious, or even a duty, not to pay them (at least to an ecclesiastic in mortal sin). The reasons given varied from largely negative considerations to positive alternatives: they made priests proud and lecherous; God had no part in them . . . ; and the money should be given instead to the poor. (16)

For example, William Hardy admitted to the belief

> that it is meritorie and charitable all men to withdrawe and withhold from the prestes and curates all offringes and tithes, for offringes and tithes make prestes proude and lecherous and vicious, and therefor it were more meritorie to spende suche good in other use. (153)

Anti-clerical literature makes much of the curses and litigation heaped upon delinquent parishioners, including desperately poor peasants, by priests who demanded prompt payment of the tithe. The author of *The Office of Curates* writes of churchmen, "yif a man be bihynde of tithes & othere offryngis & custumes maad of sinful men, he schal be sompned, ponyschid & cursed" (Matthew 151). Such strong-handed techniques were keenly resented and prompted much of the anti-clerical violence of the Fourteenth and Fifteenth Centuries. Resentment of the tithe and of Church pressure to tithe is particularly

emphasized in Cain's reluctant and drawn out counting of his wheat. Critics
have noted the stinginess of Cain's accounting, and rightfully so, but few
have stressed the constant badgering by Abel to "tend," or tithe, correctly.
The word "tend" or "teynd" is used twenty one times during the 131 lines of
the offering scene alone, usually in the context of argument between Cain
and Abel over what constitutes a proper tithe. Cain's argument, as we shall
see, is principally that of an overworked and struggling farmer, hardships
Abel consistently ignores.

In reminding Cain, and therefore the audience, of these obligations, Abel
stands for the clerical hierarchy of the Church. He summons Cain to worship,
advises Cain to do his confession, and reminds Cain of his obligation to tithe.
His thoughtful and measured observations resemble priestly homilies more
than brotherly advice. Indeed, when Cain's sacrifice refuses to light, Deus's voice
speaks directly in support of Abel: "Cam, whi art thou so rebell/ Agans thi
brother Abell?" (ll. 293–4). Aside from identifying Cain as a symbol of usurpation, Deus' comment reinforces and supports Abel, making Abel, in practice,
God's representative on earth. In other words, Abel is overtly developed as a
priestly figure in the play, a priest representative of deeply resented religious obligations. Indeed, Cain recognizes him as a priest and makes several comments
on his preaching and "sermonyng" (l. 88). Abel's occupation as a shepherd is a
further link to the clergy. In religious typological tradition, priests were often
thought of as spiritual shepherds, and much in the play symbolically connects
him with the medieval clergy.[6] Further, Abel's ability to make the only effica-
cious sacrifice in the play is particularly stressed. This issue of efficacy was particularly relevant to the medieval audience. For example, Wycliffe and many
later Lollards had held that corrupt priests could not truly consecrate the host
and that Christ was not present in the host when such priests performed the
service. Although Lollardy had long been branded a heresy, the issue of efficacy
remained topical, and Abel's ability to initiate an acceptable sacrifice certainly
identifies him as a priest. Abel, the shepherd who speaks for God and reminds
Cain and the audience of their religious obligations, is thus a clear symbol of the
orthodox priesthood. As the representative of the church, Abel is placed in direct opposition to Cain, the disruptive symbol of festive celebration. Therefore,
the natural hostility between these two influential cultures is embodied in the
primary characters of the play, and any conflict between these characters is symbolic of the conflict between these cultures.

Along the same theoretical axis, we may see another contrast between the
two, one more dependent upon festive forms. Cain's relationship with the corn
is especially well developed by the playwright, and this in at least one sense connects him with another festive character, namely the "spirit of the corn" or a

"jack of the harvest" figure. Such figures were essential parts of festive summer celebrations. They most commonly took the form of human figures fashioned from sheaves of wheat,[7] but their role was often taken by humans and incorporated into Lord of Misrule activities.[8] Chambers description of typical harvest activities is helpful here:

> A large garland, often with an anthropomorphic representation of the fertilization spirit in the form of a doll, parades the street, and is accompanied by a 'king' or 'queen,' or a 'king' and 'queen' together. Such a garland finds its place at all the seasonal feasts; but whereas in spring and summer it is naturally made of the new vegetation, at harvest it as naturally takes the form of a sheaf, often the last sheaf cut, of the corn. Then it is known as the 'harvest-May' or the 'neck,' or if it is anthromorphic in character, as the 'kern-baby.' (117)

The relevance of such a custom to the *Mactacio Abel* lies in the drama's focus upon the individual sheaves of grain and particularly in Cain's reluctance to part with them:

> Oone shefe, oone, and this makys two,
> Bot nawder of thise may I forgo.
> Two, two, now this is thre:
> Yei, this also shall leif with me,
> . . .
> Wemo, wemo! Foure, lo, here!
> Better greved me no this yere.
> . . .
> Foure shefys, foure—lo, this makys fyfe:
> Deyll I fast thus, long or I thrife!
> Fyfe and sex, now this is sevyn;
> Bot this gettys neuer God of heuen,
> . . .
> Sevyn, sevyn, now this is aght
> . . .
> We! Aght, agth, and neyn, and ten is this:
> We! This may we best mys.
> Gyf hym that that ligys thore?
> It goyse agans myn hart full sore. (ll. 194–7, 200–1, 206–9, 212, 220–3)

This petulant accounting, which continues until Cain has placed eighteen sheaves for sacrifice, is fairly typical of Cain's standard characterization as a miser. However, in this play, the detailed emphasis with which each sheaf is tenderly and sadly laid out also smacks of the veneration accorded to the "harvest-May," "kern baby," or "jack-o-th'-harvest," and this painstaking attentiveness

thus firmly associates Cain both with wheat as a farmer and with wheat sacrifice. In other words, Cain is blatantly connected, in a symbolic sense, with the
"spirit of the corn." The resulting implications are striking. If Cain is, as it
seems, a figure with the typical characteristics of a summer Lord of Misrule, and
if, as it seems, his entry with plough animals is particularly reminiscent of the
festive plough play, then his carrying of and tending to sheaves of wheat within
a sacrificial context identify him as a festive character. This festive link is further
cemented by the circumstances of the failed sacrifice.

Ritual fires were a central element in summer festive occasions. Indeed,
their significance as a bringer of fortune survives even today, as the bonfire preceding modern American homecoming games will attest. Bonfires are often associated with other festive elements, like the sacrificial burning victim (often
an anthropomorphic figure made of vegetation) which we still see in the Guy
Fawkes celebrations. Such customs were widespread in medieval England, always connected specifically with festive occasions. Chambers notes,

> The Midsummer or St. John's fires are perhaps the most widely spread and
> best known of surviving heat-charms. But they can be paralleled by others
> distributed all over the summer cycle of festivals, at Easter and on May-day,
> and in connection with the ploughing celebrations on Epiphany,
> Candlemas, Shrovetide, Quadragesima, and St. Blaize's day. (126)[9]

Chambers explains the significance of fires to festive observances:

> The magical notions which, in part at least, explain the garland customs
> of the agricultural festival, are still more strongly at work in some of its
> subsidiary rites. These declare themselves, when understood, to be of an
> essentially practical character, charms designed to influence the weather,
> and to secure the proper alternation of moisture and warmth which is
> needed alike for the growth and ripening of the crops. . . . To achieve
> rain, water must be splashed about, or some other characteristic of a
> storm or shower must be reproduced. To achieve sunshine, a fire must be
> lit, or some other representation of the appearance and motion of the sun
> must be devised. (121)

We will return in the next chapter to the significance of water charms and
their relevance for the *Processus Noe*. For this chapter, the importance of fires,
and particularly of smoke, to festive celebrations is more immediately appli-
cable because of its occurrence in the *Mactacio Abel*. Chambers writes,

> The ordinary form of heat-charm was to build, in semblance of the sun,
> the source of heat, a great fire. . . . [I]n order that they may receive the

full benefits of the heat-charm, they must come into direct physical contact with the fire, by standing in the smoke, or even leaping through the flames, or by smearing their faces with the charred ashes. The cattle too must be driven through the fire, in order that they may be fertile and free from pestilence throughout the summer. . . . The fires were built on high ground, that they might be visible far and wide. Or they were built in a circle round the fields, or to windward, so that the smoke might blow across the corn. (124–5)[10]

Cain's association with the sacrificial fire bears a striking resemblance to "heat-charm" activities as described by Chambers. While Abel's sacrifice is quickly over, Cain's preparation, including counting out the sheaves and deciding which should be burnt, takes up a significant amount of the text. The actions accompanying the text must surely have involved arrangement of the sheaves. As we have noted, Cain speaks specifically of each sheaf as he lays it down.[11] When he attempts to start the blaze, he is almost overcome by the smoke which clearly engulfs him. A number of scholars have dwelt upon the emphasis of smoke in the play, and several have mentioned the suggested associations between this smoke and Hell Mouth (Helterman 43), but none has noticed the parallels between this event and the numerous festive fires in medieval England. Interestingly, the fire is extra-biblical; fire is not a part of the account of Cain and Abel in Genesis. Note that Cain is literally covered in the smoke. He says,

> Now will I set fyr on myne.
> We! Out, haro! Help to blaw!
> It will not bren for me, I traw.
> Puf! This smoke dos me mych shame—
> . . .
> Almost had myne breth beyn dit;
> Had I blawen oone blast more,
> I had beyn choked right thore.
> It stank like the dwill in hell,
> That longer ther myght I not dwell. (ll. 276–9, 282–6)

This emphasis upon the smoke engulfing the participants, while comic, is also similar to festive, mock-sacrifice bonfires. Therefore, the Towneley Cain embodies a number of characteristics and associations that we can assume the audience would have recognized as festive.

Cain's festive character is particularly significant because his brother is a shepherd associated with lambs, which connects him typologically with the priesthood. Considering this well developed contrast within a set of Christian

mystery plays, one would expect a spirited defense of Orthodox Church values
and a repudiation of the festive. However, this is not the case. Abel's explanation
of obligation is standard and competent, but it borders on the callous and is
hardly convincing. God gives us all our living, and God's grace is but a loan;
therefore the tithe really belongs to him (ll. 100, 118–9). When this argument
fails to convince Cain, who suggests that tithes go to the priest rather than to
God, Abel resorts to nagging, reminding Cain that they are brothers and that
their father would not want them to "go in sonder" (l.157). Whenever there is
an opportunity for Abel to make a good point, he fails to do so. When Cain declares his reluctance to go hungry, for example, Abel responds by fearing public
reproach (ll. 141–7). Hanks notes of Abel that

> he gets almost as short shrift from the playwright as he does from Cain.
> He has only seventy-four lines, as compared to sixty-eight for Pikeharnes
> and over three hundred for Cain. Moreover, the content of his lines is no
> more than the bare needful. (50)

Abel in this play is a straw man for Cain to denounce. He parrots the party
line of the medieval Church, demanding compliance with unreasonable sacrifice even in the face of Cain's struggles. Eleanor Prosser calls him "a stuffed
shirt" (78) and says, "It is he who points toward the moral, who exhorts again
and again. . . . [T]he impression of a pompous do-gooder is made inevitable
by the author's treatment of him" (76). Thus, Church obligations, represented
here by Abel, are accurately but unsympathetically described. They seem mere
abstractions, an intellectually created duty to an uncaring and rigid Church.

Cain's complaints, on other hand, are original and more thoughtfully
developed. Within the context of the play, they evoke more empathy than
Abel's "sermonyng." Diller notes that

> [Cain's] reactions and attitudes are . . . of a sort that the medieval
> burgesses have no difficulty recognizing themselves in them. Though
> Cain, as unwilling to sacrifice, is clearly marked as evil, he does offer ar-
> guments which at least sound plausible. . . . His complaints about the
> burden of his labor must also have rung familiar with a large part of the
> audience—all the more so since the offering of tithes is clearly brought
> into connection with the demands of the contemporary Church. (*Middle
> English Mystery Play* 228)

Cain convincingly argues he is so hard pressed that he has no time to spare
from work to attend worship (ll. 93–96). He points out that his produce is
the result of long labor upon which he has broken his body (ll. 188–91). He

argues that he never borrowed anything from God or anyone else; he did the work himself (ll. 101–2, 116–7). When he had great need, God gave him nothing; why should he now give away his hard earned gains? (ll. 126–31). Indeed, he has only "soro and wo" (ll. 97–8). When he reluctantly agrees to sacrifice, he resists giving the best tenth of his crop, thinking it ludicrous to burn up and therefore waste the best portion of his hard-earned sustenance (ll. 190–95, 209–11, 214–9). These are points that the audience would have found compelling, and their association with Cain has caused critical dissent over how sympathetic a character Cain really is. Critics such as Diller recognize the appeal of Cain's argument. On the other hand, as Clifford Davidson notes, Cain's actions ultimately mark him as an evil character: "Cain's mistreatment of those under him or equal with him and also his rebellion against the God who is over him separate him from the sympathy of those watching the play" (67). I suggest this problem is easily resolved by recognizing the festive character of Cain. As a Lord of Misrule, he is expected both to usurp authority and abuse those around him; however, he is also allowed to speak truth, truth the audience can recognize and embrace, even as they celebrate his ultimate uncrowning. Diller and Davidson are both correct; Cain may be an evil character in the orthodox context of the play, but as a festive character, his arguments are a genuine reflection of the hardships faced by his medieval audience.

More significantly, Cain's complaints draw specifically and anachronistically upon the distrust and resentment the medieval peasant felt towards the relatively corrupt clergy of the time. As he discusses the ethics of rendering a tithe to God, Cain says, "My farthyng is in the preest hand/ Syn last tyme I offyrd" (ll. 106–7), pointing out that the tithe goes to priests rather than directly to God himself. This seems out of place since the story deals with burnt offerings and involves no priests, but it is appropriate to a discussion of the medieval tithe. Medieval peasants were painfully aware that tithes and offerings, levied in the name of God, were used to support a variety of classes of clergy and preachers, many of whom were corrupt and lived lives of luxury and immorality. We see such awareness and hostility in Chaucer's portrayal of the worldly Prioress and Monk and in the corrupt Friar and Pardoner. The Prioress and Monk each live in aristocratic style and luxury, comfortably oblivious to their religious duty. The Friar and Pardoner are even worse. In "The Summoner's Tale," for example, the Friar unctuously manipulates sincere hopes and dreams to support his own lustful materialism. In "The Pardoner's Tale," the Pardoner openly admits his greed and lust; he loves luxurious living and only preaches to separate simpletons from their money. Cain refers to the same predatory tactics when he says about Abel, "How! Let furth youre geyse; the fox will preche" (l. 86). In other words, the priest calling for tithe from the peasants, here represented by Abel, is no better than the fox leering hungrily at geese. As mentioned in Chapter One, this is a common metaphor for corrupt clergy, bent on enriching themselves through religion at the expense of the populace. In particular, medieval anti-clerical literature uses the image of the fox in relationship to wealthy religious possessioners. The anonymous tract, *Of Prelates,* for example, declares that "Prelatis . . . ben malicious foxis & rauyschynge wolues," while the author of *Of Clerks Possessioners* accuses possessioners of feigning holiness, "as the fox feyneth hym dede til the briddis comen to his tounge, & thane he schewith hym on lyue deuourynge & swelwynge of hem" (Matthew 103, 123). Thus, Cain's references evoke the deep resentment felt by much of the medieval populace towards the abuses of the clergy.

In addition, as I have noted, Abel's role as a shepherd is deliberately parodied by Cain's profanity. When he says, "Go grese thy shepe vnder the toute" (l. 66), he turns Abel's role as shepherd, which is typologically related to the role of the priest, upside down. The reversal can be read two ways; by Stevens and Paxson's reading, it becomes another dark parody of the priest and the mass, as the shepherd/ priest offers the shepe/ congregation their grese/ sustenance (in this case the host) at their collective "toute." However, if "grese" refers to ointment or salve, the reference evokes a far more common complaint made against medieval pastors, one that we will examine in detail in Chapter Five. In brief, many anticlerical works pointed out that the primary role of priests, as spiritual shepherds, was to tend to the needs of their flock, and priests were often accused of neglecting the spiritual instruction of their parishioners, leading to spiritually diseased, or "scabby" sheep. The author of *De Officio Pastoralis* argues that one of the most important duties of a parson is "to greese ther scabbid sheep & to telle hem medicyn of goddis lawe" (Matthew 439). Cain's declaration, "Go grese thy shepe," thus implies that Abel, as priest, is neglecting the spiritual care of his flock; notably, the "shepherd" Abel seems to have no business with his flock during the play, spending his time exclusively in repeatedly exhorting Cain to tithe. The implication echoes accusations made against the medieval priesthood; the author of *The Order of Priesthood* states that priests seek "here owene worldly honour & wynnynge more than goddis, & helthe of mennys soulis; for thei traueilen fast aboute here owene worldly honour and lucre . . . , but of goddis worschipe & helthe of cristenis soulis chargen thei ful litel" (171–2). Cain's implication is raised again during their argument over his tithe. As Abel exhorts him to give more generously, Cain says, "How that I tend, rek the neuer a deill,/ Bot tend thi skabbid shepe wele" (ll. 249–50). Cain's pun specifically connects the generousity of his "tend," or tithe, with the quality of Abel's "tend," or care, for his flock; this is a curious

connection to make unless one takes into account the extremely common assertion that tithes should be given only to priests who actually perform their
duties conscientiously. Cain makes the same connection, once more with reference to a neglected and diseased flock, when Abel yet again exhorts him to
give more: "Bot change thi conscience, as I do myn—/ Yit teynd thou not thi
mesel swine?" (ll. 265–6) Cain's answer is the typical response of the medieval
laity to the priest's demand for tithe, as we see in *De Officio Pastorali*: "cristen-
men of this ground thenken that pariyshens shulden drawe fro presouns of-
feringis & dymes [tithes] & othere godis whanne they faylen opynly in ther
offiss" (Matthew 418).

The exchange between the two brothers, therefore, is constructed so as
to direct festive hostility and scorn towards orthodox religious obligation and
to draw empathy to Cain's complaints, even if the audience does not fully embrace him in his role as Lord of Misrule. Thus when Abel is murdered, the
deed is not an unthinkable one. Abel's self-righteousness is inevitably joined
to the tithe and to the oppressive authority of the Church. Cain's murder of
Abel is brother to the audience's own deep anger and unrest, and even though
an audience might celebrate Cain's damnation, they could also enjoy the ritual death of Abel. As the representative of unpopular religious obligation,
Abel is a killjoy, a nag, a shrew to be overthrown with festive abuse. After Cain
kills him, he says, "So, lig down ther and take thi rest;/ Thus shall shrewes be
chastysed best" (ll. 328–9). Hanks writes,

> Cain, to be sure, is a villain, but the audience must have seen him as the
> villain we all carry under our skins. Abel's constant virtue *is* irritating, the
> tithe *is* onerous, crops *do* fail and lead farmers to question providence.
> Cain, then, is almost as much Everyman as murderer. (52)

Cain is, of course, damned for his fratricide, thus completing the orthodox
theme, but this is also the expected conclusion of a Lord of Misrule's role, one
that does little to diminish the subversive impact of his accusations against orthodox religious obligation.

Moreover, God's condemnation of Cain, while less than impressive, leads
to a comprehensive usurpation and a key turning point in the play. Damned by
Deus, Cain affects a complete role reversal, claiming fraudulently and comically
the role of official authority. Like a Boy Bishop or Comic King, he is the least
suited for the claim, having both denounced authority and rebelled against it. It
is a profoundly festive reversal, one that changes both Cain's character and the
audience's reaction to him. Indeed, it is a mistake to see Cain's role before the
murder in the same light as his actions after. For one, as Helterman has argued,

any sympathy felt by the audience during the dispute over the tithe surely dimin- ishes upon Cain's murder of Abel and subsequent damnation. This shift is obvi- ous in Pikeharnes' shocked reaction when he returns to the stage. Cain has done the unthinkable, especially in his defiance of God; he has become a true villain rather than merely a disgruntled tither, and Pikeharnes quickly distances himself and begins to mock his fraud. More significantly, however, after killing his brother, Cain assumes the mantle of authority once worn by Abel and becomes, instead of the voice of rebellious protest, the target of it. Such reversal seems con- tradictory, but it is a natural part of festive observance; the old order overthrows the new, only to assume the forms and practices of the old in burlesque form.

The most apparent aspect of this usurpation and role reversal is Cain's perversion of God's condemnation. Stevens and Cawley note, "God's refusal to allow the murderer himself to be murdered in punishment for his crime (373–5) is twisted by Cain into a royal proclamation of pardon" (446). Brockman notes that contemporary royal pardons led to notorious abuses, so much so that the issue was a frequent and hotly debated topic in fourteenth century parliaments and was a common subject for contemporary writers (701–704). Indeed, Brockman writes, "the royal prerogative of pardon was one of the most widely known and deeply resented aspects of the administra- tion of justice in late medieval England" (701). Cain's claim of the pardon, as well as his issuing a series of commands "in the kyngys nayme" (l. 421), per- verts God's judgment to assume the direct power of royal prerogative, specif- ically an element of that power resented by the audience. With this fraudulent assertion of authority, Cain thus shifts from the initiator to the object of par- ody and festive abuse, as we see in Pikeharnes's mockery:

> *Caym:* I commaund you in the kyngys nayme
> *Garcio:* And in my masteres, fals Cayme.
> *Caym:* That no man at thame fynd fawt ne blame,
> *Garcio:* Yey, cold rost is at my masteres hame.
> *Caym:* Nowther with hym nor with his knafe,
> *Garcio:* What! I hope my master rafe
> *Caym:* For thay ar trew full manyfold.
> *Garcio:* My master suppys no coyle bot cold.
> *Caym:* The kyng wrytys you vntill,
> *Garcio:* Yit ete I neuer half my fill.
> *Caym:* The king will that thay be safe.
> *Garcio:* Yey, a draght of drynke fayne wolde I hayfe. (ll. 421–32)

Cain asserts his authority in the king's name, but Pikeharnes undermines that authority between every breath.

However, Cain's and Pikeharnes's pronouncements also signal a reversal of religious roles. Where before Cain scorned the act of sacrifice and the paying of tithe, he now performs a mock mass over the body of Abel and demands payment, upon the completion of the consecration, from the audience. As Cain utters commands, Pikeharnes changes the subject with reference to food, such as "cold rost" and "a draft of drynke" (ll. 424, 432). As Cain continues, he says, "My stomak is redy to receyfe" (ll. 434). This focus upon eating seems unusual in the aftermath of a homicide, and odd as part of a declaration of pardon, but it fits the festive pattern. The feast is the center of the festive world and consonant with the actions of misrule. Yet the feasting references are also a dark parody of the Eucharist. At the end of his feasting references, Pikeharnes says, "Now old and yong, or that ye weynd, / The sam blissyng withoutten end" (l. 446-7). The second phrase, "blissyng withoutten end," is, as Stevens and Cawley point out, a variation on the phrase "at the end of the Consecration of the Mass," (447). Cain gives the exact translation a few lines further, at the end of the play: "Warld withoutten end" (l. 468). Thus, the feast images themselves actually compose a deliberate parody of the Mass, connecting Cain with the orthodox Church. As noted previously, Abel uses almost the same words as Pikeharnes when he first urges Cain to sacrifice. If they sacrifice, Abel says, "Then blis withoutten end / Get we for oure seruyce" (ll. 83–4). Pikeharnes repeats the same words, "blissyng withoutten end," used originally in reference to the rewards of sacrifice, after Cain has murdered Abel. The echoes connect the sacrifice, the murder, and the parody together. Cain's sacrifice, or "seruyce," is his murder of Abel, and the host of the parodic Mass is none other than the victim of Cain's sacrificial service, the still unburied body of Abel. Helterman notes this textual connection between Abel and the sacrifice:

> When Garcio mocks, 'My stomak is redy to receyfe' (432), he becomes for Cain the equivalent of the sacrificial altar, which also was ready to accept Cain's offering. The phrase recalls Cain's irate wish that Abel were the altar for his foul sacrifice: 'I wold that it were in thi throte/ Fyr, and shefe, and ich a sprote' (289–90). The pair even conceive of Abel's death in terms of food imagery. Since neither of them understands anything of the spiritual, the joking 'yey, cold rost is at my masteres hame' (422) fit the dead body precisely. (46)

It follows that if Abel is repeatedly connected with the sacrifice and at the same time with food, and if this all takes place within the context of a mock mass, then Abel's body, the sacrificial "cold rost," is also a parody of the host. In thus engaging in a mock religious service, Cain has usurped in burlesque

form the role of the Church once symbolized by his murdered brother, a reversal typical of festive culture.

The parody seems odd, connecting, as it does, the service of the Church
with the damned Cain, a connection made even more explicit with admission
of Cain's thralldom to Satan as he ends the play with another parody of the
end of the Mass:

> Now fayre well, fellows all,
> For I must nedys weynd,
> And to the dwill be thrall,
> Warld withoutten end; . . . (ll. 465–8)

The connection between Cain, Satan, and religious order is again emphasized
through puns when Cain says, speaking still of his allegiance to the "dwill,"
"Ordand ther is my stall" (l. 469). On a surface level, Cain is admitting his
place is reserved in hell, but his words, "ordand" and "stall," also carry religious connotation, ordination being the mark of priesthood, and a stall being
the station of a priest's worship.

Cain's mock priestly role, one clearly associated with usurpation and satanic evil, is confusing within an orthodox Christian matrix, but it closely parallels the common accusation made by medieval anti-clerical writers that
corrupt clergy are satanic usurpers and the spiritual descendants of Cain . For
example, one contemporary tract, suggestively entitled "Hou sathanas & his
prestis & his feyned religious casten bi thre cursed heresies to distroie alle
good lyuynge & mayntene alle manere of synne," accuses the ecclesiastical hierarchy of being servants of Satan who aim to usurp the true priesthood
(Matthew 264–74). Another, helpfully entitled "Hou sathanas & his children
turnen werkis of mercy vpsodom & disceyuen men ther-inne & in here fyue
wittis," explicitly develops festive imagery in its description of the deliberate
reversals of Christian living by the clergy (Matthew 210–18). This tract refers
specifically to the connection between the Cain legend and the worldly
Church (Caym's Castel), charging that the satanic clergy spend their time "for
to gete worldly muk by false disceitis & carien it home to caymes castelis"
(Matthew 211). Indeed, the Caym's Castel references common in anti-clerical literature make explicit the association between a damned Cain, a corrupt
Church, and the reversal or usurpation of the priestly role, associations that
are developed through festive forms in *Mactacio Abel.*

However, the parody thus links Cain with the very structure of authority he has so railed against and, in the murder of Abel, overthrown earlier in
the play. Cain, the profane but empathetic rebel at the beginning of the drama
assumes a new role and becomes the pompous and mocked authority figure

of the ending. In this way, the complaints over the tithe and clerical corruption so convincingly put forth by Cain before the murder of Abel are ironically linked with Cain's satanic mock priesthood. As he comes to the end of his parodic mass, Cain instructs Pikeharnes to take an offering from the audience: "Byd euery man theym pleasse to pay" (440). It is a futile attempt, doomed, like the Pardoner's attempt to sell pardons to Harry Bailey, by the audience's knowledge of Cain's falsity, and by the very force of Cain's earlier rhetoric. Like Chaucer's Pardoner, Cain has convincingly laid out the argument against religious offerings for corrupt clergy; like the Pardoner, he can only sputter furiously when his request is dismissively mocked by those who know his true nature.

The festive components of the play thus allow for a fundamental reinterpretation of the significance of the conventional plot. Abel is still slain, and Cain is still damned, but the didactic meaning is muted, if not lost. Comic mockery transforms Abel from a righteous victim into a nagging symbol of deeply resented religious obligation, a shepherd away from his flock whose only apparent concerns are a generous tithe. Seen through the prism of festive forms, his death becomes as much a ritual uncrowning as a homicide . Festive patterns of disorder, reversal, and parody allow Cain initially to undermine religious obligation and later, as a condemned usurper, to claim and discredit it even further. Cain remains an evil character, but his role as a Lord of Misrule shifts the significance of his evil, and the audience is left with a dramatic illustration of Caym's Castel. By destabilizing the conventional significance, festive elements thus allow criticism of Church worldliness within an ostensibly Christian play, a trend we will see continued in the *Processus Noe*.

Chapter Four
The Shrewish Bride of Christ

In the Noah play, the Wakefield Master chooses another subject that is particularly resonant with festive culture. Structurally speaking, the story of Noah and the flood matches festive cyclic patterns exactly: order is interrupted by deliberate chaos, overthrow, and death; when the flood waters recede, order is reestablished and life returns. The flood is also regenerative; a world suffering from decay and corruption is wiped clean through death to make room for revitalized life. Indeed, flooding and immersion in water was a common theme in pagan rituals and remained a popular element of many festive observances.[1] Chambers notes the importance of bathing, sprinkling, and dunking in festival customs both ancient and modern. He observes that many such customs are

> charms designed to influence the weather, and to secure the proper alternation of moisture and warmth which is needed alike for the growth and ripening of the crops. . . . To achieve rain, water must be splashed about, or some other characteristic of a storm or shower must be reproduced. (121)

Perhaps the most universal of these customs is ritualized dunking. Chambers notes the popularity of this particular observance among Western European cultures:

> The image or bough which represents the fertilization spirit is solemnly dipped in or drenched with water. Here is the explanation of the ceremonial bathing of the goddess Nerthus recorded by Tacitus. It has its parallels in the dipping of the images of saints in the feast-day processions of many Catholic villages, and in the buckets of water sometimes thrown over May-pole or harvest-May. (122)

Another form of festive dunking expressed itself as a type of ritual violence. Chambers writes that most forms were either "horse-play or else a rough-and-ready form of punishment for offences, real or imaginary, against the rustic code of conduct. The churl who will not stop working or will not wear green on the feast-day must be 'ducked'" (122). In other words, dunking and sprinkling is on many levels an expression of festive celebration. The importance of water in festive celebrations is also evident in the veneration of holy wells, themselves a clear pagan survival. Chambers writes that

> the efficacy of some wells is greatest on particular days, such as Easter or the first three Sundays in May. And in many places the wells, whether ordinarily held 'holy' or not, take an important place in the ceremonies of the village festival. The 'gospel wells' of the Rogation processions, and the well to which the 'Bezant' procession goes at Shaftesbury are cases in point; while in Derbyshire the 'well-dressings' correspond to the 'wakes,' 'rushbearings,' and 'Mayings' of other districts. (124)

Given this fondness for baptism, dunking, sprinkling, and well-veneration in festive celebrations, the appeal of a flood story which emphasizes cyclical regeneration to a festive culture is self-apparent. As with the *Mactacio Abel,* the Wakefield Master has chosen here to revise a story with inherent festive significance.

As recorded in the scriptures, however, and particularly as interpreted within the orthodox Judeo-Christian tradition, the Noah story assumes a distinctly different meaning. Elements which can be interpreted as festive or pagan are marginalized, and the story is cast in orthodox patterns. For example, the Christian version is linear, a symbol of salvation history. Rather than emphasizing the cyclic, as genetic cousins of the Noah tale do, the story stresses the uniqeness and singularity of the flood. Of particular import here is the rainbow and the promise it symbolizes. In Genesis, God promises never to bring another flood, and as a symbol of this promise, He places a rainbow in the sky. Therefore, the flood is a one-time event, with a beginning, middle, and end, and it will never again be duplicated. Instead of one cycle in a cyclic pattern, it is an independent, completed, linear story.

In addition, the flood has little or no regenerative meaning; it is pure damnation, a just punishment for a sinful population, the eventual result of constantly ignoring the timeless laws of God. In the medieval typological tradition, it is a type for the final doom; the earth is purified, and the unbelievers are destroyed, while believers are saved through provident intervention. More importantly, Noah is a type of Christ, providing for the coming doom in a disbelieving and recalcitrant world, and serving as the vehicle of God's mercy. The ark itself is often a type of the Church, the protective structure by which humanity is saved from destruction. John Gardner writes of this typology, "Noah is a type or presignification of Christ; the ark is a type of the

church; the flood adumbrates the Last Judgment and at the same time looks
back to the fall" (43).

The Wakefield Master makes substantial use of this orthodox typology.
As he did in *Mactacio Abel* and will do again in the later plays, he harnesses
orthodox typology for the significance it holds for the audience, and he art-
fully enhances this typology to ever more creative levels. Scholars have recognized the liberal use of types in the play. Martin Stevens and A. C. Cawley
echo Gardner as they write, "the play enacts the allegorical meaning of the
flood as a type of Baptism and the Ark as a type of the Church, which symbolically brings sinners like Noah's Uxor to redemption" (447). Gardner, in
particular, has completed a thorough study of the typological significance of
this play, and I will draw much from Gardner's work here.

However, despite the typological tradition and the seemingly obvious
typological references, reading the *Processus Noe* typologically has always been
hazardous. For example, if Noah is a type of Christ, then Uxor, the bride of
Noah / Christ can logically be inferred to be the Church. Yet Uxor's peevish
disobedience seems inappropriate for the actions of the Church, and the violent behavior of Noah seems equally unsavory as a representation of Christ.
Since the burlesque elements of the play interfere with and alter the overall
lessons that can be drawn from the typology, previous scholars have limited
the typological import to the beginning and end of the play and rationalized
away apparent thematic failures or contradictions. Stevens and Cawley write,

> The Wakefield Noah, while portrayed as a type of Christ . . . is also un-
> usually boisterous and belligerent. In other cycle plays, particularly those
> of York and Chester, Noah is portrayed as the henpecked and relatively
> passive victim of a shrewish wife. The Wakefield Noah, in contrast, not
> only beats his wife but also offers the first blow. The playwright thus hu-
> manizes the patriarch and provides dramatic contrast between the dis-
> cord of everyday life and the harmony in a divinely ordered world.
> Typologically, Noah can be seen not only as a Christ figure but also as a
> fallen man (reminding us of Adam) who must be cleansed by the water
> of baptism before he can be saved. (447)

Interpreting Noah as typic of both Christ and sinner seems contradictory,
however, especially since Christ was supposedly without sin. Gardner has the
same difficulties reconciling the obvious typology with Noah's actions.
Despite listing multiple typological references to Noah as Christ, he writes,

> The Wakefield poet's method is not simple allegory in which Noah equals
> Christ. Noah is a man, at once typic of Christ and, in his mere humanness,

comically unlike the Savior he foreshadows. Whereas Christ is omnipotent
lord of His bride, the church or fellowship of Christians, Noah shudders
to think what his wife will say and do to him when he tells her he has to
build an ark. (43–4)

Since typological interpretation threatens to deviate from orthodox doctrine,
especially in the combative relationship between Noah, the type of Christ,
and Uxor, his bride, the significance of Noah's role is given a split personality,
and his wife's potential as a type is utterly dismissed.

Yet the typology in the *Processus Noe* does in fact provide a coherent message when it is applied without consideration to orthodox doctrine. Indeed,
beyond the orthodox circles of the official Church, many people would have
considered Uxor to be an accurate symbol of the medieval Church, and
Noah's violence an apt vision of divine retribution.[2] I propose we read Uxor's
rebellion as symbolic of ecclesiastical rebellion. If Uxor, as the bride of Noah
/ Christ, represents a rebellious Church, then the anger of Noah / Christ
seems typologically justified. In fact, the typology is especially meaningful in
light of the overwhelming festive flavor of the play and the effect that the festive forms have upon audience expectations of renewal and change. While he
has maintained much of the traditional typology, the Wakefield Master has
substantially changed the structure and content of the orthodox version of the
Noah story, and these changes have recast the flood into a cyclical form which
reflects the values of a festive, regenerative world view. The flood becomes a
powerful metaphor for change and revitalization, and the Wakefield Master's
use of traditional typology within this context signifies a ritual cleansing and
renewal of a rebellious Church hierarchy.

When the Wakefield Master wrote *Processus Noe,* he made three major
changes (along with one minor but significant one) from his biblical and contemporary sources. First, he let Noe review the history of the world to that
point and, in effect, call down the wrath of God. Second, he made Noe's wife
stronger, cheekier, and more independent. Third, he added a shocking
amount of chaos and spousal violence. Each feature is a distinctly festive one.
Noe's judgment of the earth establishes a cyclical pattern of human sin and divine punishment. Noe's wife introduces central festive themes of usurpation
and overthrow, themes that alter the significance of conventional Noah typology. The violence and chaos create a general atmosphere of festive license and
disorder and contribute to the patterns of overthrow and renewal. Taken individually, each change causes a significant shift in the aesthetic development
of the play. However, as interlocking festive elements, they also function together to shape the Noah story into a festive cycle of renewal. Those elements

which are?

or medieval
commonplace.

that are old, stale, or corrupt, are washed away by the destructive flood and replaced with symbols of change and vitality. With these few changes, the Wakefield Master creates in the tale a powerful sense of regeneration and re-birth in the face of decay and corruption.

He begins by reemphasizing the cyclic and regenerative nature of the story. In the *Processus Noe,* both the death and rebirth of God's creation and the cyclical nature of historic events are vividly emphasized. Noe opens the play with an unusual 104 line review of the history of creation. This review is unique to the Wakefield play. In fact, it is curiously redundant in a cycle play. All previous biblical and ecclesiastical history would just have been performed in the preceding cycle plays, and, therefore, a recitation here is redundant. This review stresses the theme of regeneration in two ways, however. First, the recitation serves to add a sense of life span to the entire creation. Josie Campbell notes that the "prayer is a recapitulation of the history of mankind, . . . and Noah's story is that of a second creation" ("Idea of Order" 76). Creation has gone through birth, loss of innocence, and maturity. The corruption of humanity signals old age and sets up a natural movement towards flood and death. The flood kills, but it also prepares the way for rebirth and a new, revitalized creation by wiping away the corruption of sin. After the flood, Noe says,

> Behald on this greyn!
> Nowder cart ne plogh
> Is left, as I weyn,
> Nowder tre then bogh,
> Ne other thyng,
> Bot all is away;
> Many castels, I say,
> Grete townes of aray,
> Flitt has this flowyng. (ll. 772–80)

A fertile and natural world, "this greyn," has replaced the signs of social development, the "Cart" and "plogh," "castels," and "Grete townes of aray." Specifically, the two are related by the main event of the play, the destructive flood. Stress is not placed upon the ruin of civilization and the tragic loss of life. Rather, the emphasis is upon the wonder of the new, green, regenerated world, a world created through the death of the old. Now that the earth is a clean slate, growth and hope are renewed. Within the context of the life of creation, the flood becomes more of a festive, regenerative event than a symbol of doom.

In addition, the recitation of previous biblical events establishes a clearly cyclical pattern to the history of creation. It lists a series of biblical and apocryphal stories which all display the pattern of rising and falling action, a pattern which, as John Gardner points out, is centered around the notions of order and chaos (39–43). Placed back-to-back as they are in Noah's speech, the individual stories merge into a cyclical movement. Specifically, they stress the tendency of God's creation to fall away from his will, thus necessitating divine punishment and renewal. Lucifer and his angels are created to serve God in heaven (generation and order). They rebel against God and are cast into hell (chaos and destruction). Adam and Eve are then created to serve God in Eden (regeneration and order). They disobey and are cast out into the world (chaos and destruction). The pattern becomes almost seasonal in its regularity (generation / order / chaos / destruction / regeneration / order / chaos / destruction / etc.), and Noah's story is firmly placed within, and as a part of, the cycle. After Adam's fall, God established worldly authority (regeneration and order), but humanity has rejected God's laws (chaos), and God will now destroy human corruption in the flood (destruction) and start over with Noah's family (regeneration).

The Wakefield Master also introduces usurpation and reversal to the Noah story. Neither the biblical version nor contemporary renderings focus so intensely on usurpation. In the *Processus Noe,* however, there are two clear usurpations. When Noe lists the sins of man, condemns man, and predicts the coming judgment of man, he highlights mankind's rebellion against God's authority. Noe says of humanity,

> Bot now before his sight
> Euery liffyng leyde,
> Most party day and nyght,
> Syn in word and dede
> Full bold:
> Som in pride, ire, and enuy,
> Som in couetous and glotyny,
> Som in sloth and lechery,
> And other wise manyfold.
> Therfor I drede lest God
> On vs will take veniance,
> For syn is now alod,
> Without any repentance. (ll. 70–82)

When Deus appears, he repeats and agrees with everything Noah has just said, specifically echoing Noe's words:

> And now in grete reprufe
> Full low ligys he,
> In erth hymself to stuf
> With syn that displeasse me
> Most of all.

Veniance will I take
In erth for syn sake; (ll. 122–28).

By confirming Noe's earlier comments, Deus once more places particular
stress on human rebellion and on the need for punishment and renewal.

Humanity's usurpation of God's authority is paralleled by Uxor's
usurpation of Noe's. Kolve notes this reversal when he says, "God's great
world is turned upside down just as is man's little world, and for the same reason: proper *maistrye* has been destroyed" (150). The disobedience of Noah's
wife was a standard tradition, as was her blow to Noah's noggin (Beadle and
King 7), but the Towneley Uxor is a far stronger character than contemporary
examples. Noe cannot uphold his authority over her; she stubbornly resists all
of his attempts to master her. When he tries to reprove her with threats of
punishment, she responds in kind: "By my thryft, if thou smyte, / I shal turn
the untill" (ll. 315–6). When he hits her, she hits him back. All of this is a clear
reversal of roles. In most versions of the story, Noe calmly reasons with his
wife while she babbles on and finally strikes him. This pattern of an unreasonable, physically abusive, shrewish wife and a victimized, peace-seeking husband is also typical of other medieval drama contemporary with the play. In
the *Processus Noe*, however, the wife is dismissive and aloof, and Noe is the one
who becomes frustrated by her lack of obedience. This pattern clearly parallel's humanity's stubborn rejection of God's commandments, emphasized in
the beginning of the play. Uxor repeatedly voices her desire to escape Noe's
mastery and rule her own destiny, even when this is not in her best interests.
As the flood waters rise and Noe urges her to board the ark, she stubbornly rejects any advice: "Now will I downe set me; / Yit reede I no man let me, / For
drede of a knok" (ll. 492–4). Reversal and usurpation continue in the ark.
Spousal violence illustrates this principle, but so too does the scene in which
Uxor sits on Noe while telling him to get off of her. While such self-will may
not appear to be unusual to modern audiences, it is, in the medieval Christian
view, a clear usurpation of the natural order. Only when Uxor submits to
Noe's authority, at which point the order of the world is restored and the seven
planets are again aligned, do Noe and his wife resume their traditional roles.

Violence is also a notable part of the *Processus Noe*. Such violence, especially at this level, was not a traditional part of the Noah story. Noah's wife hits
him in some versions, but in the York and Chester plays, she only hits him
once, and it is only a box on the ear. In the *Processus Noe*, however, the frequency and severity of the violence are drastically increased. When Noe first
encounters his wife, he strikes her three times, and she strikes him back three
times. Hans-Jürgen Diller recognizes the increased realism of the Wakefield

Master's portrayal of human relations (245–59), but this violence goes beyond realism to develop its own symbolic value and play a pivotal role in the
development of dramatic tensions. For example, the first fight coincides with
and helps to dramatize Uxor's usurpation of Noe's authority; in this sense, it
serves the same purpose as ritualized violence in folk culture. It is also symbolic, as Kolve points out, of the greater violence God is about to inflict upon
the world (146–47), the heart of the festive uncrowning.

Noe's and his wife's second dust-up, when they are in the ark, is equally disturbing. This violence also serves a festive purpose by coinciding with and stressing both the reversal of roles and the chaos of the world's "death." Furthermore,
as is evident in the speech of Noe and his wife, the violence is particularly exaggerated, and the accompanying dialogue contains anatomical reference:

> *Noe:* In this hast let us ho,
> For my bak is near in two.
> *Vxor:* And I am bet so blo
> That I may not thryfe. (ll. 595–8)

As we have noted, mock festive beatings were exaggerated as outlandishly as
possible, and because they represented the death of a physical body, they were
usually accompanied by specific anatomical references. Such reference is apparent in the threats exchanged between Noe and Uxor. When Uxor antago-
nizes Noe early in the play, Noe says "Haue at the, Gill! / Apon the bone shal
it byte" (ll. 318–19). Later, he threatens, "Thi hede shall I breke!" (l. 559). As
his anger grows, he says, "I shall bete the bak and bone, / And breke all in sonder" (ll. 588–9). The type of exaggerated harm from comic violence that we
see in *Processus Noe* is especially characteristic of folk and festive culture.

The *Processus Noe* also substantially increases the level of chaos evident in
the flood. In Genesis, Noah and his family ride out the flood secure in the
knowledge of God's promise and unbothered by the mayhem around them.
The other cycle plays portray equally peaceful passages for Noah and his family.
The characters typically recite lines which indicate their secure trust of God's divine order. The journey of the Towneley Noe, however, is anything but peaceful. The worst spousal violence happens during the flood, parallel to the ritual
death of the earth, and the violence is particularly chaotic and disturbing, as can
be seen in the desperation of this dialogue, spoken as Noe and Uxor fight:

> *Vxor:* Out, alas, I am gone!
> Oute apon the, mans wonder!
> *Noe:* Se how she can grone,
> And I lig vnder! (ll.590–93)

In addition, Noe and his wife are frequently afraid for their safety during the flood, as the following piece of dialogue demonstrates:

> *Noe:* This is a grete flood,
> Wife, take hede.
> *Vxor:* So me thoght, as I strode.
> We are in grete drede;
> Thise wawghes ar so wode.
> *Noe:* Help, God, in this nede!
> . . .
> *Vxor:* This is a perlous case.
> Help, God, when we call! (ll. 612–17,623–4)

In fact, the entire universe has dissolved into chaos. Kolve notes that Noe has added to the Vulgate account of open cataracts the information that "The seven planets have left their places in the sky; all is chaos and lack of order" (150). Gardner notes that such disorder is almost exclusive to the central flood section, whereas the beginning and ending of the play are marked by harmony and planetary order (41–47). In other words, the Wakefield master specifically increases the overall sense of chaos connected with the flood beyond scriptural or contemporary treatments of the story.

Critics have long noted the contrasting effects or duality of the play. It opens in relative peacefulness and harmony; it then sinks into chaos and violence, both through the flood and chaos in the world and in the conflict between Noe and his wife, and it finally returns again to peace and harmony.[3] Yet this so-called "duality" is in fact part of a clearly cyclical pattern; several critics have pointed out that the chaos functions as an illustration of the decay of God's ordered world (Campbell 76). Fewer critics stress the other half of the equation, the regeneration illustrated by the return of order and the establishment of a previously missing marital accord. When the flood subsides, order and harmony have returned to Noe's and his wife's relationship as well as to the natural world. Kolve points out that with "the restoration of domestic order and degree, the seven planets again find their place in the universal order, and man and the universe move together toward the rightness of new beginnings" (150). This pattern of emphasizing the chaos and disorder of the flood before a return to order serves to further align the play with festive themes of renewal. The flood becomes a massive overthrow of all order, but that overthrow is temporary and is soon followed by a return to proper order.[4] The introduction of these festive elements, therefore, namely the unruly wife, the reversals, the chaos, and the violence, have in fact completely reworked the atmosphere of the play so that it structurally and thematically projects a *which are?*

cycle of death and seasonal renewal. Furthermore, the disruptive festive chaos of the play is temporally connected with the inherently festive element of the story, the flood.

In addition to the major changes noted above, the Wakefield Master makes one additional minor, but significant, change. The Wakefield *Processus Noe* leaves out all mention of the rainbow and of God's promise not to repeat the flood. All other cycle play treatments of this story finish with a sustained emphasis upon the rainbow. The Wakefield deletion of this central symbol is thus a major departure from biblical and contemporary sources. Without the symbolic rainbow, the traditional sense of the singularity of the flood is lost in this play; the destruction represented by the flood becomes cyclical in nature rather than a one-time catastrophe. In this respect, the *Processus Noe* mirrors the structure of festive regeneration rituals and suggests that the action in the play is part of a cyclical renewal of the relationship between God and his creation. With the major changes initiated by the Wakefield Master, *Processus Noe* develops overall structural, linguistic, and symbolic patterns clearly parallel to and reminiscent of festive regeneration rituals. That which is sickly is renewed, and that which is corrupt is cleansed. However, this pattern of decay and renewal is not simply a random expression of festive culture. It is clearly focused on the central relationship in the play; the most obvious renewal in the story occurs in the relationship between Noe and his wife.

see above

Noe's and Uxor's relationship is the most striking part of *Processus Noe;* in fact, it is the element most mentioned by critics of the play. Their relationship stands out for its uniqueness, humor, and sheer dramatic force. The play could be titled "Noah and His Wife" without misrepresentation. Furthermore, as we have seen, this relationship develops parallel to the other major movements in the play and reflects, in miniature, the great and catastrophic changes happening in the world beyond Noe's ark. Therefore, any analysis of the overall significance of the play and the ritual of regeneration must first consider the significance of the relationship between Noe and his wife.

On a surface level, Noe's and Uxor represent the tensions existing between husband and wife in medieval society. Such gender interaction is a popular topic in contemporary texts, as we see in "The Wife of Bath's Tale," and the Wakefield Master explores it again in *Secunda Pastorum.* The bitter contention and fighting is also traditional, especially within a festive context. As I have noted, the beatings exchanged by the pair fulfill the role of ritual festive violence, and the constant bickering matches festive patterns of reversal. On an immediate level, therefore, the central conflict between Noe and Uxor is a traditional dramatization of gender conflict, and the festive reversals and violence initiated by the conflict are stock elements which the audience would have enjoyed. Yet, as with

most of the Wakefield Master's plays, the entertaining comic action has second-
ary significance, and the characters of Noe and Uxor represent more than is immediately apparent.

As noted above, the Wakefield Master casts Noe as a type of Christ.
Such typology is not unusual; Noe is traditionally interpreted as Christ in orthodox Christian exegesis, and critics have noticed this typology in the
Wakefield Noe. In his chapter, "Christology in the Noah," John Gardner
traces the elaborate use of typology in the Noah tale by contemporary authors
such as Richard Rolle and the Pearl Poet and ancient authors such as
Augustine, concluding that the typology of Noe as Christ is conventional and
commonplace (43). Frederick S. Holton examines in detail the particulars of
the typology in the play, arguing that "the [Towneley] *Noah* has a clearly
Christological emphasis, looking forward to the Incarnation" (57).[5]

If, as Gardner, Stevens, Cawley, and Holton argue, Noe is a type of Christ
and the ark is a type of Christ's sacrifice through which humanity is redeemed,
then Uxor, the wife saved by the ark, is also a type of the Church, the bride of
Christ redeemed by Christ's sacrifice. The Wakefield Master drops many hints
that suggest this is so. In her initial conversation with Noe, while speaking of
"husbandys," Uxor says, "I haue oone, bi Mary, / That lowsyd me of my bandys!"
(ll. 301–2). On a surface level, the statement is rather odd; it seems to be the conventional reference to Christ, the one who has freed Christians from their bonds
of sin, and this is how critics have generally interpreted it. As Gardner points out,
this statement "is simply an oath of sorts, . . . but the line means also 'I have one
[a husband or bridegroom] by Mary [he is the son of Mary] who has freed me
from my bonds [death]'" (45). Notably, Uxor says this as she first describes her
relationship with her husband, Noe, suggesting an early typological connection
between Noe and Christ; however, this reference within the context of Noe and
Uxor's marital relationship also typologically connects Uxor with the bride of
Christ, or the Church. While Uxor may not match our concept of the ideal, even
ethereal, bride of Christ, the housewife is a commonly used metaphor for the
Church. For example, the anonymous author of *Tractatus de Regibus* writes,
"God seis that holy chirche is a gode howswife" (Hudson 128). Indeed, Uxor's
words frequently allow alternate readings that suggest the relationship between
Christ and the Church. When Noe initially greets her, for example, she responds
to him angrily:

> Where has thou thus long be?
> To dede may we dryfe,
> Or lif, for the,
> For want.
> When we swete or swynk,

> Thou dos what thou thynk;
> Yit of mete and of drynk
> Haue we veray skant. (ll. 276–86)

Gardner notes that the lines suggest humanity's relationship with Christ and his crucifixion:

> Uxor's "where has thou thus long be?" plays on the idea of the long wait of man for the Redeemer. It is indeed "for the"(because of Thee) that "To dede may we dryfe, or lif." Uxor's "mete" and "drynk" ironically suggest the bread and wine, body and blood, traditionally associated not only with the Mass but also with the celestial banquet (cf. *Pearl,* line 1064). (44)

More broadly, the "swete" and "swynk" of which the wife complains is a traditionally accepted symbol of mankind's fall, as Adam and Eve are expelled from the Garden of Eden. Notably, the play has begun with a long and detailed review of the sins of mankind. Fallen humanity must live by "swete or swynk," but God promises that a savior will come to redeem mankind. Moreover, the "mete" and "drynk," are unavailable to Uxor at this point, just as the Eucharist that signals salvation is unavailable to mankind before Christ's sacrifice. Thus, before Noe's building of the ark, Noe's wife speaks to him in language highly suggestive of both the lost state of humanity before Christ's crucifixion and of the eucharistic symbols of redemption that result from Christ's crucifixion. When Noe immediately responds with, "Wife, we ar hard sted / With tythyngys new." (ll. 287–8), his words suggest the new covenant of Christ's redemption, or as Gardner interprets it, "New Tidings, the Gospel" (45).

Noe's departure to build the ark and his return afterwards also parallel the events before and after Christ's Crucifixion and resurrection. As he leaves, Noe says,

> We! Farewell, lo;
> Bot wife,
> Pray for me beselé
> To eft I com unto the. (ll. 346–9)

Noe's words recall Christ's attitude among his disciples before the crucifixion and his words in the Garden of Gethsemane. As he begins to build the ark, Noe drops several typologically significant puns that suggest the crucifixion. He says, for instance,

> To begyn of this tree,
> My bonys will I bend;

> I traw from the Trynyté
> Socoure will be send. (ll 365–8)

The passage could have been drawn directly from Christ's passion. Gardner notes that these lines parallel "Christ 'bent' on the cross" (46). Interestingly, most of the mystery cycle representations of the crucifixion, including the Towneley *Processus Crucis,* emphasize in detail the agonizing stretching and bending of Christ to fit the cross. As Noe begins to shape the wood of the ark, a vehicle of salvation, he speaks of bones being bent upon a tree, which evokes images of Christ's crucifixion, another means of salvation. In addition, Noe's call for succor from the trinity echoes Christ's cries for heavenly help from the cross. Further, as Noe removes his gown for better movement ("Now my gowne will I cast, / And wyrk in my cote" [ll. 378–9]), he evokes the image of the soldiers casting lots for Christ's gown, another popular staple in mystery cycle representations of the crucifixion. Holton finds another parallel with the crucifixion in the image of Noe casting his gown: "In the Old English Dream of the Rood, Christ strips before ascending the cross, and in early Judaeo-Christian legends of the ascent of the soul, a change in garments—trading earthly clothes for heavenly—is necessary before the soul may enter the highest heaven" (62). Noe also places stress upon the driving of nails into the wood[6]:

> To drife ich a nayll
> Will I not forsake.
> This gere may neuer fayll,
> That dar I vndertake
> Onone.
> This is a nobull gyn:
> Thise nayles so thay ryn
> Thoro, more and myn,
> Thise bordys ichon. (ll. 395–403)

The particulars of nailing Christ to the cross, along with the stretching of his body, is yet another important and emphasized part of the mystery cycle crucifixions. Thus, Noe's building of the ark, which traditionally typifies Christ's incarnation and sacrifice, repeatedly connects him with Christ and the crucifixion. Noe's running monologue is also appropriate to Christ's agony on the cross. After "cast"ing his "gowne," Noe complains of fatigue like a man near death:

> A! my bak, I traw, will brast!
> This is a sory note!
> Hit is wonder that I last,
> Sich an old dote,
> All dold,

> To begyn sich a wark.
> My bonys are so stark:
> No wonder if thay wark,
> For I am full old. (ll. 382–90)

The near breaking of Noe's back, here the result of work, is also appropriate to
Christ's stretched and dislocated skeleton in contemporary contemplations of
the crucifixion, as are his stark bones. When Noe returns from the building of
the ark, a type of the crucifixion, his commands to make haste shock Uxor:

> Whi, syr, what alis you?
> Who is that asalis you?
> To fle it avalis you
> And ye be agast. (ll. 426–9)

Clearly Uxor is shocked, but the final line puns on Noe looking aghast, or
"like a ghost," which parallels the reactions of the disciples when they see
Christ after the resurrection. Noe may strike Uxor as aghast because of his
frightening news, but he is also a type of Christ risen from the dead, who
seemed to many of the disciples to be a ghost. When the wife dissolves in
panic at the news of God's imminent judgment, Noe reassures her: "Be not
aferd. Haue done" (456); this parallels Christ's reassurances towards his disciples in Matthew 28:10: "Do not be afraid."[7] When they arrive at the ark, Noe
again uses language that identifies the ark with salvation; he says to Uxor,

> Dame as it is skill,
> Here must vs abide grace;
> Therfor, wif, with good will
> Com into this place. (ll. 482–5)

The reference to abiding, or awaiting, grace echoes Ephesians 2:8: "For by
grace you have been saved through faith: and that not of yourselves, it is the
gift of God." In both cases, salvation is not an earned benefit; it comes
through the grace of God. This reference also anticipates a much more overt
reference to Christ and grace after the flood (ll. 795–805). Just as Uxor must
await the "grace" of God (salvation from the destruction of the flood) in the
ark, the vehicle of their salvation, so it is by Christ's crucifixion, the vehicle of
human salvation from spiritual damnation, that humanity receives spiritual
grace. When Noe brings his wife to grace through the ark, therefore, he symbolizes Christ bringing humanity to grace through his own sacrifice.

Thus, the play presents a consistent pattern of typing. Noe represents the
Christ, and the ark represents his sacrifice and new covenant by which humanity

is saved. Uxor originally represents fallen mankind, or humanity separated from God and doomed to death by its own sin; after Noe builds the ark and thus symbolically offers himself, as Christ, upon the cross, Uxor becomes humanity redeemed by Christ's new covenant, or, in other words, the fellowship of Christians known as the Church.

Even as the relationship between Noe and Uxor deteriorates into arguing and fighting, such puns continue. When Uxor sits down to spin, she says to Noe,

> Sir, for Iak nor for Gill
> Will I turne my face,
> Till I haue on this hill
> Spon a space
> On my rok. (ll. 486–90)

Literally, Noe's wife is spinning upon a staff, her "rok"; within the context of typology, however, the phrase also recalls Christ's foundation of his church upon the "rock" of Peter. The Catholic Church traced its authority and its ecclesiastical tradition back to this moment, when Christ renamed Simon "Peter," or "rock," and declared his intention to build his church upon Peter's leadership. Thus, when Uxor sits down to spin upon her "rok," the play suggests that she also makes a symbolic transition into the ecclesiastical body of the Church. This significance is echoed by similar references a few lines later. Uxor repeatedly resolves to keep spinning "In fayth" (ll. 519, 526). As she refuses to enter the ark, wanting to continue spinning "Apon this hill" (l.529), Noe explodes with an oath: "Peter! I traw we dote" (l. 531). On a literal level, Noe's words are mere frustration, but he is also calling his wife "Peter," the root of all papal and ecclesiastical tradition. The pun, "Apon this hill," is particularly apt, since the papacy (descended from Peter) ruled from the Vatican hill in Rome, the site of St. Peter's tomb and the site of St. Peter's cathedral. These hints of Uxor's role as the Church continue. When Uxor finally enters the ark, for example, Noe says, "It bees boght full dere" (l. 540), parroting the common reference to Christ, who dearly bought the souls of believers.

Yet the relationship between Noe and his wife is quite different from the orthodox interpretation of the Church's relationship with Christ. Uxor is rebellious and dismissive, alternately offering to fight and completely ignoring her husband. She is contemptuous of him and scornful of his values and his loyalty to Deus. Clearly, the Towneley Uxor would not be the orthodox choice for a type of the Church, and herein lies the obstacle to full application of the typology. However, as I have pointed out, the festive culture that dominates the plays is naturally hostile to the orthodox Church, and the Wakefield

Master seems inclined to point out many of the medieval Church's flaws. If we apply the typology consistently, Uxor portrays a Church in rebellion against Christ, an accusation common in a great deal of literature on the Church at this time. In fact, her rebellion has distinct patterns, patterns which make coherent and damning accusations against the orthodox ecclesiastical structure of the Church, and patterns that parallel accusations made against the Church in the anti-clerical and anti-ecclesiastical literature of the day.

Uxor, the type of the Church, chafes under the mastery of Noe, the type of Christ, and seeks to throw off his mastery in favor of her own self-determination. As she stubbornly refuses to enter the ship, for example, she says,

> Well were he myght get me!
> Now will I downe set me;
> Yet reede I no man let me,
> For drede of a knok. (ll. 491–4)

Uxor's obstinacy here makes little sense. Noe has given good advice; the floods are coming, and the safest place is in the ship. For Uxor, however, the very notion of Noe telling her anything is distasteful. As she says, she will let no man give her advice, even if, as in this case, it is good advice. Her flaw is pride in her own self-sufficiency, and she yearns to be free of Noe's mastery. Even after she finally enters the ship and is saved by finally following Noe's advice, she openly expresses her desire for independence, going so far as to wish for Noe's death:

> Lord, I were at ese
> And hertely full hoylle,
> Might I onys haue a messe
> Of wedows coyll.
>
> For thi saull, without lese,
> Shuld I dele penny doyll;
> So wold mo, no frese,
> That I se on this sole
> Of wifys that ar here,
> For the life that thay leyd,
> Wold thare husbandys were dede;
> For, as euer ete I brede,
> So wold I oure syre were! (ll. 560–72)

Uxor's words are humorous and develop the conventional and popular themes of gender conflict. She wishes to sample the food, or state, of a widow, and she tells Noe she would be happy to spend a penny on a prayer for his soul, as would many other women. Yet her comments, which clearly express a desire to be rid of the mastery of a husband, also drip with puns referring to the orthodox Church and its relationship to Christ. While she prefaces her words with "Lord" as a type of oath, she also thus addresses Noe as "Lord" . When she yearns for a "measse / Of wedows coyll," her words pun upon desiring to have "Mass" as a widow. While such an attitude from the orthodox Church towards Christ may seem odd, it is echoed again in lines 570–1, when Uxor says that as ever she eats bread (typologically significant as the Eucharist), she wishes her husband was dead. In other words, the act that is the symbolic and spiritual center of the orthodox Church, the celebration of the Mass, is twice here connected with the desire for a husband's death. Further, these two puns bracket a separate and much more overt reference to Mass and dead husbands; the "penny doyll," which Uxor says she will gladly pay (ll. 565–6), refers to the price paid by a widow to have her dead husband's name inserted into a Mass. All three of these statements, therefore, connect Uxor with the formal, symbolic liturgy of the Church and with the desire to be rid of a husband. Typologically, the puns suggest that the ecclesiastical authority, the "bride" of Christ, wishes to fulfill the material and social role of the Church without the interference of its spiritual master, the 'husband' of the Church, or Christ. This is a common accusation made against the Church hierarchy in contemporary literature. The pseudo-Chaucerian *The Plowman's Tale,* for example, argues that the Church hierarchy has replaced submission to Christ with self-agrandization:

> Her heed loveth all honour,
> And to be worshypped in worde and deed.
> Kynges mote to hem knele and coure:
> To the Apostles, that Chryst forbede.
> To popes hestes suche taketh more hede
> Than to kepe Chrystes commaundement.
> Of gold and sylver mote ben her wede,
> They holdeth him hole omnipotent.
> . . .
> So semeth he above hem all,
> And Christ aboven hym nothyng;
> Whan he sytteth in his stall,
> Dampneth, and saveth, as him thynk.
> Suche pryde to-fore God doth stynk. (ll. 205–12, 221–25)[8]

The ecclesiastical hierarchy is particularly condemned for the vicious infighting over power that resulted from the Great Schism: "Betwene hem now is great stryfe./ Many a man is kylled with a knyfe,/ To wete which of hem have lordship shall" (ll. 240–42). Moreover, the poem argues, the Church hierarchy would kill Christ if he were to return to earth, because they have long rejected his teachings:

> Were Christ on erthe here efte sone,
> These wolde dampne Hym to dye;
> All Hys hestes they han fordone,
> And sayn His sawes been heresy. (ll. 629–32)

The motivations for the Church's or ecclesiastical structure's rebellion from and rejection of Christ is also developed in Uxor's behavior. Uxor's rejection of authority is driven by the love of the world and scorn for privation and hardship. When they first reach the ark, for example, Uxor is repulsed by the spartan conditions proposed by Noe:

> I was neuer bard ere,
> As euer myght I the,
> In sich an oostré as this!
> In fath, I can not fynd
> Which is before, which is behynd.
> Bot shall we here be pynd,
> Noe, as haue thou blis? (ll. 475–81)

Uxor is drawn to salvation, but she is unwilling to endure privation to reach her goal. This particular attitude is often noted in the medieval clergy by contemporary writers; Chaucer, Gower, and Langland portray clergy who wish to be in the Church but have no intention of suffering any material discomfort. In the *Canterbury Tales,* for example, the Monk enjoys the security and importance that belonging to the monastery brings, but he has no interest in honoring the principles of self-denial and privation upon which the monastic tradition is founded (A ll. 177–88).[9] Most of Chaucer's other ecclesiastics show a similar lack of concern, and in some cases even scorn, for the founding principles of the Church. They serve the Church as a means to material gain, and they refuse to relinquish their worldly comforts. Many of the clergy, such as the Friar, who in fact has taken a vow of poverty, use their material gain as a means to social status and look contemptuously upon the poor (A ll. 208–69). Chaucer's criticism of Church corruption is not unusual; if anything, it is rather mild. Speaking of clergy in general, the "Pellycane" in *The Plowman's Tale* says,

> They forsake, for Christes love,
> Traveyle, hungre, thurst, and colde;
> . . .
> For Chryst her kyng they woll forsake,
> And knowe Hym noughte for His poverte.
> For Christes love they woll wake
> And drynke pyement and ale aparte.
> Of God they seme nothyng aferde. . . . (ll. 421–22, 429–33)

The 14th Century poem, "The Simonie," makes similarly sarcastic and vicious attack upon the worldliness of monks and religious orders in general:

> This is the penaunce that monekes don for ure Lordes love:
> Hii weren sockes in here shon, and felted botes above.
> He hath forsake for Godes love both hunger and cold;
> But if he have hod and cappe fured, he is noht I-told
> In convent;
> Ac certes wlaunkness of wele hem hath al ablent.
> Religioun was first founded duresce for to drie,
> And nu is the most del i-went to eise and glotonie.
> Where shal men nu finde fattere or raddere of leres?
> Or betre farende folk than monekes, chanons, and freres?
> In uch toun
> I wot not eysiere lyf than is religioun. (ll. 145–56)[10]

The Church hierarchy and the wealthy possessioners in particular were frequently accused of rejecting Christ's poverty in favor of wealth and luxury. The author of *Of Prelates* writes,

> Prelatis also setten more pris bi a litel styngynge drit of worldly goodis
> than thei don bi the moste holy gospel of ihu crist; for the grete bysynesse
> that thei han abouten worldly goodis & the litel traueile & studyyng
> abouten cristis gospel prouen wel that thei louen more this worldly muk
> than the gospel of ihu cristis. (Matthew 70)

The author of *Of Clerks Possessioners* makes a similar accusation against possessioners:

> Also thes possessioneris seyn in dede that cristis lif & ensaumpel ther-of is
> insufficient & lif sikerere bi worldly lawes is betre; for thei forsaken pore lif
> & meke aftir crist & his apostlis, & taken worldly sykernesse for the betre;
> & her thei blasphemen crist & ben out of rigt faith. (Matthew 118–19)

As this brief sampling indicates, the Church in the late medieval period was widely perceived as overly worldly and materialistic.

Resentment over these perceptions manifested itself in a variety of schemes and yearnings for change from within the Church and from without. Church reformers such as Robert Grosstette met with only limited and temporary success, and the mendicant revolution of St. Francis was perceived by many to have become just as corrupt as the conventional priesthood. More radical and apocalyptic were the mystics and visionaries who prophesied punishment from above. In her study of medieval reformist apocalypticism and its influence upon

Piers Plowman, Kathryn Kerby-Fulton notes that the sentiment that the Church
was corrupt and rebellious was a common theme in medieval Europe. Writers
such as Hildegard of Bingen, Robert of Uzès, and Bridget of Sweden had sav-
aged the Church with vicious condemnation and predictions of divine punishment; however, these writers also looked forward to a renewal of the Church
after divine chastisement:

> The motivating factor for each prophet [is] an overwhelming concern
> with Church reform and the question of renewal: can there be a renewal
> of the Christian Church or is it already too late? . . . [They] feel that there
> has been a crisis of leadership, especially in religious affairs, and that lead-
> ers from the Pope down to the parish priest have failed the Church. . . .
> Apostolic poverty and simplicity of life and belief become ideological
> tenets as apocalyptic reformers yearn to rid the future Church of the ex-
> cess baggage of worldly wealth, on the one hand, and what they see as
> overweaning intellectualism on the other. (4–5)

The zeal of Church reformers was matched by the population's hostility,
which often resulted in direct action. Lollards, as we have seen, determined to
remove their tithes in order to inspire change, and taking their cue from
Wyclif, they continued to advocate the disendowment of the Church. During
the Norwich heresy trials of 1428–31, for example, John Skylan admitted,

> Also that it is leeful every man to withdrawe and withholde offrynges and
> tithes from prestes and churches.
> Also that all temporel lordis and every temporell man is bounde a peyne
> of dedly synne to take alle possessions and all temporell godis, hors, har-
> neys and juwell from the covetouse bisshops and proude prelates of the
> Churche, and yeve thair good to the pore puple, and compelle thaym to
> sustene thaymself with labour of here owyn handes.
> Also that it is no synne to do the contrarie of the preceptes of holy
> Churche. (147)

While Lollards were a relatively small segment of the population, their statements nonetheless represent a general anti-ecclesiastical fervor that has nothing
to do with Lollardy and often manifested itself in violence against the ecclesiastical hierarchy. Peasant riots repeatedly targeted the wealthy clergy, who owned
considerable estates and could serve in secular positions of authority. Anti-clericalism was at the heart of the revolt of 1381, with John Ball and others calling
for the clergy to be stripped of their large manorial estates and to be relieved of
their temporal offices. Clergy were also targets of the rebels' violence. At the
height of the disruption, Wat Tyler and several of his followers broke into the

Tower of London, seized "Archbishop Sudbury, who was Chancellor, and Sir John Hales, Prior of the Hospitallers, who was Treasurer," and beheaded them on the spot (Previté-Orton 988). Anti-clericalism was also central to the abortive revolt of 1431, which was largely sponsored by Lollards and / or Lollard associates. The bills spread around by the rebels called for the disendowment of the clergy and "for the use of the Church's temporalities to relieve taxpayers" (Harvey 24). According to I. M. W. Harvey,

> their alleged plan of action was to make an energetic assault on Salisbury cathedral in order to raze its buildings to the ground and to carry off its goods and relics. It was intended that this should set the pattern for a country-wide purge of the possessions of Abbeys and priories. . . . According to one chronicler, the rebels at Abingdon said that they would have three priests' heads for a penny. (26–7)

Many of the men suspected in the 1431 revolt, which was entirely anti-clerical, were later part of Jack Cade's 1450 revolt (30). Cade's revolution was caused by a combination of mismanagement and social unrest, but anti-clericalism was still a dominant feature. John A. F. Thompson tells us that "in the diocese of Salisbury, there was anti-clerical rioting in 1450 which reached its peak in the murder of Bishop Ayscough at Edington in Wiltshire, but there is no reliable evidence that Lollard teaching was in any way responsible" (38). Thompson further writes,

> Sherborne, another of the places where there were riots and where the Bishop's manor was despoiled after his murder, had never been a Lollard centre, and it is significant that the Sherborne annalist, who was free with his abuse of the rioters, did not accuse them of being heretics. The indictments for participation in these disorders also avoid any charges of heresy, the worst that was said of the rioters being that they were acting as if they were heretics. (38)

Therefore, there is much evidence to believe that the general public was thoroughly annoyed by the materialism and corruption of many members of the ecclesiastical authorities.

Symbolically, Noe's wife parallels the general perception of a corrupt and worldly Church hierarchy. Although she seeks salvation out of fear, she steadfastly refuses to leave the comforts of the world beyond the ark. She says to Noe, "Yei, Noe, go cloute thi shone! / The better will thai last." (ll. 510–11). The comment is insulting and dismissive. By telling Noe to repair his shoes (by stuffing rags in holes or "clouting" them), she equates him with

still not proven

the poor and the deprived, who cannot afford new shoes and thus must repair their old shoes. Significantly, however, she is also connecting Noe's proposed lifestyle with that of the ideal spiritual guide, whose worldly poverty is often held up as example in the anti-clerical literature. Chaucer's one ideal cleric, for example, is the "povre persoun," the brother of a simple plowman, whose material poverty is directly related to his spiritual richness (A ll. 477–28). Piers, the one spiritual guide in *Piers the Plowman's Crede* who is able to teach the narrator his crede when all the wealthy orders have failed, is described in exaggerated terms of poverty, stressing, by chance, his clouted shoes:

> His cote was of a cloute that cary was ycalled,
> His hod was full of holes, and his heer oute,
> With his knopped schon clouted full thykke.
> His ton toteden out as he the londe treddede. . . . (ll. 422–25)[11]

Uxor's comment to Noe, "go cloute thi shone!" indicates that she scorns joining Noe in such poverty and privation, preferring instead to remain in the world and spin, symbolically seeking profit through commerce. Her attitude parallels that which is frequently ascribed to the Church hierarchy by anti-clerical literature. The "Gryffon" in *The Plowman's Tale,* for example, who represents the voice of the ecclesiastical authority in the poem, responds to the Pellycane's criticism of Church worldliness with similar scorn for a life of poverty:

> And the Pope were purely poore,
> Nedy, and nothynge ne hadde,
> He shulde be dryven from dore to dore,
> The wycked of hym nolde not be dradde.
> . . .
> Yf the Pope and prelates wolde
> So begge, and bydde, bowe, and borowe,
> Holy Churche shulde stande full colde,
> Her servauntes sytte and soupe sorowe.
> And they were noughty, foule, and horowe,
> To worshyppe God men wolde wlate. (ll. 1085–8, 1093–8)

Uxor's refusal to enter the ark thus corresponds directly to contemporary portrayals of a corrupt Church hierarchy refusing to accept clerical poverty as advocated by Christ.

These moments of obstinate worldliness correspond directly with the puns that connect her with papal and ecclesiastical authority. Following her haughty rejection of the spartan ark, she determines to spin "On my rok" (l. 490). When Noe and the first two sons urge her to enter, she says, "In fayth, yit will I spyn" (519), connecting, therefore, faith and commercial profit. When Noe and the third son urge her again, she says,

> Wheder I lose or wyn,
> In fayth, thi felowship
> Set I not at a pyn.
> This spyndill will I slip
> Apon this hill
> Or I styr oone fote. (ll. 525–30)

Her comment places the fellowship of Noe, the type of Christ, and her spinning, representing material gain, in direct opposition. Within her "fayth," she cares nothing about fellowship with Noe, and she determines to continue spinning, "Apon this hill," which, as I have noted, is symbolically suggestive of Vatican hill, the root of Papal and ecclesiastical authority. Noe's next word is "Peter!" (l. 531).

Within this typological matrix, the beatings exchanged between Noe and his wife make a great deal of sense. The notion that God had punished, was punishing, or would punish a sinful and corrupt Church was widespread in medieval Europe. Each successive catastrophe, ranging from Muslim victories and Bulgar invasions to natural disasters and the Black Plague, was attributed to the righteous scourging of an indignant God. The anonymous author of "The Simonie" opens his attack upon religious corruption with apocalyptic imagery, listing an array of disasters and attributing them to a general lack of Church faithfulness, or "treuthe":

> Whii were and wrake in londe and manslaught is I-come,
> Whii hungger and derthe on eorthe the pore hath undernome,
> Whii bestes ben thus storve, whii corn hath ben so dere,
> Ye that wolen abide, listneth and ye mowen here
> The skile.
> I nelle liyen for no man, herkne who so wile.
> God greteth wel the clergie, and seith theih don amis,
> And doth hem to understonde that litel treuthe ther is;
> For at the court of Rome, ther Treuthe sholde biginne,
> Him is forboden the paleis, dar he noht com therinne
> For doute;
> And thouh the Pope clepe him in, yit shal he stonde theroute.
> Alle the Popes clerkes han taken hem to red,
> If Treuthe come amonges hem, that he shal be ded. (ll. 1–14)

After relating an impressive account of ecclesiastical abuses, which he names "shrewedom," the author returns to his theme of divine punishment, emphasizing in particular weather that equates well to Noah's flood:

So that for that shrewedom that regneth in the lond,
I drede me that God us hath for-laft out of His hond,
Thurw wederes that he hath I-sent cold and unkinde.

. . .

God hath wroth wid the world, and that is wel I-sene;
For al that whilom was murthe is turned to treie and tene. (ll. 373–5, 379–80)

Noe's beating of an obstinate wife who prefers the world to his safe mastery therefore closely parallels Christ's punishment of a worldly and disobedient Church. In fact, Noe's words imply just such a relationship between religion, disobedience, and punishment: "In fayth, and for youre long taryyng / Ye shal lik on the whyp" (ll. 545–6).

Uxor's beatings of Noe make equal sense in this context. Standard theology held that since Christ suffered for humanity's sins, each sin committed by a Christian added to the pain suffered by Christ. Hebrews 6: 6, for example, states that believers who sin "again crucify to themselves the Son of God, and put Him to open shame." The Pellycane of "The Plowman's Tale" uses a similar image in his criticism of the Church's use of violence:

These wollen make men to swere
Ayenst Christes commaundement;
And Christes membres all to-tere
On Roode, as He wer newe yrent. (ll. 253–6)

Thus, when a beaten Uxor pleads for an end to the fighting, calling Noe "mans wonder" (l. 591), another reference to Christ, Noe replies, "Se how she can grone, / And I lig vnder!" (ll. 592–3). Noe's position at the bottom of the scuffle reflects the topsy-turvy sense of the festive cycle, but his words also suggest Christ's burial position under the earth after his crucifixion. Although the Church groans at the punishment received from Christ, its sins continue to crucify Christ anew and to subject him to suffering again and again. When Uxor finally submits to the mastery of Noe, they are both better off, neither being subjected to the abuse of the other. This equates to the harmony possible between Christ and his Church if the Church will submit to Christ's authority.

When analyzed within the context of overwhelming structural, linguistic, and thematic renewal in the play, therefore, the struggles between Noe, the type of Christ, and Uxor, a type of the orthodox Church, imply that the Church itself, or the relationship between the Church and Christ, is in need of regeneration. Through the actions of Noe and his wife in the context of the festive, regenerative flood, the Church is ritually cleansed and renewed. However, as with all of the Wakefield Master's plays, the satire here is playful and parodic. By placing criticism of the Church within the context of a conflict between a husband and his shrewish wife, the Wakefield Master lowers this serious (and dangerous) indictment of corruption into the festive realm of ridicule and innuendo. In addition, since the parody deals with Church corruption within the Noah story, it places it within the borders of festive behavior, where beatings, laughter, and other traditional forms of ritual renewal can be brought to bear upon the Church. Placing Christ and the Church in such a context allows renewal that would otherwise not be aesthetically possible. Renewal is the traditional ending for the flood and for the conflict between husband and wife; by equating these with Christ and the Church, the Wakefield Master is able to project a positive sense of renewal and regeneration onto the future of a corrupt and rebellious Church.

Chapter Five
Foolish Shepherds and Priestly Folly[1]

Much about *Prima Pastorum*[2] suggests it is more than a conventional shepherd's play. In fact, like *Secunda Pastorum*, most of *Prima Pastorum* is entirely irrelevant to and unconcerned with the nativity. Further, the play is filled with nonsense and absurdity. Shepherds play the fool, perform irreverent parodies, and eat an excessive Yuletide feast. As with *Mactacio Abel* and *Processus Noe*, festive elements cause a reinterpretation of serious religious symbols. Irreverence and folly establish a festive world, a world immune to order and conventional wisdom. The play presents a scandalous and clever parody of the clergy, equating the shepherds with priests, shepherds with fools, and, by extension, priests with fools. In so doing, the play satirizes and undermines the orthodox clerical authority. Yet as in *Secunda Pastorum*, the festive currents do not completely repudiate the serious message of the play. In both plays, the atmosphere changes as the nativity approaches. All parody and folly end, and irreverence is muted. Indeed, both plays are sharply divided into sections of initial festive parody and subsequent serious reverence. None of the other plays contain this sharp separation, which suggests that the plays are intended to distinguish between objects of folly and objects of reverence. And the objects between which this distinction is drawn say much about the Wakefield Master and the festive stance in the plays. Priests and their vocations are mocked in the first play, with non-existent congregations, parodic sermons, and mock masses. The second play mocks not only corrupt priests but predatory clergy. However, neither play disrupts the sense of quiet reverence at the nativity itself. This division between the initial festive parody and the subsequent serious reverence indicates that while the play mocks the shepherds of the Orthodox Church, they do not mock Christ. Rather, Christ, the *pastor bonus,* is held up as an ideal by which contemporary spiritual pastors are measured. The plays become a message of social and religious reform and a festive affirmation of hope in a bleak world.

Orthodox versions of the shepherds' story are typically short, serious narratives in which angels announce Christ's birth and the shepherds travel to the nativity. In the York play, "The Shepherds," for example, the first shepherd speaks only four lines before he begins recounting in detail the prophecies of Christ's birth in Bethlehem (l. 5–12).[3] The other two shepherds repeat and expand this discussion of the prophecies through line 35, at which point they observe and are awed by the star in the east. After a presumed appearance by the angels (a leaf is missing from the text), the shepherds sing as they travel to Bethlehem, observe Christ "Betwyxe two bestis tame" (l. 94), and give homage to Christ. It is all over (except for the missing leaf) in 131 lines. The N-Town play, "The Shepherds," begins with an introduction by *Angelus* (ll. 1–13).[4] The three shepherds then see the star and relate the prophecies concerning Christ's birth (ll. 14–61). The *Gloria in Excelsis Deo* is sung (the text does not indicate by whom); the shepherds are amazed, and they sing as they travel to Bethlehem (ll. 62–89). They pay homage to Christ, are addressed by Joseph, bid Christ farewell, and are dismissed by a blessing from Mary (ll. 90–154). Like the York play, it is short and to the point, lasting only 154 lines.

There is a reason for such brevity and seriousness. The nativity represents the fulfillment of God's promise to Adam to redeem his descendants. The child Christ is God become flesh to be sacrificed for humanity's salvation, and most orthodox treatments strictly maintain this weighty context. Emphasis is usually placed upon the history leading up to the incarnation, and upon the many prophecies foretelling Christ's birth. Because of its import, the nativity and the announcement to the shepherds are treated with a profound sense of reverence and seriousness. Most versions avoid detailed examination of the shepherds except as conduits for this good news. Personal details about the shepherds are left to a minimum. They hear, bear witness to, and relate the birth of Christ, but they are not major players in this cosmic drama. The conventional focus is on the nativity and on the birth of the savior; shepherds are mere decoration.

The majority of the *Prima Pastorum,* however, focuses upon the seemingly irrelevant lives of the shepherds. 425 out of 724 lines in the play are spoken before angels ever appear. What's more, the majority of the play is steeped in the topsy-turvy world of festive absurdity. As in *Mactacio Abel,* where horses and servants defy their master, or as in *Processus Noe,* in which the seven planets have left their orbit, the Wakefield Master creates in *Prima Pastorum* another environment which is disordered and makes no sense. Two shepherds drive non-existent sheep back and forth. Another shepherd demonstrates the folly of the first two by pouring his own sack of wheat all over the ground. All three shepherds gluttonously partake of a lavish but completely imaginary feast. These absurd and disparate episodes are unified only by the overriding sense of folly that pervades the first part of the play. In fact, the only consistent theme of this first part is folly.

The heart of the play is a widely-known tale of folly borrowed from the legendary fools of Gotham, which Martin Stevens and James Paxson paraphrase thus:

> [A] man sets out to buy sheep at a market and is confronted by another man who declares that he will not allow him to cross the bridge when he returns with his newly-acquired sheep. They quarrel as if there were actual sheep until a third man comes along who mediates the quarrel by emptying a bag of meal into the river, observing that the two quarrelers have as much wit in their heads as he now has meal in his sack. The emphasis here is on the alleged wisdom of folly, though the most foolish character may well be the one who poses as the wiseman, for he has lost the most tangible possession. (76–7)

With minor elaborations, lines 145 through 253 of *Prima Pastorum* follow this source faithfully, and Iak Garcio makes specific reference to the "foles of Gotham" (l. 260). The Wakefield Master seems intent upon incorporating the Gotham fools into the *pastores* play. The effect of this addition is to stress human folly and particularly the folly of wisdom.

This emphasis upon fools and folly is characteristic of festive culture. The fool is indeed a festive figure, more representative of festive culture than any other character type. He is the central character in the feast of Fools and later in the "Societè Joyeuse" (Chambers 372–89). As a festive character, the fool serves the primary purpose of burlesquing that which is serious. He is the epitome of topsy-turvydom, the center of nonsense, the symbol of reversal and change in the festive celebration. Folly is the reversal of known truth and wisdom, and reversal of any kind symbolizes the cycles of change central to festive existence. Indeed, the play opens with a monologue by Gyb, the first shepherd, which serves to introduce this theme of cyclic change. He begins with a discussion of past generations and proceeds to establish the ever-changing nature of life.

> Now in hart, now in heyll,
> Now in weytt, now in blast;
> Now in care,
> Now in comforth agane;
> Now is fayre, now is rane;
> Now in hart full fane,
> And after full sare.

Thus this warl, as I say,
Farys on ylk syde,
For after oure play
Com sorows vnryde. (ll. 7–17)

The lines reflect Gyb's dismay at the variable nature of life. One moment we
are content; the next we are driven to despair. JeffreyHelterman writes, "The
dismaying change of seasons, which nearly overwhelms the first shepherd,
symbolizes the mutability of 'this world here'" (74). This theme of variability,
while odd in a nativity play, is central to festive culture. Cycles of degeneration and regeneration are the foundation of the festive calendar, and festive
expression largely consists of symbols that represent cyclical reversal and overthrow. Herein lies the root of festive folly; conventional wisdom, which in-
vests time and energy in eternal verities and social prosperity, is overthrown
when these elements are themselves overthrown by time and change. In his
opening monologue, Gyb says,

For he that most may
When he syttys in pryde,
When it comys on assay
Is kesten downe wyde. (ll. 18–21)

In its initial discussion of the folly of life's achievements and the folly of wisdom, the play is strongly evocative of Ecclesiastes. The primary theme of
Ecclesiastes is the folly of life in a changeable and oppressive world, as we see
in 1:14: "*Vidi cuncta quae fiunt sub sole,/ Et ecce universa vanitas, et afflictio
spiritus.*" "I have seen all the works which have been done under the sun, and
behold, all is vanity and striving after wind."[5] The preacher also stresses the
folly of aspiring toward wisdom, as we see in 1:17: "*Dedique cor meum ut
scirem prudentiam, atque doctrinam, erroresque et stultitiam: et agnovi quod in
his quoque esset labor, et afflictio spiritus*" "And I set my mind to know wisdom
and to know madness and folly; I realized that this also is striving after wind."

The similarities with Ecclesiastes are not just thematic, however. Gyb's
opening monologue is replete with close paraphrases of sections of
Ecclesiastes which are, in turn, central to the message of the play. Take, for example, Gyb's summary of the folly of life:

This is seyn:
When ryches is he,
Then comys pouerte:
Horsman Iak Cope
Walkys then, I weyn. (ll. 22–6)

The quotation is profoundly festive; those in society who are rich or power-ful are overthrown. Yet the quotation is also reminiscent of Ecclesiastes 10:6–7: "*Positum stultum in dignitate sublimi, et divites sedere deorsum. Vidi servos in equis, et principes ambueantes super terrum quasi servos.*" "Folly is set in great dignity, and the rich sit in low place. I have seen servants upon horses, and princes walking as servants upon the earth." Again, the ever-changing na-ture of existence makes any worldly achievement temporary and elusive.

Another paraphrase may be seen in Gyb's determination to replace his dead sheep:

> Thus sett I my mynde,
> Truly to neuen,
> By my wytt to fynde
> To cast the warld in seuen. (ll. 53–6)

Gyb's statement has been interpreted as a reference to gambling (Stevens and Cawley 483).[6] Yet it is remakably close to Ecclesiastes 11: 1–2: "*Mitte panem tuum super transeuntes aquas: quia post tempora multa invenies illum. Da partem septem.*" "Cast your bread on the surface of the waters, for you will find it after many days. Divide your portion to seven." Beyond containing linguis-tic parallels, this verse reinforces many of the festive themes of the play. Casting bread upon the water to receive it after many days is a cyclic image that parallels the dumping of the wheat into the river by the fools of Gotham. Like the fools of Gotham episode, the verse also stresses the folly of reliance upon self and upon conventional expectations. The wise man will abandon striving after wind or non-existent sheep and cast his expectations on chance.

A final parallel appears in the social evils that serve as a backdrop for the play. The presence of the shepherds would undoubtedly have reminded the audience of the new practices of enclosure, a bitterly controversial practice in which traditionally common lands were enclosed by the aristocratic landown-ers, usually so that large herds of sheep could be grazed for the growing wool industry. This practice apparently loomed large in the consciousness of the medieval peasant. Enclosure is consistently attacked by medieval writers as an avaricious abuse of power (Tate 44–5), and indeed it did lead to harsh condi-tions for the peasants. The enclosure practice is savagely criticized in *Secunda Pastorum,* and in *Prima Pastorum,* Iohn Horne rails against the agents of the aristocracy who enforced the new practices "with thare long dagers" (l. 81). Iohn Horne says that it would be better to be slain than to refuse to obey these argumentative and raging men, who go about just looking for someone to beat and rob:

> Sich wryers and wragers
> Gose to and fro
> For to crak:
> Whoso says hym agane
> Were better be slane;
> Both ploghe and wane
> Amendys will not make. (ll. 85–91)

These conditions are reflected best in Gyb's statement that the dead are "weyll" because they don't have to experience the evils of the world:

> Lord, what thay ar weyll
> That hens ar past
> For thay noght feyll
> Theym to downe cast.
> Here is mekyll vnceyll,
> And long has it last. (ll. 1–6)

The general situation and Gyb's specific words recall the words of the preacher in Ecclesiastes 4:1–2:

> *Verti me ad alia, et vidi calumnias, quæ sub sole geruntur, et lacrymas inno-*
> *centium, et neminem consolatorem: nec posse resistere eorem violentiæ, cunc-*
> *torum auxilio destitutos. Et laudavi magis mortuos, quam viventes.*
> Then I looked again at all the acts of oppression which were being done under the sun. And behold I saw the tears of the oppressed and that they had noone to comfort them; and on the side of their oppressors was power, but they had noone to comfort them. So I congratulated the dead who are already dead more than the living who are still living.

This is an important theme in Ecclesiastes—and in *Prima Pastorum*. Life is folly because it is full of hardship and oppression.

These paraphrases, spoken by a shepherd in a *pastores* play, are the first indications that the main characters might be read as more than secular shepherds. In fact, their actions and words also suggest spiritual shepherds, or priests. The Latin word "*pastor*" is more commonly used to denote clergy than keepers of livestock, and the metaphor of clergy shepherding the believers is common in medieval expression. As Christ is the good shepherd to the church, so too are clergy to shepherd their congregations to wholesome nourishment. This theme is perhaps best known to modern readers through Chaucer's portrayal of his poor Parson, but the metaphor dates back to Old Testament texts, is used by Christ in John 10, and is developed at length by Gregory the Great in his *Cura Pastoralis*. Chaucer's description of the Parson uses this metaphor repeatedly. Chaucer says, "He was a shepherde and nought a mercenarie" (A l. 514) and gives nine direct references to the Parson's protective role as shepherd to his flock. Reformers of all types drew upon the passage in John and upon related passages in *Cura Pastoralis* to blast corruption among the clergy. The role of the priest was compared to that of the shepherd to evoke the ideal priest, usually when other priests were far from ideal. John Gower uses the pastoral metaphor extensively in books III and IV of *Vox Clamantis* to comment upon corruption in all ranks of the clergy. In fact, religious homilies often treated the nativity shepherds in particular as types of priests. Margery M. Morgan points out that the metaphor is developed explicitly in the Chester *Adoration of the Shepherds:*

> As they cross the *platea* once more, the dialogue records their conversion from the care of sheep to the cure of souls: the Second and Third Shepherds declare their intention of preaching the gospel, the First Shepherd chooses to be a wandering hermit, and the boy, Trowle, resolves to be an anchorite. . . . [T]he Chester Shepherds talk of the nature and purpose of their work, and they do so in terms familiar in metaphorical application to the ministry of Christ. (682)

The shepherds in *Prima Pastorum* are particularly priestlike. They speak blessings and use Latin phrases. They know a great deal about religious music (Carpenter 699). They know and quote a great deal of scripture and related religious material. For instance, they list Isaiah, David, the Erythraean Sibyl, Nebuchadnezzar, Jeremiah, Moses, Habakkuk, Eli, Elizabeth, Zachariah, John the Baptist, Daniel, and Virgil as prophetic predictors of the coming of Christ. Martin Stevens and A. C. Cawley write, "The learning displayed by the Wakefield Shepherds is no doubt due to the medieval tradition of scriptural exegesis which made the shepherds that find Christ types of the clergy" (490). Indeed, these shepherds tease each other about being clergy because they speak so learnedly to one another. During the feast, for example, Gyb accuses Slawpase of being a priest because of his use of French words: "Yee speke all by clerge, / I here by youre clause" (ll346–7). A few pages later, however, Iohn Horne indicts Gyb as a priest because Gyb quotes Virgil:

> Weme! Tord! What speke ye
> Here in my eeres?
> Tell vs no clerge!
> I hold you of the freres;
> Ye preche.
> It semys by youre Laton
> Ye haue lerd youre Caton. (ll. 560–4)

Yet the shepherds are most like clergy in their sermon-like monologues. Gyb, preaching of the vanities of life with Ecclesiastes as his text, represents a spiritual shepherd, or priest, as much as he does an agricultural shepherd. And the other shepherds follow suit.

Thus, when Iohn Horne, the second shepherd, enters the play, he sounds more like a medieval preacher blessing and speaking to an audience than a cold shepherd alone on the moors:

> Benste, benste
> Be vs emang,
> And save all that I se
> Here in this thrang!
> He saue you and me,
> Ouer thwart and endlang,
> That hang on a tre,
> I say you no wrang.
> Cryst sane Vs
> From all myschefys. (ll. 66–75)

Iohn Horne then delivers a monologue, focussing upon the oppressive agents of the aristocracy:

> Both bosters and bragers
> God kepe vs fro,
> That with thare long dagers
> Dos mekyll wo;
> From all byll-hagers
> With colknyfys that go. (ll. 79–84)

Iohn Horne's complaints reflect contemporary social and economic hardships and parallel the discussion of oppression in Ecclesiastes 4:1 : "Then I looked again at all the acts of oppression which were being done under the sun. And behold I saw the tears of the oppressed and that they had noone to comfort them; and on the side of their oppressors was power, but they had noone to comfort them."

In both references, to expect justice in an unjust world is folly; this explains why the dead are more fortunate than the living. Both references suggest festive themes, but both are also ethical instruction, a moral statement against the oppressors. Indeed, beyond the general blessings, Iohn Horne's monologue falls into the typical pattern of a medieval sermon. He begins with a theme: Christ saves all. He then progresses through stages of elaboration upon the theme: Christ saves you and me from all types of "myschief," especially robbers and thieves and men who oppress us. He then gives a series of exempla of exactly what mischief and what kind of men Christ saves us from: the "bosters and bragers" and "wryers and wragers" who serve the aristocracy and go about with long knives stealing "ploghe and wane" from whomever they please.

Iohn Horne specifically catalogues the deadly sins of these men. Stevens and Cawley note that "bosters and bragers" parallels "bostaris, braggaris" from Dunbar's *Dance of the Sevin Deidly Synnis* (484), following a conventional formula for listing deadly sins. Horne does not list the entire set, but rather focuses upon those sins consonant with the themes of the play. He proclaims that the men sin through wrath, covetousness, sloth, and pride. He especially focuses upon their pride:

> He will make it as prowde
> A lord as he were,
> With a hede lyke a clowde,
> Felterd his here.
> . . .
> I wote not the better,
> Nor wheder is gretter—
> The lad or the master—
> So stowtly he strydes. (ll. 92–3, 101–4)

These references on one level project reversal and usurpation of authority, perennial festive values; however, they also illustrate the pride of man. This emphasis suggests Proverbs 16: 18: "Pride goeth before destruction, and an haughty spirit before a fall." The topic is both appropriate for priestly discussion and resonant with the festive themes of reversal and uncrowning. Thus, when Horne prays for the men, he simultaneously evokes the overthrow traditional in festive culture and closes his sermon with a conventional formula:

> Help that thay were broght
> To a better way
> For thare sawlys;
> And send theym good mendyng
> With a short endyng. (ll. 111–5)

Slawpase, the third shepherd, also delivers a sermonlike monologue, but his comments return to the theme introduced by Gyb: the folly of striving after that which is intangible. When he enters the play and encounters the first two arguing over imaginary sheep, he chastises them:

> God gyf you wo
> And sorow!
> Ye fysh before the nett,

> And stryfe on this flett;
> Sich folys neuer I mett. (ll. 199–203)

Note here the semantic parallels between striving over the "flett," or petty argument, and striving after the wind, the image used in Ecclesiastes to indicate the true nature of folly. Slawpase then proceeds to give a sermonlike speech upon folly. He tells Gyb and Iohn Horne to "lere at my lawe" (l. 234); "lere" here means "learn," and "lawe" is glossed by Stevens and Cawley as "faith" or "religion" (685). The reference suggests religious instruction, therefore, and not mere homespun wisdom. After introducing the theme, Slawpase elaborates with a series of figurative examples of folly. Such wit for ballast would "Make a shyp be drownde" (l. 210). Fighting over nothing has the same effect as commanding an egg to move (ll. 214–17). Slawpase then gives an exemplum and follows it with exegetical illustration. The exemplum relates the story of Mowll (or Moll), a maid who is so distracted by shearing imaginary sheep that she forgets about the pitcher she is carrying and subsequently breaks it:

> Ye brayde of Mowll
> That went by the way—
> Many shepe can she poll,
> Bot oone had she ay.
> Bot she happynyd full fowll
> Hyr pycher, I say,
> Was broken.
> . . .
> The mylk-pycher was layde,
> The skarthis was the tokyn. (ll. 220–6, 229–30)

The moral, again, is that obsession with intangible materialism (such as Gyb and Iohn Horne have displayed) causes one to neglect that which is real. The exegetical illustration consists of Slawpase emptying the bag of meal:

> This sek thou thrawe
> On my bak,
> Whylst I, with my hand,
> Lawse the sek-band.
> Com nar and by stand,
> Both Gyg and Iak.
> Is not all shakyn owte,
> And no meyll is therein? (ll. 238–45)

The illustration, as exegesis typically does, works on at least two levels. The action of emptying the bag immediately illustrates Gyb's and Iohn Horne's lack of wits. Slawpase says, "So is youre wyttys thyn, / . . . /So gose youre wyttys owte" (ll. 247, 250). Yet Slawpase has also unintentionally illustrated the very folly he criticizes. He has given insight into wisdom, an intangible benefit, but he and the other shepherds are now without any meal. As Iohn Horne notes, he has given them "Wysdom to sup," at best a light dinner (l. 236). Slawpase's monologue mimics the structure of medieval homilies, tieing in to the typological relationship between the nativity shepherds and the priesthood.

Yet while the shepherds in this play are symbolically and typologically connected to the clergy, and while they perform the actions of priests, they also fulfill the roles of fools. I have noted the extreme foolery of the three, particularly their topsy-turvy evocation of festive life and their re-enactment of the tale of the fools of Gotham. Like their cousins, the festive fools, the shepherds are the center of topsy-turvy nonsense and symbols of reversal and change. They question authority, reverse expectation, exchange sense for nonsense, and generally engage in absurd behavior.[7] Their folly is further stressed by the echoes of Ecclesiastes. Ecclesiastes examines the many faces and actions of vanity and folly, as the preacher reiterates in 2:12: "So I turned to consider wisdom, madness, and folly". In such a context, the shepherds, through their ridiculous behavior, become visible symbols of this folly.

Indeed, the three go out of their way to call each other fools and to treat each other as fools. When the third shepherd, Slawpase, enters to find Gyb and Iohn Horne fighting over the non-existent sheep, he describes them as fools: "Sich folys neuer I mett" (ll. 201–3). When Iak Garcio, another traditional servant fool figure, enters after Slawpase has emptied his bag of meal onto the ground, he says of the shepherds,

> Now God gyf you care,
> Foles all sam!
> Sagh I neuer none so fare
> Bot the foles of Gotham.
> . . .
> Of all the foles I can tell,
> From heuen vnto hell,
> You thre bere the bell; (ll. 257–60, 266–8)

When Iohn Horne accuses Gyb of speaking like a friar or a clergyman, Gyb retorts that the other two are fools: "Herk, syrs! Ye fon" (l. 567). Indeed, *Prima Pastorum* uses the term "fool" more than any other play in the Towneley cycle. Thus, while the shepherds clearly represent priests, they also represent fools and folly.

The result of this dual symbolic value is that priests and their actions are lowered into the realm of fools and folly. If we return to Gyb's quotation at the beginning of the play, we see just such a correlation:

> When ryches is he,
> Then comys pouerte:
> Horsman Iak Cope
> Walkys then, I weyn. (ll. 22–6)

[handwritten marginalia: "= Jack Plenty", "you would never call a priest a priest Cope"]

The name Iak Cope is itself suggestive of both fool and priest. Jack is a common term for fool, and a "Cope" is a mantle worn by priests during ceremonious occasions. Therefore, Jack Cope, the rich authority figure degraded in the reference, is actually a type for the priest/fool. However, this raises an important question: why would the play relate priests with fools?

The answer lies in the three central scenes of folly in the play, which are also symbolic of priestly action. In the first scene, Gyb laments the loss his flock to disease and sets about getting a new, imaginary flock. This image evokes a metaphor common in the medieval discussions on the duties of a spiritual pastor to his parishioners, and on the consequences of failing to carry out those duties. One of the principal obligations is spiritual instruction, without which the flock is susceptible to the disease of sin. A Lollard sermon written for the second Sunday in Advent speaks of the "cloudes" of spiritual disease that follow on such ignorance and drives men "wode," or mad:

> Suche cloudes gendren gostli pestilence and deth of mannes soule for ignorance or necligence of suche prechynge. The deuel spredeth aboute corupte eire of his temptacions of synnes and, whanne men recyeuen hem, than bi processe thei gendren togydere manie foule corupcions of lustus and likyngis that thei han to thoo synnes. And so, at the last, of hem growth in mannes herte a ful consente, whiche is a foule pestilence boche in the sigt of God almyti, and this is gret tokene of gostli deth. But whanne the blake spottis ben borsten oute (of foule horribile synnes, as pride, wrath, and enuye, couetise, gloterie) into dede, thane a man mai haue ful knowing that suche a man is at the deth. And, in suche pestilence, the grete hete of the ague that thei han smyteth vp into her heed, and so it maketh hem raue and speke thane as wode men. (Cigman 19)

Metaphorically, Gyb's folly matches with the madness brought on by the "ague" of sin, but the focus here is on his flock. As noted in Chapter Three, it is the pastor's duty to protect the flock from the pestilence of sin: "to greese ther scabbid sheep & to telle hem medicyn of goddis lawe wherby that they may be hool" (Matthew 439). We have seen the same reference in *Mactacio*

Abel, when Cain, tired of being berated by the priestlike shepherd Abel for reluctant tithing, tells him to tend his "skabbid" sheep. Naturally, the result of
a pastor failing to care for his flock is spiritual disease, the "foule corupcions"
that lead to spiritual, or "gostli" death. Therefore, on a metaphorical level,
Gyb represents a neglectful priest whose flock has succumbed to the "gostli
pestilence" of sin from lack of pastoral care.

Gyb's response to the death of his flock also matches contemporary anti-
clerical criticism of priestly neglect. He sets off to town to procure an imaginary flock, which he and Iohn Horne fight over. These actions equate well
with the widely-deplored practice of priests vying for positions in well-en-
dowed chantries or monastic orders while neglecting the spiritual needs of the
populace. Chaucer speaks of this abuse when he notes that his poor parson
was too dedicated a shepherd to abandon his flock for such gain:

> He sette nat his benefice to hyre
> And leet his sheep encombred in the myre
> And ran to Londoun unto Seinte Poules
> To seken hym a chaunterie for soules.
> Or with a bretherhed to been withhoulde;
> But dwelte at hoom, and kepte wel his folde. (A ll. 507–12)

Chantries involved priests saying a certain number of daily prayers for the
souls of the dead, an intangible flock at best.[8] Priests employed in such work
often came from poor or underpopulated parishes; thus, their tangible flock
was abandoned, as Chaucer says, "in the myre," while the priests wrangled for
the lucrative rights to shepherd a non-existent flock. The scene where two
foolish shepherds argue over pasturage for an imaginary flock which has replaced the diseased and dead flock, therefore, is a parodic satire of a very real
and widely-criticized priestly abuse, an act of sheer folly for any true shepherd.

The second scene parodies another priestly folly. When Slawpase comments upon the folly of Gyb and Iohn Horne, he gives instruction upon abstract benefits at the expense of concrete prosperity. With his sack of meal,
Slawpase has the ability to alleviate the suffering of two poor shepherds, one
of whom is completely destitute; yet his lesson has the opposite effect. Once
his meal is dumped out, he is satisfied that his point has been made.
However, while Gyb and John Horne may be somewhat wiser, they are still
without food. Slawpase's action is another obvious act of folly. This scene is
significant in light of the incredible material wealth invested in the Church
during the latter part of the Middle Ages. Yet even as the Church grew
wealthy, many among the working classes began to suffer from extreme
poverty and hardship. Jerome Blum, Rondo Cameron, and Thomas G.

Barnes note that Europe suffered a tremendous depression in the fourteenth and fifteenth centuries:

> The economic expansion of the twelfth and thirteenth centuries slowed down or leveled off in the first half of the fourteenth century and about the middle of the century gave way to a long depression, lasting in most parts of Europe approximately one hundred years. . . . Evidence . . . can be found in the movement of population and prices, in the changes in agriculture, commerce, and industry, and in social unrest and political disturbances. (35–6)

While the depression had many causes and effects, agrarian disruption was a dominant feature of both. Grain prices in England fell inexorably, dropping in the period from 1451–1475 to 54% of the price in the period from 1351–1375, all during a period of steady inflation (Blum, Cameron, and Barnes 39). Landowners who felt the pinch of the market frequently raised rents or enclosed common lands to raise sheep. The practice of enclosure led to widescale displacement of the peasantry. This is precisely the oppression mentioned at the beginning of the play, the root cause of the shepherds' misery. With its vast material resources, the Church could have easily helped alleviate the widespread suffering and poverty of late medieval England, but it didn't. Calls for the Church to devote more of its resources to the poor were common, as were calls for disendowment. The anonymous author of *The Clergy May Not Hold Property* blasts the clergy for ignoring Christ's commands to help the poor: "in worde & ensaumple he taugte his prestis to be procuratouris for nedy people & pore at the ryche men, & specifyed thes pore, & taugte how thai that wer mygty schuld make a purviance for syche pore folke" (Matthew 387). The "Lollard Disendowment Bill," introduced into Parliament in 1406 argues that among other things the wealth of the church can be used more profitably in setting up alms houses across England (Hudson 135). To be fair, the Church sponsored a variety of charities, but against the wealth and possessions of the clergy, this was perceived by the populace as only a fraction of what should have been done. Churches became far more ornate, the living conditions of clerics were more luxurious, and the spiritual services of the Church encompassed more of medieval life, but with a few notable exceptions, the Church ignored the physical condition of its flock. When Iohn Horne says, "He has told vs full plane / Wysdom to sup" (ll. 255–6), he parodies this tendency. The clergy dispense abstract wisdom, but in the end their flocks go hungry, an act of sheer folly.

The third scene of folly, following upon Iohn Horne's ironic comment, turns the satire of abstract nourishment into a full-blown parody of the Mass. The feast is a parody of the body and blood of Christ; the phrase "boyte of

oure bayle," usually used to refer to Christ, the cure for our suffering, is here used by Gyb to refer to "Good holsom ayll" (ll. 357–8).[9] Yet the feast differs from the mass in two ways. First, it is extravagant, more like a holiday feast than a simple meal. Holiday feasts are the center of the festive world. They are marked by excess and abundance. Participants gorge themselves upon a menu of unusual variety, with emphasis placed upon exotic organs and body parts. Conceptually, feasting celebrates the material body and its consumption. It is the ultimate symbol of becoming, change, and development. Bakhtin says,

> Eating and drinking are one of the most significant manifestations of the grotesque body . . . ; the body transgresses here its own limits: it swallows, devours, rends the world apart, is enriched and grows at the world's expense. (281)

The shepherds' mock mass has all the marks of a festive feast. The shepherds mention nineteen dishes, including such exotic ones as cow's foot, blood pudding, swine groin, goose leg, ox tail, and calf liver. They mention at least three bottles of wine. They drink and eat and laugh and joke and argue and generally have a raucously good time. Thus, the feast appropriates the Mass into a festive form.

Metaphorically, this again equates well to popular perceptions of the priesthood. Many contemporary writers complain that the clergy spend their time engaging in gluttonous revelry while ignoring their flocks. The author of *Of Clerks Possessioners* writes of the clergy, "whanne thei schulden be gostly ligt of the world bi opyn ensaumple of holy lif & trewe prechyng of holy writt, as crist comaundid to alle his apostlis & disciplis, thei hidden hem self in gay cloistris & lyuen in lustis of flech & glotonye, drounknesse & ydelnesse & sleep" (Matthew 116–7). These are indeed the actions of the three shepherds, far from their flocks, eating, drinking, lounging, and sleeping. As a mock mass, the feast parodies the actions of the medieval clergy, whose duties should be the spiritual and Eucharistic nourishment of their flocks, but who instead engage in gluttonous feeding of their own appetites.

The other difference between this feast and the mass is that most scholars interpret the feast to be completely imaginary. A. C. Cawley, for example, argues, "The playwright's mixing of high-class and low-class table delicacies makes a ludicrous gallimaufry that can never have existed except in his imagination" ("Grotesque Feast" 215). As they begin to eat, Slawpase says to Iohn Horne, "I fare full yll / At youre mangere" (290–1). As Stevens and Cawley note, "mangere" is a pun; it "may be used here as a foreshadowing of the Eucharist with reference to both 'crib, manger' and 'feast'" (487). Yet Slawpase's statement also indicates that the feasting is not satisfying, not filling, and lacking substance. Moreover, the shepherds laugh and joke about speaking or conjuring the food and drink into existence. Gyb says, for example, "Cowth ye by your gramery / Reche vs a drynk" (ll. 348–9). Iohn Horne says, "Be thou wyn, be thou ayll" (l. 370). When Iohn Horne presents a bottle, Slawpase says, "That is well spoken" (l. 379). Helterman writes that the Wakefield Master "wishes to show the shepherds' imagination at work creating this feast. The shepherds' creative approach is seen in the apostrophe to the cup, . . . which, in the context of an imaginary feast, is a fiat" (85). Speaking food and drink into imaginary existence parodies transubstantiation and the Eucharist, which is much of the joke in this scene, but simple parody is not the main point. The shepherds have entered a festive paradox in this Yuletide feast; they are eating gluttonously, yet they are not eating at all.

This last paradox ties all of the folly together. The shepherds earlier strove mightily over the flock, but they strove over nothing. Slawpase exhorted Gyb and Iohn Horne to leave their folly and embrace his wisdom, but his wisdom was folly. Here, the shepherds work energetically at feasting, but no actual nourishment is consumed. This final folly, an exotic mock mass with no actual host, is the most satiric of all. It parallels much of the scepticism the populace felt towards the mystical treatment of the sacraments of the Church. Many medieval Christians questioned the orthodox doctrines surrounding transubstantiation. The Lollards, for example, either ruled out transubstantiation altogether or accepted a heretical compromise, consubstantiation. In the Norwich heresy trials, for example, John Peert admitted the following belief: "Y held, beleved, and affermed that no prest hath poar to make Goddys body in the sacrament of the auter, and that aftir the sacramental wordis said of a prest at messe ther remayneth but oonly a cake of material bred" (Tanner 170).

Yet while the feast parodies the claims of transubstantiation, it also parodies the exotic and multi-faceted structure into which the Church had been transformed. The medieval Church had increased in power, wealth, and diversity. A bewildering variety of monks, friars, pardoners, and parish priests swarmed across medieval England.[10] Great cathedrals rose to proclaim the glory of God. Great universities taught priests the many facets of God. Religious learning, art, and music flourished. And in many ways the ecclesiastical structure began to exist separate from and independent of the body of believers it was intended to guide. Just as the shepherds imagine myriad ways of eating, yet have no actual food, the Church devised ever more exotic levels of spiritual service, yet no longer met its primary responsibility—to shepherd the faithful.

And herein lies the overall satire of *Prima Pastorum* and the significance of the echoes of Ecclesiastes: sheep, the very reason for the existence of shepherds, never actually appear in this shepherds' play. There is constant interaction with sheep in *Secunda Pastorum,* but none in this play. Surely shepherds without sheep are a folly, a symbol of life without purpose, a vanity of vanities. The only reference to sheep in the play, other than to Gyb's dead flock, comes before the feast when Gyb asks Iak Garcio, the "boy fool," how the sheep are pastured: "How pastures oure fee? / Say me, good pen" (ll. 270–1), The boy answers that "Thay are gryssed to the kne" (l. 273), a statement with at least two possible interpretations. "Gryssed" in this case surely refers to the act of being nourished, as in "gressen," where animals eat grass or graze to become fat or "*gras*." The boy's statement could indicate that the sheep are well nourished in grass up to their knees; yet given Garcio's attitude towards the shepherds, it is just as likely a ridiculous exaggeration or even an outright lie. The shepherds accept the first interpretation without checking for themselves. It is the answer they want to hear as they sit down to their lavish imaginary feast. They leave their primary duties, the maintenance of their flocks, to Iak Garcio, a type of the disobedient servant /boy prankster, who scorns the shepherds as fools and mocks their abstract folly. Helterman notes Garcio's mocking function:

> Garcio's brief appearance needs some study. His name suggests that he is the mischievous boy of many of the plays, like Pikeharnes in *Mactacio Abel* or Froward in *Coliphizacio*. The boy's typical role is that of deflator of swollen egos, and he is as close to a skeptic as one can find in the plays. (79)

Indeed, Garcio's skepticism as to the shepherds' wisdom carries over to their skill as shepherds. As he leaves, Iak Garcio says, to no one in particular, "If ye will ye may se; / Your bestes ye ken" (ll. 274–5), or "If you really want to know, you can see for yourself; you know your sheep." The statement is an ironic rebuke to the foolish, neglectful shepherds, who clearly don't know where their sheep are or what condition they are in, but it is also an indictment of clergy who are unaware of the needs of their flocks. This compares sadly with Christ's statement of pastoral responsibility in John 10:14: "I am the good shepherd; I know my sheep and my sheep know me." Christ knows his flock, and they know him; these shepherds are fools; they neither know nor are known by their flocks. Using the pastoral metaphor, the author of *De Officio Pastorali* writes that the spiritual shepherd "moten haue his presence with his sheep; for who can preche to his sheep, or defende hem fro wolues, or heele hem as curatis shulden , but yif he be present with his sheep? . . . Yif he waste tyme in this absence & profite not to hooly chirche, thys los of tyme accusith him before crist, the firste herde" (Matthew 454). The connection between mercenary shepherds and Christ, the first shepherd whose example all shepherds should follow, is explicit. So too is the ironic contrast between the folly of Gyb, Iohn Horne, and

Slawpase and the potential inherent in the birth of the original *pastor bonus* at the end of the play.

This contrast explains the change in tone at the end of the play. When the shepherds awaken after their post-feast stupor, the angels arrive to sing and announce the birth of Christ. Folly and parody disappear from this point on in the play, but festive themes remain. The shepherds discuss the prophecies of Christ's coming and then travel to visit him. They are certainly playful with each other, but they are also respectful and reverent, and their visit generally fits the standard nativity pattern; however, this does not mean that the influence of festive culture disappears. In fact, while the final nativity scene evokes the conventional, orthodox themes of salvation, it also fulfills the festive cycle.

The structural correlation of the feast and the angels' announcement is particularly important here. Following as it does the chaotic folly of the shepherds' feast, Christ's birth fits into the festive pattern of spring renewal and the regeneration that follows Winter death. Thus, at this point in the play, the central Christian message of the nativity and the values of the festive sub-culture become synchronized. Christ is the renewal of humanity, and his birth symbolizes the renewal expected after a winter feast. Thus, festive regeneration occurs only through Christ's incarnation. Similarly, note that structurally, Christ's birth follows only after the imaginary festive feast / mock mass has been celebrated. Symbolically, this implies that true incarnation and salvation occur only when the symbols of priestly abuse are degraded through parody and folly. In other words, the festive cycle brings Christian incarnation, and Christian incarnation is the fulfillment of the festive cycle. The same structural splicing occurs in *Secunda Pastorum*.

This synchronization of the two structural patterns in the play, namely the festive Yule cycle and the Christian nativity, ultimately binds the symbolic significance of festive celebration to Christ. In essence, the festive elements appropriate Christ and the meaning of his incarnation. This is best seen in the holiday (yet not parodic) atmosphere at the end of the play. The shepherds leave for the nativity in a lively, yet no longer foolish, mood. They perform the standard functions of relating the prophecies of Christ's birth, but their mood is neither serious nor reverential. Instead, they banter back and forth playfully and sing songs in imitation of the angels. Certainly this reflects the conventional orthodox sense of joy at such an occasion, but the shepherds display none of the serenity typical of joy; they are having fun and happily teasing each other:

> *1 Pastor:* Breke outt youre voce!
> Let se as ye yelp!
> *3 Pastor:* I may not for the pose,
> Bot I haue help.

> *2 Pastor:* A, thy hart is in thy hose!
> *1 Pastor:* Now, in payn of a skelp,
> This sang thou not lose! (ll. 608–14)

The three act like friends going to see an exciting attraction at the fair, and when they reach Christ, their playfulness continues. As they stumble around at the entrance to the nativity and wonder who should enter first, Iohn Horne teases Gyb about his age: " Ye ar of the old store; / It semys you, iwys" (ll. 658–9). Stevens and Cawley write, "In this context *old store* (used literally of livestock) is humorously applied to the First Shepherd, who is an older man than the Second" (493). Just as the old year meets the new in the guise of an old man welcoming a child, so the oldest of the foolish shepherds is first to greet the infant *pastor bonus.*

Further, the shepherds are playful even with their gifts to Christ. Scholars have given various interpretations as to the spiritual significance of the coffer, the ball, and the bottle, and I do not intend to disagree with these interpretations.[11] Yet the gifts, if spiritually significant, are also profoundly festive. Helterman notes that they "reflect on a literal level the shepherds' new sense of abundance, their understanding of a world which offers song and play as well as backbreaking work, and especially their homely joy in seeing the Child" (91). The gifts reflect the mirth and celebration of a festive occasion, but they also have individual festive significance. The "spruse cofer" (l. 672) is a little wooden box, but, as Helterman points out, it is very close (symbolically and linguistically) to a coffin (91). The gift therefore prefaces Christ's sacrifice and resonates as a festive symbol of death and regeneration. The ball is an unmistakeable symbol of play, (the essence of the festive spirit) as Iohn Horne emphasizes: "This wyll I vowchesaue, / To play the withall" (ll. 684–5). The third gift, a "botell" (694), evokes festive feasting, something we have already seen in great detail. It suggests drinking, as does Slawpase in his quotation of a popular proverb:

> It is an old byworde,
> 'It is a good bowrde
> For to drynk of a gowrde'—
> It holdys a mett potell. (ll. 695–8)

This suggestion of drinking with reference to the Christ perhaps smacks of irreverence in a conventional sense, but within the festive appropriation of the nativity, it only makes sense. Feasting is a celebration of abundance, and if Christ is the fulfillment of the festive cycle, then his association with the earthier elements of festive celebration becomes proper.

In this way, the shepherds inject festive mirth and imagery into the conventionally serious nativity. Gyb's final words underscore the festive appropriation even further. His welcome of Christ's birth is phrased in the form of holiday celebration rather than orthodox religious observance:

> To ioy all sam
> With myrth and gam,
> To the lawde of this lam
> Syng we in syght. (ll. 721–4)

The orthodox sense of serene joy remains, but it is joined to mirthfulness and the games of Yule. Christ the lamb is appropriated into the festive world view, while the folly of the orthodox clergy is exposed, mocked, degraded, and finally rehabilitated in the potential of the *pastor bonus*.

In all three episodes of folly, we see a common satirical thread; the clergy strive after the intangible to the detriment of that which is real. Priests bickering over lucrative chantries neglect the living flock. Priests care for the abstract soul but neglect to feed the living body. The church flourishes, but the flock is not nourished. In working solely for the intangible, priests strive after the wind. Their actions have become, to quote Ecclesiastes, vanity, emptiness, and folly. Yet priests are not the final measure of Christianity in the play. Christ, who was a lamb before becoming the good shepherd, offers hope to the disillusioned. The child Christ, born into the festive cycle as a symbol of renewal and as a New Year miracle, is the real foundation and hope, the means of peace and plenty not provided by foolish shepherds.

Chapter Six

Stripping Away the Wolf-Skin of False Shepherds[1]

The second play of shepherds in the cycle, traditionally called *Secunda Pastorum* or *Second Shepherds' Play*,[2] has a great deal in common with the first. Shepherds open with festive monologues, and the bulk of the play is marked by festive puns and parody before it ends with a more respectful nativity. In fact, *Secunda Pastorum* seems largely modeled after *Prima Pastorum*, with the notable change that the three shepherds tend their flocks conscientiously. Mak, however, has the traits of a false shepherd, like Gyb, Iohn Horne, and Slawpase in *Prima Pastorum*. Indeed, Mak seems to refer directly to the *Prima Pastorum* shepherds, claiming Iohn Horne and another Gyb, Gybon Waller, were the god-parents of his new "child." While it is perhaps a stretch to suggest that the themes of the one play directly inspired those of the other, the structural and thematic relationship between the two plays is clearly close, and critics have understandably sought after the nature of this relationship. John Gardner, for example, asks and answers this question:

> 'Why did the Wakefield Master need to compose, himself, two separate shepherds' pageants?' The answer is virtually implied by the question. The first pageant gave him the idea for the second, an idea he liked so well he decided to use it. . . . Much of what happens in *Secunda Pastorum* is drama-tization in new form of ideas worked out in this earlier pageant. (77)

The play certainly repeats much of what was said in *Prima Pastorum*, but what is repeated is as important as the repetition itself. All three shepherds open their monologues with passages which echo Gyb's opening monologue in *Prima Pastorum*, part of which I repeat here:

Here is mekyll vnceyll
And long has it last

Now in hart, now in heyll,
Now in weytt, now in blast;
Now in care,
Now in comforth agane;
Now is fayre, now is rane;
Now in hart full fane,
And after full sare.
Thus this warld, as I say,
Farys on ylk syde,
For after oure play
Com sorows vnryde; (*Prima* ll. 5–17)

In *Secunda Pastorum,* Coll says in his first stanza,

For I am al lappyd
In sorow.
In stormes and tempest,
Now in the eest, now in the west,
Wo is hym has neuer rest
Mydday nor morow! (ll. 8–13)

Gyb complains in his first stanza,

Now in dry, now in wete,
Now in snaw, now in slete,
When my shone freys to my fete
It is not all esy. (ll. 88–91)

The first stanza of Daw's opening remarks include,

Whoso couthe take heed
And lett the warld pas,
It is euer in drede
And brekyl as glas,
And slythys.
This warld fowre neuer so,
With meruels mo and mo:
Now in weyll, now in wo,
And all thyng wrythys. (ll. 174–82)

All three shepherds repeat the festive theme of variability with specific linguistic and semantic echoes of *Prima Pastorum.* The world is a shifting reality, or as brittle as glass, and this is best seen in the series of oppositional, topsy-turvy situations: *now in this, now in that.* Both plays also use the violent changes in weather that plague poor shepherds as examples of the world's changeability.

Sounds more like a lament

This theme resonates well with the cyclic world view of festive culture. It is particularly appropriate to a festive observation of Yule, which begins with Winter disruption and looks forward to the regeneration of spring.

The individual monologues, although they begin with the same theme, quickly diverge to different subject matter, but these subjects are also explored from a distinctly festive perspective. Coll begins by attacking the current enclosure practices of the landed aristocracy. No wonder, he says, if farmers are poor; they are prevented from tilling the land by the agents of the aristocracy (ll. 18–21). The landowners and their agents pile burden after burden upon the poor peasants:

> We ar so hamyd,
> Fortaxed and ramyd,
> We ar mayde handtamyd
> With thyse gentlery-men. (ll. 23–6)

Coll complains long and hard about enclosure:

> Thus thay refe vs oure rest,
> Oure Lady theym wary!
> These men that ar lord-fest,
> Thay cause the ploghe tary. . . . (ll. 27–30)

Like Iohn Horne in *Prima Pastorum,* Coll points out the excessive pride, unreasonable demands, and mindless violence of the agents of the landowners (indicated by colored sleeves or brooches):

> For may he gett a paynt slefe
> Or a broche now-on-dayes,
> Wo is hym that hym grefe
> Or onys agane-says!
> Dar noman hym reprefe,
> What mastry he mays. . . . (ll.40–5)

> . . . .

> There shall com a swane
> As prowde as a po;
> He must borow my wane,
> My ploghe also;
> Then I am full fane
> To graunt or he go.
> Thus lyf we in payne,
> Anger, and wo,

By nyght and day.
He must haue if he langyd,
If I shuld forgang it;
I were better be hangyd
Than oones say hym nay. (ll. 53–65)

These comments and complaints are typical of the festive perspective. As
noted in Chapter Two, rejection and overthrow of conventional authority is
an important festive practice. Coll's complaints amount to a verbal overthrow of the moral authority of the landed class. He attacks the actions of
the land owner's agents, but he also implies that the root cause lies with the
seigneurial system:

He can make purveance
With boste and bragance,
And all is thrugh mantenance
Of men that ar gretter. (ll. 49–52)

Coll's monologue follows festive patterns of rejection of authority and suggests the shepherds exist in a moral winter as well as a meteorological one.
       Gyb enters after Coll with a lament over the miseries of married men:

We sely wedmen
Dre mekyll wo:
We have sorow then and then;
It oft fallys so. (ll. 94–7)

Gyb uses the metaphor of a hen laying an egg to describe how the production
of offspring heralds great hardship in a married man's life:

Sely Copyle, oure hen,
Both to and fro
She kakyls;
Bot begyn she to crok,
To groyne or to clok,
Wo is hym is our cok,
For he is in the shakyls. (ll. 98–104)

As a result of children, Gyb tells us, married men lose their will, being con-
strained to labor without rest for the maintenance of their families:

These men that are wed
Haue not all thare wyll;
When they ar full hard sted,

Thay sygh full styll.
God wayte thay are led
Full hard and full yll. . . . (ll. 105–10)

Gyb repeatedly warns young men against the burden of marriage, and to drive
his point home, he gives a frightening description of his own drunken, repul-
sive, and ill-tempered wife:

As sharp as a thystyll,
As rugh as a brere;
She is browyd lyke a brystyll,
With a sowre-loten chere;
Had she oones wett hyr whystyll,
She couth syng full clere
Hyr Paternoster.
She is as greatt as a whall,
She has a galon of gall. . . . (ll. 146–54)

Gyb's monologue makes use of several festive themes. The constant childbirthing
of wives fits the general theme of regeneration. So, too, does the reversal inherent in an abusive and domineering wife who makes life miserable for her hen-
pecked husband. Gyb's wife is also a particularly festive character since Gyb's
description of her is excessive and grotesque and focuses upon her drinking.
Overall, however, Gyb's attack upon marriage fits the festive pattern of abolish-
ing normal social constraints and restrictions for a temporary festive moment.

Daw's monologue elaborates upon the bad weather with a twist, evok-
ing Noah's flood to characterize the current rains:

Was neuer syn Noe flode
Sich floodys seyn,
Wyndys and ranys so rude,
And Stormes so keyn. (ll. 183–6)

Daw's usage of the great flood is curious here because there is no such flooding in the biblical or dramatic accounts of the nativity. Stevens and Cawley
credit the reference to Noah's typological significance as Christ (498), but
Daw's reference makes no mention of salvation. Rather, the flood he describes
has a destructive effect only:

These floodys so thay drowne,
Both in feyldys and in towne,
And berys all downe;
And that is a wonder. (ll. 191–5)

However, the reference recalls the terrible disruption of natural forces in the *Processus Noe,* which is an appropriate theme of Yule celebration.

After an initial greeting of the first two shepherds, Daw's monologue continues, developing the theme of oppression begun by the first two, but reversing the relationship such that Coll and Gyb become the oppressors. When Gyb and Coll scorn and reject his request for food and drink, Daw says,

> Sich seruandys as I,
> That swettys and swynkys,
> Etys oure brede full dry,
> And that me forthynkys.
> We are oft weytt and wery
> When master-men wynkys,
> Yit commys full lately
> Both dyners and drynkys;
> Bot nately
> Both oure dame and oure syre,
> When we haue ryn in the myre,
> Thay can nyp at oure hyre,
> And pay vs full lately. (ll. 222–34)

Daw's complaints have a topsy-turvy effect upon the previous two monologues. Coll has just complained about the oppressive practices of his masters. Gyb has just explained how his wife abuses him. In Daw's monologue, however, Coll and Gyb are cast as the oppressive and abusive ones, reversing roles in a typically festive pattern.[3] Thus, all three opening monologues evoke festive qualities and themes, suggesting more of a festive Yule celebration than a reverent nativity, a suggestion that the subsequent comedic action of the play, in the story of Mak and Gyll, confirms.

The first two speeches also have another festive purpose. They use a series of puns to create a parallel symbolic relationship between children and sheep, husbands and farmers, wives and fields, and more. These puns are an important foundation to the later parody of the play, but they also constitute a subtle and irreverent parody of contemporary land management practices.

Double meaning begins in the first line with a pun on the word "weder." The first shepherd, Coll, begins the play with the words, "Lord what these weders are cold!/ And I am yll happyd" (ll. 1–2). "Weder" in this context seems to mean weather, as in "the weather is cold."[4] When Gyb enters, he uses the term in just such a context:

> Lord, thyse weders are spytus
> And the wyndys full kene,[5]
> And the frostys so hydus

Thay water myn eeyne,
No ly. (ll. 83–7)

On a surface level, both shepherds are complaining about the bitter winter weather.

Yet the same word is used with another meaning, both in this play and in *Prima Pastorum*. In the first play, Gyb uses the word "weder" in reference to a sheep (l. 164), as in "wether," or "bell-wether" (the leader of the flock to whom a bell was attached). Coll uses the word in the same context in *Secunda Pastorum* when he discovers the lost sheep: "A fat wedir haue we lorne" (l. 651).

These homonyms, which cannot be distinguished by the liberal spelling conventions of the day (both denotations are spelled "weder" and "wedir" in the Towneley plays), can usually be distinguished by context. In this context, "weather" seems to be implied; despite the plural form of the word. Yet the shepherd is surrounded by sheep, or wethers, and the reason the shepherds are out of doors in such bad weather lies with the sheep, or wethers—the shepherds are in fact plowmen who have been forced to give up farming and tend to flocks of sheep by the practice of enclosure, as Coll divulges a few lines later:

Bot we sely husbandys
That walkys on the moore,
In fayth we ar nerehandys
Outt of the doore.
No wonder, as it standys,
If we be poore,
For the tylthe of oure landys
Lyys falow as the floor,
As ye ken. (ll. 14–22)

Martin Stevens and A. C. Cawley note that "the decision by landowners to let their arable land lie fallow as a preparatory step to its enclosure for pasture brought on the conversion of husbandmen to shepherds" (495). Peasants who had farmed common manor lands for as long as they could remember were suddenly fenced off of these lands so the Manor Lords could raise the more lucrative sheep, and the only work available to the ex-plowmen was that of the shepherd.

The threat of enclosure loomed large in the consciousness of medieval peasants because it diminished their economic worth and reduced their ability to support themselves. In his landmark text on the enclosure movement, W. E. Tate notes that enclosure meant at best reduced (and undesirable) forms of employment and at worst complete expulsion from the land:

It might be profitable on enclosure to convert it to pasturage for the rearing of sheep (or more rarely of cattle). If this happened, however, without other lands being taken into cultivation, the corn acreage would be diminished. There would be a shortage of employment (since the same area gave much more employment when it was under the plough than when it was in grass). . . . The former villagers might be expelled from the place and driven into vagrancy. If as vagrants they begged, they were liable to be whipped and branded, and if they stole they might suffer death. (62)

Indeed, enclosure is the bane of the plowman-turned-shepherd's existence in the *Secunda Pastorum*. Coll complains at length, although without any specific accusations, about the abuses and predations of the large land owners, especially about their brutal denial and rejection of what peasants considered their traditional rights to farm the land.

Thus when Coll speaks of "weders," in the context of something causing hardship and misfortune, he both means the obvious weather and implies the less obvious sheep, or rather the oppressive practices that have driven the men into being caretakers of the sheep. This pun is insignificant by itself, but it introduces a series of puns that together create an artful and subtle parody of the very enclosure practices obliquely criticized by Coll.

The second pun is upon the word "husbandys." As it is used above (line 14), the term implies farmers, as practitioners of the art of husbandry. Specifically, the word refers to those plowmen, traditionally tillers of the soil, who have been turned into shepherds by enclosure. Lines 20–21 specify this when Coll mentions that his fields lie fallow at the order of "gentlery-men" (l.26). Coll immediately reiterates this situation, again with the word "husband":

> These men that ar lord-fest,
> Thay cause the ploghe tary;
> That, men say, is for the best—
> We fynde it contrary.
> Thus are husbandys oppresst,
> In ponte to myscary
> On lyfe. (ll. 29–35)

Again, Coll emphasizes that the natural inclination of the husband or farmer, tilling the land with his plow, is prevented by the agents of the aristocracy.

As with "wedirs," however, the word "husbandys" also has another, more ancient meaning. From the Anglo-Saxon for "house" and "bond," the word also means husband in the modern sense, the male partner of the wife. In fact, the word is rarely used to denote a farmer; the word seems so unusual in this context that a scribe has replaced it with "shepardes" in line fourteen even though this breaks the clear feminine rhyme of the stanza. Concerning this switch, Stevens and Cawley write, "There can be no doubt, in view of the rhyme sequence, that husbandys (suggested in J. M. Manly's edition) is intended here" (495). Since the use of "husband" to denote farmer is so rare in the Towneley cycle, and since even the scribe apparently found the term to be inappropriate in this context, the audience would have surely caught the implied second meaning, that of a husband in a marital relationship. Note also that the word is used within the context of "opprest" husbands (l. 33), which, if the term implies the male marriage partner, evokes a stock tradition in folk drama, one that the Wakefield Master uses extensively in this play. In fact, oppressed husbands are central to the play. Mak's character derives from this stock type of the oppressed husband. Furthermore, this concept of the henpecked husband is at the heart of the next monologue and the next pun.

The third pun, which ties the first two together, is introduced by Gyb. When he enters the play, he twice within two lines repeats the same sentiment about the terrible "weders," although modern editors replace one of these "weders" with "wyndys" (ll. 83, 84) because repetition of "weders" seems unnecessary. Gyb then says,

> We sely wedmen
> Dre mekyll wo:
> We haue sorow then and then;
> It fallys oft so. (ll. 94–7)

Stevens and Cawley gloss the word "wedmen" as "married men," and Gyb's long monologue on the sad plight of married men supports this interpretation (724). As he relates the miseries of being bound in wedlock to a domineering wife, Gyb continues to use the two parts of this word ("wed" and "man") in varying combinations. After his metaphorical lament over the miseries initiated by the birth of children, he says,

> These men that ar wed
> Haue not all thare wyll;
> When they ar full hard sted,
> That sygh full styll. (ll. 105–9)

This loss of "wyll" in the married state is at the heart of his complaints. Marriage forces a young man to exchange liberty for servitude, choice for obedience. Gyb recommends that young men in the audience avoid marriage altogether, because later regrets will not help them escape:

> Bot, yong men, of wowyng,
> For God that you boght,
> Be well war of wedyng,

And thynk in youre thoght:
'Had-I-wyst' is a thyng
That seruys of noght. (ll. 131–6)

Yet the term "wedmen" also suggests a second meaning, namely the shepherds themselves, men who take care of weders. The reference occurs directly after Gyb has twice (within two lines) mentioned the miseries of weders (weathers), a repetition so strange that modern editors have removed the second "weders." Further, the plight of the shepherds (weder-men) directly parallels the plight of husbands (wedded men). Both have lost their independence to irreversible trends. The married man has lost his will to "wedyng" (l. 133), or marriage; the shepherd has lost his will to "wedyng" also, at least in the sense of the practice of replacing his traditional and preferred livelihood with the onerous duty of caring for "weders." Further, just as the production of children who must be cared for and provided for puts the husband (wedded man) "in the shakyls" (l. 104), so too the increase of weders through enclosure causes the farmer (or "husbandys") to be "handtamyd" by "gentlery-men" (ll. 25, 26). Weders symbolize their servitude and remind them of their lost independence, just as children do to husbands such as Gyb and, later, Mak.

The puns are tied together by parallels throughout, such as the lament for married men at the end of Gyb's monologue:

Mekyll styll mowrnyng
Has wedyng home brought,
And grefys,
With many a sharp showre. (ll. 137–40)

The "wedyng," or marriage, brings to the married man the same "grefys" and "mowrnyng" as weders (in both senses) bring to the shepherd. Furthermore, "wedyng" exposes "wedmen" to "many a sharp showre." In this case the showers probably denote insults or items thrown at the husband, but they parallel the showers of rain and sleet that all three shepherds complain of as they enter the play.

The interconnection of these puns reveals more when viewed overall. The first shepherd, Coll, muses upon the miseries of farmers turned shepherds, but he does so using the language of married men, namely referring to the farmers as "husbandys." The second shepherd, Gyb, muses upon the miseries of lovers turned fathers, or husbands, but he does so using language that could also refer to shepherds. The two monologues cross-reference each other and thus create a humorous symbolic relationship. The farmer deprived of his lands and forced to tend sheep resembles the husband deprived of his will and forced to tend his children.

The comparison is further enhanced with festively *risqué* details. In Coll's speech, the farmer is prevented from tilling his lands. His fields are enclosed, and he is forced to endure hardship as he tends sheep. In spite of the farmer's, or husband's, natural inclination to plow his fields, the landowners "cause the ploghe tary" (l. 30). Gyb's speech contains many parallels; when wives give birth, husbands are forced to endure hardships and provide for their families. Yet Gyb implies a closer parallel. He suggests that husbands, or wedmen, "Haue not all thare wyll; / . . . In bowere nor in bed" (ll. 106, 111). In other words, when children enter the husband's life, he no longer has his will in sexual matters. Metaphorically speaking, he can no longer use his "ploghe." Gyb's comparison of childbirth with "Sely Copyle," the hen, laying an egg, implies this relationship more forcefully:

> Bot begyn she to crok,
> To groyne or to clok,
> Wo is hym is our cok,
> For he is in the shakyls. (ll. 101–4)

The signs of birth, in this case the groaning and clucking of a hen laying an egg, are also signs that the cock, or rooster, has been bound into servitude, and this image appears again in the description of Gyll's childbirth. Yet the word "cok" has long had another meaning, namely "penis," and the cock in shackles after the production of offspring directly parallels the "oppresst" "husbandys" "ploghe" being caused to tarry after enclosure.[6]

These puns thus create an elaborate and clever burlesque of the practice of enclosure. The farmer forced from the tilling of his lands and made to tend sheep becomes the husband forced from the sexual embrace of his wife and made to tend children. Of course the parody is important because it introduces the relationship between children and sheep, and between shepherds and husbands, relationships essential to the later, well-known parody of the nativity. However, these puns are significant in their own right because they create a clever and festive parody of an abusive aristocratic practice. By comparing the hardships of the peasantry to the stock comedic woes of hen-pecked husbands, the parody redefines those hardships within the realm of joke and innuendo.

The comic portrayal of the aristocratic landowners also undermines the authority of the aristocracy. If husbands are farmers and children are sheep, then the landowners and agents who enclose the fields and force plowmen into shepherding can be equated to the fat, drunken, and obnoxious wife described by Gyb. Note that this wife matches a typically male character type; she is hairy, rough, large, loud, and mean (ll. 145–54). This description seems particularly masculine, as suitable for describing an ill-tempered, domineering overseer as for describing a wife. Whereas the agents of the land owners hold the powers of life, death, failure, and prosperity, this stock shrewish wife presents the audience with a familiar and non-threatening nag to mock and belittle.

Moreover, Gyb's stock comic dig at those men who are foolish enough to engage in bigamy places in a comic context the hardships faced by those peasants who are forced by enclosure to peddle their labor from one landowner to another, or are forced to be subservient, like Coll, to a variety of aristocratic agents. Gyb says,

> Bot now late in oure lyfys—
> A meruell to me,
> That I thynk my hart ryfys
> Sich wonders to see;
> What that destany dryfys
> It shuld so be—
> Som men wyll haue two wyfys,
> And som men thre
> In store; (ll. 118–26)

Gyb's joke is conventional; with a wife like his, only a fool would want more than one.

However, the comic relationship between wives and landowners extends the humor of this folly to the plight of landless laborers, who, like bigamous husbands, must now negotiate with multiple masters rather than with one. We hear the anguish of their perspective when Coll says, "Thus hold thay us hunder,/ Thus thay bryng vs in blonder" (ll. 36–7), or "Thus lyf we in payne,/ Anger, and wo./ By nyght and day" (ll. 59–61). Yet this anguish is somehow mitigated, and even absorbed, by Gyb's parallel image of a husband subjected to the mastery of several wives:

> Some ar wo that has any.
> Bot so far can I:
> Wo is hym that has many,
> For he felys sore. (ll. 127–30)

Gyb's stock commentary on the folly of polygamous husbands, especially piquant from the perspective of the hen-pecked husband, subtly highlights the immorality and folly of enclosure practices, but it also renders them ridiculous and, hence, non-threatening within stock festive conventions.

The parody thus redefines frightening social change and aristocratic abuse within a stock comic scene. A peasant thrown off of land that has been farmed by his family for centuries is unthinkable, but a husband thrown out of his bedroom by an abusive wife is familiar and funny, and contemplation of the second somehow makes the reality of the first more bearable. The plight of farmers forced to tend sheep seems less devastating when compared to the stock comedic complaint of husbands besieged by hungry children.

Yet this early parody is also significant because it introduces the relationship between children and sheep, the foundation of the main parody in the play. This parody, whereby the story of Mak, Gyll, and the stolen sheep parallel the nativity scene, is the central dramatic episode and the element around which the rest of the play is built. The parody is set up when Mak approaches the singing shepherds, who immediately become suspicious of his motives and force him to sleep between them. Once they are asleep, he rises, casts a spell on them, and steals a fat sheep which he takes home to his wife, Gyll. Mak conspires with Gyll to hide the sheep in the baby cradle and pretend she has just given birth; he then returns to lay down with the shepherds. The shepherds awaken, Daw panicking because he has dreamed of Mak in a wolf skin, and find Mak apparently sleeping. Later, when the shepherds realize a sheep is missing, they go to Mak's and Gyll's home to search for their charge. The two thieves successfully deceive the shepherds, Gyll complaining loudly about being disturbed after childbirth, until the shepherds return with a gift for the "child" and discover its remarkable similarity to their missing sheep. The shepherds toss Mak in canvas and return to their herd, where the Angels appear with the news of Christ's birth.

The plot, while immensely entertaining drama, seems little connected to the final nativity, but it introduces themes of pastoral care and predation which are. When Daw, the third shepherd, declares he has dreamt of Mak "lapt / In a wolfe-skyn," (ll. 530–1), modern students may be reminded of Wile E. Coyote hiding beneath a sheepskin as he tries in vain to slip past the ever vigilant sheepdog. For medieval audiences, however, Daw's comment, along with the first shepherd's reply that "So are many hapt / Now, namely within" (ll. 532–3),[7] would have evoked a completely different set of images. Portrayals of shepherds, of sheep, and of wolves in shepherds' clothing who prey upon sheep are repeatedly used in medieval literature to comment upon the clergy and priestly corruption. Heretofore, scholars have largely ignored the import of the pastoral metaphor in their analysis of the play. However, Mak's portrayal as a wolf-like pseudo-shepherd, especially one who feigns camaraderie as he plots to beguile the shepherds and ravage their flock, closely parallels the common medieval metaphor of clergy as false, predatory shepherds and would seem to offer the best key with which to interpret the middle section of the play. The pastoral metaphor pervades Fourteenth and Fifteenth Century English writings on the clergy, and, as noted in Chapter

Five, the nativity shepherds in particular are commonly treated as types of clergy. Like their colleagues in *Prima Pastorum,* these shepherds speak Latin and display an impressive knowledge of the scriptures (ll. 972–84, 998–1010). Unlike Gyb, Iohn Horne, and Slawpase, however, these shepherds tend their flocks with care, searching near and far for their lost sheep, illustrating the shepherd in Christ's parable of the lost sheep:

> *Quis ex vobis homo, qui habet centum oves: et si perdiderit unam ex illis,*
> *none dimittit nonaginta novem in deserto, et vadit ad illam quae perierat,*
> *donec inveniat eam? Et cum invenerit eam, imponit in humeros suos gau-*
> *dens: et veniens domun convocat amicos et vicinos, dicens illis:*
> *Congratulamini mihi, quia inveni ovemmeam, quae perierat?*
> What man among you, if he has a hundred sheep and has lost one of
> them, does not leave the ninety-nine in the open pasture, and go after the
> one which is lost, until he finds it? And when he has found it, he lays it
> on his shoulders, rejoicing. And when he comes home, he calls together
> his friends and his neighbors, saying to them, 'Rejoice with me, for I have
> found my sheep which was lost!' (Luke 15: 4–6)

Mak, however, plays the role of a predator upon the flock, one who stops at nothing, including sorcery, to beguile the shepherds and take their sheep for slaughter. His predatory nature is surely key to interpretion of the central sheep-stealing episode, and perhaps of the entire drama. Mak is, after all, the dominant character of the play; he is the lynchpin connecting the discussions on the moors, the theft of the sheep and parody of the nativity, and the final nativity scene.[8] His central role suggests that his corrupt character and larcenous actions, so contrary to the promise of hope and salvation inherent in the birth of Christ, should be considered a central focus and theme of the play. Specifically, his role evokes a multitude of anti-clerical metaphors criticizing corrupt, wolvish clergy who subvert the work of good shepherds in order to exploit and defraud the flock. Reading Mak as a type of these false, predatory clergy reconfigures the cultural significance of the play. Perhaps most significantly, such a reading offers an explanation as to why the Towneley Master places a long tale of delusion, fakery, larceny, and exploitation into the heart of his second nativity play.

The bulk of the *Secunda Pastorum,* between the shepherds' monologues and the final *Gloria* and nativity scene, is focused upon the sheep-stealer Mak. While the sheep-stealing plot has several analogues in medieval ballads, it is an unusual focus for a shepherds' play.[9] As Morgan notes, most medieval shepherds' plays contain only two main scenes, "one set in the fields, where the Angel proclaims Christ's birth to the Shepherds, and the other set in the stable, where the Shepherds do homage to the newborn Child" (676). Aside

from the Towneley plays, only the Chester shepherds' play has a central section unrelated to the scriptural nativity, and this merely involves bickering
among the shepherds. In *Secunda Pastorum,* however, the Towneley Master in-
serts a raucous and lengthy story that takes up lines 274–906 of this 1088-line
play, and it introduces themes of theft and fraud that contrast sharply with the
conventional nativity at the end of the play.[10] Especially striking is the contrast between the birth of Christ, the archetypal good shepherd, and the actions of the larcenous Mak, an apparent model trickster who exploits the flock
for selfish ends.[11]

While Christ is the true *pastor bonus,* the good shepherd of the Church,
Mak is an inverted or false shepherd, the wolf in shepherd's clothing that
poses as a shepherd even as he preys on the sheep. This is a familiar concept
in Christian tradition, which often combines the roles of the mercenary shepherd and the ravaging wolf from scriptural sources. In John 10, when Christ
speaks of himself as a shepherd, he also speaks both of false shepherds and of
wolves who come to prey upon the sheep:

> *Amen, amen dico vobis, qui non intrat per ostium in ovile ovium, sed ascendit*
> *aliunde, ille fur est et latro. Qui autem intrat per ostium, pastor est ovium.*
> 'Truly, truly, I say to you, he who does not enter by the door into the fold
> of the sheep, but climbs up some other way, he is a thief and a robber,
> but he who enters by the door is a shepherd of the sheep.' (John 10:1–2)

> *Alienum autem non sequuntur, sed fugiunt ab eo, quia non noverunt vocem*
> *alienorum.*
> 'And a stranger they simply will not follow, but will flee from him, be-
> cause they do not know the voice of strangers.' (John 10:5)

> *Fur non venit nisi ut furetur, et mactet et perdat. Ego veni ut vitam habeant*
> *et abundantius habeant. Ego sum pastor bonus. Bonus pastor animam suam*
> *dat pro ovibus suis. Mercenarius autem, et qui non est pastor, cuius non sunt*
> *oves propriae, videt lupum venientem, et dimittit oves, et fugit: et lupus rapit,*
> *et dispergit oves.*
> 'The thief comes only to steal and kill and destroy; I came that they
> might have life, and might have it abundantly. I am the good shepherd;
> the good shepherd lays down his life for the sheep. He who is a hireling,
> and not a shepherd, who is not the owner of the sheep, beholds the wolf
> coming and leaves the sheep, and flees, and the wolf snatches them, and
> scatters them.' (John 10:10–12)

In these passages, Christ contrasts the good shepherd with the pretender, the
one who climbs into the fold rather than entering through the door, and who

comes "to steal and kill and destroy." Mak is just such a pretender. He arrives surreptitiously, seeking to sneak around the shepherds to steal their sheep. When they see him, he attempts to fool them into thinking he is an agent of the king. Later, when they are asleep, he says:

> Now were tyme for a man
> That lakkys what he wold
> To stalk preuely than
> Vnto a fold. (ll. 387–90)

Mak's stated intentions directly echo Christ's portrayal of the pretender in John. Further parallels with the passage can be seen in Daw's dream of Mak lapped "In a wolfe-skyn" (l. 531); Daw awakens in a panic, seeking to bar the door, perhaps the door to the fold spoken of in John (ll. 517–26). Similarly, the frightened reaction of the sheep to Mak's foreign presence also parallels verse five, in which Christ speaks of the sheep fleeing from the voice of a stranger: "If the flock be skard, / Yit shall I nyp nere. / How! drawes hederward!" (ll. 417–9)

However, while Mak is a distinct type of predator, one suggestive of the wolf who preys on the sheep in the shepherd's flock, his character also resembles that of a shepherd. Like Gyb, Coll, and Daw, he roams the moors, hungry and cold and complaining about it. Like Coll, he bemoans his lack of "will," or of control over his own destiny (ll. 284–6). Like Gyb, he complains of a brutal, lazy, drunken wife and of too many children. These are striking parallels that emphasize the similarities between Mak and the shepherds. Indeed, Mak technically becomes a shepherd, albeit a predatory and dishonest one, when he steals the sheep and attempts to keep it. He says as much about himself: "Was I neuer a shepard, / Bot now wyll I lere" (ll. 415–6).

Mak's "shepherding," however, seems a photographic negative of that of the real shepherds in the play, who, unlike their brethren in *Prima Pastorum*, are conscientious pastors. Despite the general similarities of form, Mak is an uncanny inversion of Coll, Gyb, and Daw in his treatment of the flock. Whereas they watch over the sheep, he stalks them. While the shepherds protect, he devours. This inverse relationship is perhaps best demonstrated in Mak's horrible piping and singing. As they pass the night away, the shepherds sing harmoniously to their sheep in the best pastoral tradition:

> *1 Pastor:* Yit I wold, or we yode,
> Oone gaf vs a song.
> *2 Pastor.:* So I thoght, as I strode,
> To myrth vs emong.
> *3 Pastor:* I grauntt.
> *1 Pastor.:* Lett me syng the tenory.

> 2 *Pastor.*: And I the tryble so hye.
> 3 *Pastor* Then the meyne fallys to me.
> Lett se how ye chauntt. (ll. 265–73)

However, when Mak enters directly after their song, the shepherds notice dissonant notes. Coll says, "Who is that pypys so poore?" (l. 283). This question could refer to Mak's initial whining complaints, but in the context, it could also mean shepherd pipes, bagpipes, or actual singing. Whichever it is, it certainly refers to an unpleasant sound, a clear contrast to the shepherds' harmony. Later, after the angels appear and sing *Gloria in excelsis,* the shepherds emulate them, providing an inspirational preface to the true nativity:

> 2 *Pastor:* Say, what was his song?
> Hard ye not how he crakyd it,
> Thre brefes to a long?
> 3 *Pastor:* Yee, Mary, he hakt it:
> Was no crochett wrong,
> Nor nothyng that lakt it.
> 1 *Pastor:* For to syng vs emong,
> Right as he knakt it,
> I can. (ll. 946–54)

In the shadow nativity, by contrast, Mak provides a dissonant preface as he sings "lullay" to warn Gyll of the approaching shepherds (l. 638). The shepherds note his singing with distaste, horrified at the noise emanating from Mak's hut:

> 3 *Pastor:* Will ye here how thay hak?
> Oure syre lyst croyne.
> 1 *Pastor:* Hard I neuer none crak
> So clere out of toyne. (ll. 686–9)

Mak's role as both a predator upon sheep and a false or inverse image of a shepherd is significant, especially in light of John 10 and within the Christian tradition of the pastoral metaphor. When these plays were performed, as noted above, the pastoral metaphor held particular currency as a means to condemn priestly corruption and predation. Chaucer uses it in *The Canterbury Tales,* as does Gower in *Vox Clamantis.* The anti-clerical "pellycane" of *The Plowman's Tale* also uses the metaphor liberally. Speaking of the worldliness of medieval priests and prelates, the pelican says, "And all suche sheperdes God amende" (l. 676). The pelican specifically charges that the medieval clergy are "countrefete" shepherds (l. 709) who have abandoned the true shepherding traditions of Peter and instead attempt to "byte," or consume, the sheep:

> Christ bade Peter kepe His shepe,
> And with his swerd forbade hym smyte.
> Swerd is no tole with shepe to kepe,
> But to sheperdes that shepe woll byte. (ll. 573–6)

Many of the clergy are not shepherds in the tradition of Peter, the poem argues, because real shepherds would succour their sheep rather than using swords to butcher them:

> So successours to Peter be they nought,
> Whom Christ made chefe pastoure:
> A swerde no sheperde usen ought,
> But he wold flee, as a bochoure. (ll. 581–4)

Such clergy, the Pelican says, only wish to devour the sheep and exploit them for their wool, or material wealth: "He culleth the shepe as dothe the coke: / Of hem taken the woll untrende, / And falsely glose the Gospell boke" (ll. 593–5). The poem refers directly to the passage in John by accusing these clergy of being hired men, ordained only for the material rewards they can glean from the office:

> By the dore they go, nat into the folde,
> To helpe theyr shepe they nought travall;
> Hyred men all suche I holde,
> And all suche false, foule hem fall! (ll. 425–8)

Use of the pastoral metaphor to condemn the behavior of venal clergy was common among Lollards. The author of the Lollard tract *The Lanterne of Light* argues that prelates who claim the authority of heaven for their own uses are corrupt and foolish shepherds: "Art not thou thanne a wicked man, a foul-tid schepard, a cruel beest, the sone of perdicioun and Anticrist him-silf that pretendist in thee and in thi membris to bynde and lose, to blesse and curse, biside this name Jesu?" (Dean 76) The popularity of this metaphor during the time in which the play was written suggests that audiences would have understood pastoral themes as a metaphor for commentary on the clergy. This inherent implication greatly alters the significance of Mak's role as a false predator upon the flock.

As noted above, Mak parallels the predator in John in several significant ways. He plans to "stalk preuely" (l. 501), and Daw dreams of him as a wolf (ll. 530–3). Treating clergy as wolves in shepherd's clothing is a common motiff among critics of Church corruption. The author of *De Officio Pastorali*, for example, exhorts good "herdis," or priests, to keep wolvish clergy who prey upon the parishioners away from the flock:

the secounde offiss that fallith to herdis is to kepe ther sheep fro woluys, as false freris, that comen to men to robbe ther wolle & do hem harm, ben clepid of crist woluys of raueyn. and of this perel shulden persouns warne men. & what othere false prechouris that comen to men & prechen herefore, thei ben woluys or foxis or houndis, & alle thes shulden be chased fro the floc. (Matthew 438–9)

A later Lollard attack on the ecclesiastical hierarchy begins by saying, "Crist biddith vs be war with thes false profetis that comen in clothing of scheepe and ben wolues of raueyne" (Hudson 75). In like manner, a Lollard sermon repeatedly connects the wolf in John 10 to predatory clergy:

Summe been wolues withoutforth, and summe been wolues withyn and these ben more perilous, for homely enmyes ben the worste. Yuel wolues ben religious that Crist seith in Matheu book ben wolues raueschinge, al if thei comen in shepe clothis, for bi this ypocrisie thei disseyuen sunner the scheppe. (Hudson 66)

In such polemic, the false, mercenary shepherd tends to be conflated with the wolf who ravages the flock; clergy who abuse or exploit their charges are both false shepherds and rapacious wolves. The same Lollard sermon, for example, asks "hou schulde Cristis chirche fare if these heerdis weren turned to wolues? . . . Lord, if cowardise of such hynen be thus dampned of Crist, hou moche moor schulden wolues be dampned that ben putt to kepe Cristis scheep?" (65–6) Kathryn Kerby-Fulton relates how Hildegard of Bingen used the metaphor of the wolfish priest in *Liber divinorum operum*: "She opens by calling the clergy 'perversi mercenarii' (col. 1006D), who devour the goods of the people like wolves. . . . For Hildegard the avaricious clergy are wolves who tear or put to flight the 'little ones' of the flock" (35). The anonymous author of *Piers the Plowman's Crede* gives a similar interpretation of the four orders of Friars. After Peres hears of the narrator's encounters with the Friars, he condemns them as fools, false prophets, and man-wolves in sheep's clothing:

"A, brother," quath he tho, "beware of tho foles!
For Crist seyde Himselfe 'of swich I you warne,'
And false profetes in the feith He fulliche hem calde,
'*In vestimentis ovium*, but onlie withinne
Thei ben wilde wer-wolves that wiln the folk robben.'
The fend founded hem first the feith to destroie,
And by his craft thei comen in to combren the Chirche. (ll. 455–61)

Mak's character, therefore, the wolf-like false shepherd, is also a common metaphorical criticism of abusive clergy.

Indeed, much about Mak is priest-like, but in a dark and sinister way, and in this he evokes many of the harshest details of anti-clerical polemic. Like priests, he deals with the supernatural, but in Mak's case, it is with the evil supernatural. Throughout the play, he is connected with the devil, both by the shepherds and by his own wife (ll. 305, 313, 332, 477, 589, 844, 872). Such reference to the devil is typical of contemporary anti-ecclesiastical literature. The pelican in *The Plowman's Tale* calls corrupt churchmen "falser than ben fendes" (l. 536), while the author of "Freers, Freers, Wo Ye Be" calls friars "ministri malorum" and "ffalsi deceptores" (ll. 2, 41).[12] Further, in a memorable and unusual scene, Mak draws a magical circle around the shepherds and casts a spell upon them while he steals their sheep:

> Bot abowte you a serkyll
> As rownde as a moyn,
> To I haue done that I wyll,
> Tyll that it be noyn,
> That ye lyg stone-styll
> To that I haue done;
> And I shall say thertyll
> Of good wordys a foyne:
> 'On hyght,
> Ouer youre hedys, my hand I lyft.
> Outt go youre een! Fordo youre syght!' (ll. 400–10)

Mak's spell connects him with necromancy and witchcraft, typical of accusations against corrupt priests. *The Plowman's Tale*, for example, says that the corrupt cleric "sorcery uses as a wytche" (l. 891). Further, Mak's cursing of the shepherds with blindness and ignorance matches another typical anti-clerical accusation. The speaker in *Upland's Rejoinder*, for example, asserts that the friar Daw "blydest many lewde foles" (l. 218).[13] Peres in *Piers the Plowman's Crede* claims that corrupt clergy do not believe their own doctrine but "prechith it in pulpit to blenden the puple" (l. 661). Moreover, Mak's spell parallels conventional blessings given by priests to their congregations, but in an inverted way. Mak's black magic is the very antithesis of priestly sanctity. Whereas a priest raises his hands to impart blessing and protection upon his flock, Mak raises his to project mischief and malice. Whereas priests try to bring light and insight to their parishioners, Mak curses Coll, Gyb, and Daw with blindness. Mak's actions echo in form those of a priest, but they are opposite in the most essential ways. Just as he is the inverse image of a good shepherd, he also suggests the inverse image of a good priest.

This inverse nature of Mak's character closely parallels the use of the Antichrist concept in anti-clerical literature of the day. Several critics have examined the similarities between Mak and medieval portrayals of Antichrist. Noting Mak's use of sorcery, deception, and blasphemy, William Manly argues that Mak represents the Antichrist figure as he was known in medieval legends (151–55). Linda E. Marshall argues for a more specific interpretation, seeing Mak as the seven-headed beast in the Apocalypse and the sheep in the cradle as the false lamb (720–36). These interpretations reveal just how thoroughly Mak's character evokes ideas of the Antichrist, especially in his inversion of ideal or holy forms, but we need not read these associations as apocalyptic. The Antichrist was not, as in modern apocalyptic interpretation, necessarily a certain person; for medieval anti-clerical writers, the term "Antichrist" usually denoted those who were the opposite or inverse of Christ. *The Plowman's Tale* glosses the term generally as those in opposition to Christ and devoted to the opposite of Christian principles:

> What is Antichrist to saye
> But evyn Chrystes adversary?
> Suche hath nowe ben many a day
> To Christes byddyng full contrary,
> That from the trouthe clene varry. (ll. 493–7)

Specifically, the corrupt clergy, who represent the exact opposite of all of Christ's doctrines, are the real "anti-Christs":

> That lyven contrary to Christes lyfe,
> In hye pride agaynst mekenesse;
> Agaynst sufferaunce they usen stryfe,
> And angre ayenst sobreness:
> Agaynst wysdome, wylfulnesse;
> To Christes tales lytell tende;
> Agaynst measure, outragyousnesse;
> But Whan God woll, it may amende!
> Lordly lyfe ayenst lowlynesse,
> And demyn all without mercy;
> And covetyse ayenst largesse,
> Agaynst trewth, trechery;
> And agaynst almesse, envy;
> Agaynst Christ they comprehende. (ll. 501–14)

The narrator of *Jack Upland* gives a similar interpretation of "Antichrist," specifically as false priests who invert Christ's values:

> And thus bi Anticrist and hise clerkis ben vertues transposid to vicis—as mekenes to cowardise, felnes and pride to wisdom and talnes, wraththe to manhode, envye to justificacioun of wrong, slouthe to lordlynes, coveytis

to wisdom and wise purvyaunce, glotonye to largynes, leccherie to kindeli
solace, mildenes to schepisshenesse, holines to ipocrisie, heryse to pleyne
sadnes of feyth and oolde usage, and Holy Chirche to synagoge of Satanas.
(ll. 36–43)[14]

Within the context of this rhetoric, especially considering that attacks against
"Antichrist" were common, Mak's inverse relationship to the shepherds and to
priests is another clue that this is an anti-clerical parody. Mak seeks the role of
"shepherd" to exploit and devour the sheep. While claiming truth, he beguiles
his victims. He claims poverty and hardship as a means to further his indulgence at the expense of the flock. He makes a show of singing, symbolic of
providing comfort to the flock, but his singing is noisome and out of tune.
He is "devilish" and tricky. He evokes the supernatural forces of witchcraft to
separate the sheep from the shepherds. In the context of the metaphor of the
spiritual pastor, Mak is anti-shepherd and, hence, Antichrist.

In this role as false shepherd and Antichrist, Mak engages in a parody of
the Eucharist even as he and Gyll perform their famous parody of the nativity. When the shepherds enter the cottage to search for their sheep, Mak and
Gyll pun repeatedly upon the particulars of the Mass. Referring to the sheep,
or 'child,' a parody of Christ the lamb and thus a parody of the true substance
of the Mass, Mak says, 'bot we must drynk as we brew' (l. 723). He then offers the shepherds food: 'I wold ye dynyd or ye yode' (l. 725). The shepherds
reply: 'Nay, nawther mendys oure mode / Drynke nor mette' (ll. 727–8). Mak
and Gyll then try to defer suspicions with two statements about eating the
sheep/child. In response to the accusations of theft, Mak says,

> As I am true and lele,
> To God here I pray
> That this be the fyrst mele
> That I shall ete this day. (ll. 751–4)

Mak's words seem to be a denial of the truth, yet he plans to eat the sheep as
soon as the shepherds are gone. In keeping with the shadow nativity theme,
he will thus be eating the body and blood of the miraculous lamb. Gyll's statement is also parodic, playing upon the idea of Mary's blessed womb:

> A, my medyll!
> I pray to God so mylde,
> If euer I you begyld,
> That I ete this chylde
> That lygys in this credyll. (ll. 772–6)

The notion of eating a child is outrageous, and the shepherds must surely be touched by Gyll's protest. Yet she has in fact beguiled the shepherds, and her comment parodies the mass by suggesting consumption of the lamb. Stevens and Cawley write, "Gyll's vow to eat the child is, of course, a parodic antici-pation of the Eucharist" (507). That this parody of the Eucharist is performed by characters suggestive of corrupt clergy provides an interesting parallel to the Lollard criticism of corrupt priests defiling the sacraments.

As has often been noted, Mak and Gyll's attempt to hide the sheep is a grotesque parody of the conventional nativity scene, the moment of incarnation of God's son. Yet it is important to recognize that this imitation of a miraculous birth is performed specifically as a means of dishonest material gain. The mock nativity is inseparable from the fraud; in fact, it is the fraud. The main points of parodic similarity, namely the sheep in the cradle, Gyll moaning like a mother after childbirth, and Mak singing, are all intended to fool the shepherds and sep-arate them from their goods. Mak and Gyll use pseudo-religious imagery as a means to larceny, and this equates with medieval portrayals of corrupt monks, friars, and parish priests who exploit the flock merely as a means of income.

More specifically, however, Mak's fraud suggests churchmen who use fakery to separate simpletons from their money. Mak and Gyll both use claims of the false miraculous in their fraud. When the shepherds discover that the "child" looks remarkably like their missing sheep, Mak tries to put them off the scent by claiming the child was deformed through witchcraft:

> I tell you, syrs, hark!—
> Hys noyse was brokyn.
> Sythen told me a clerk
> That he was forspokyn. (ll. 883–6)

When this claim fails to convince the shepherds, Gyll tells them that the child has been bewitched by elves:

> He was takyn with an elfe,
> I saw it myself;
> When the clok stroke twelf
> Was he forshapyn. (ll. 890–3)

Mak's and Gyll's attempted use of the supernatural to defraud echoes me-dieval views of pardoners, as in *Piers Plowman,* and other predatory manipu-lators of religion, such as *Fals Semblant* in *Roman de la Rose.* In *The Canterbury Tales,* for example, the Pardoner preys upon his audience by using fraudulent claims of the miraculous and fake relics:

For in his male he hadde a pilwe-beer,
Which that he seyde was Oure Lady veyl;
He seyde he hadde a gobet of the seyl
That Seint Peter hadde, whan that he wente
Upon the see, til Jhesu Christ hym hente.
He hadde a croys of latoun ful of stones,
And in a glas he hadde pigges bones.
But with thise relikes, whan that he fond
A povre person dwellynge upon lond,
Upon a day he gat hym moore moneye
Than that the person gat in monthes tweye;
And thus, with feyned flaterye and japes,
He made the person and the peple his apes. (A ll. 694–706)

Chaucer contrasts the action of the Pardoner with the poor Parson, the type of the true shepherd that Chaucer has held up for example only 200 lines before. The Pardoner, who admits his fakery, is another inverse image of the *pastor bonus*. In his prologue, he is open about his malice and hypocrisy: "Thus spitte I out my venym under hewe / Of hoolynesse, so semen hooly and trewe" (C ll. 421–2). He pretends to carry the mantle of the priest, but his motives are purely selfish, and his actions run against the principles of a good pastor. This accusation of intentional fraud and predation is also typical of Lollard polemic against the clergy. In the Norwich heresy trials, for example, Hawisse Moone admitted her belief that

These singemesses that be cleped prestes been no prestes, but thay be lecherous and covetouse men and fals deceyvours of the puple, and with thar sotel techyng and prechyng, syngyng and redyng piteously thay pile the puple of thar good, and tharwith thay sustayne here pride, here lechery, here slowthe and alle other vices, and alwey thay maken newe lawes and newe ordinances to curse and kille cruelly all other persones that holden ageyn thar vicious levyng. (Tanner 141)

At the same trials, John Skylan admitted to the following belief:

But all persones of the Churche from the hyest to the lowest and all here techyng and prechyng and alle thair shakelment' be fals and cursed and untrewe and oonly ordeyned be these prestes to begyle and deceyve the puple, to get thaym good, to mayntene thair pride, thair slowthe and thair lecherie withall. (147)

The term "begyle," used by John Skylan to characterize the actions of corrupt priests, provides one more compelling linguistic parallel between anti-clerical literature and the *Secunda Pastorum* . The term is used frequently in the Mak episodes. Gyll addresses Mak as "Sir Gyle" when he returns from having fooled the shepherds (l.590). Gyll's name is itself a neat pun upon "gyle." When the shepherds arrive and begin to search the house, Gyll declares her innocence with the statement about beguiling that is both truth and lie:

> I pray to God so mylde,
> If euer I you begyld,
> That I ete this chylde
> That lygys in this credyll. (ll. 773–6)

Unable to find the sheep, Coll says, "I hold us begyld" (l. 797). All of these references in the mock nativity provide a grotesque contrast to Coll's statement in the nativity scene, when he says of Christ's birth (and the victory over Satan that Christ's birth foreshadows), "The fals gyler of teyn,/ Now goys he begylde" (ll. 1030–1).

Yet "begyle" is also consistently used in descriptions of fraudulent and predatory clergy. The Pelican in *The Plowman's Tale* says, "Such prestes ben Christes false traytours./ They ben false, they ben vengeable,/ And begylen men in Christes name" (ll. 804–6). The narrator of *Upland's Rejoinder* says much the same thing about Friars:

> And so as the prestes of Bel stale undir the awter,
> To bigile the kyng to thefly cache here lyflode,
> So ye forge your flashed, undir ydil ypocrisie,
> To bigile the puple, both pore and riche,
> And as the prestes fayned that Bel ete the kynges sacrifise,
> So your wikkid wynnyng, ye saye, wirchipith God. (ll. 124–9).

Similarly, Peres in *Piers the Plowman's Crede* says that corrupt clergy "serven Satanas and soules bigileth" (l. 717). The author of *Preste, Ne Monke, Ne Yit Chanoun,* sees this as typical of the friar:

> Thof he loure under his hode,
> With semblaunt quaynte and mylde,
> If thou him trust, or dos him gode,
> By God, thou art bygylde. (ll. 89–96)

The terms "guile" and "beguile" are found consistently throughout anti-clerical literature, and they serve to connect corrupt clergy with Antichrist. Christ has come to defeat the beguiler, Satan, but priests who beguile both the people and the Church invert Christ's mission, thus becoming "anti-Christs."

Thus, the motives of Mak, Sir Guile, the wolf-like, false shepherd who seeks ill-gotten gains through deceit, parallel those of the false priests and predatory preachers in Medieval literature who seek to beguile the medieval flock. Mak represents more than a simple churl who is willing to break the law to fill his belly. His fraud and the mock nativity are one. Within the context of the pastoral metaphor, he represents a spiritual predator preying upon the sheep of the Christian flock. Herein lies the primary significance of the disruptive and highly unusual central section of the play. Set as it is before the nativity, the birth of the original, ideal *pastor bonus,* who will, as Coll tells us, beguile the "fals gyler of teyn" (l. 1030) rather than beguile the pastors and flock as Mak has done, the parody provides a marked contrast between the ideal of Christian pastoral care and the perceived grotesque of spiritual predation in the Fourteenth and Fifteenth Centuries. Mak's small larcenous fraud makes fun of the larger and more devastating use of the trappings of religion for fraudulent material gain. As Mak and Gyll prey on the flock through dishonesty, trickery, theft, and a false, black nativity, they represent the ranks of mercenary medieval clergy who see the flock as a material resource and pervert Christ's Church to immerse themselves in wealth, status, and luxury at the expense of a poor and largely powerless populace. Such a parody is profoundly festive, stripping away the abstract rationale for abuse and laying bare the undisguised lust for material gain.

Yet this savage attack upon certain clergy is, like the parody in *Prima Pastorum,* a qualified one. Certainly the existence of the conscientious and kind-hearted Coll, Gyb, and Daw suggests the existence of many honest and true *pastors,* just as Chaucer's pilgrims include an honest parson. Furthermore, *Secunda Pastorum,* like *Prima Pastorum,* ends with a serious and reverent portrayal of the nativity, suggesting, again, that while certain clergy may be corrupt, the central focus of Christianity is not.

Indeed, the Christ child is again incorporated without qualification into a festive context. As the shepherds make their way to Bethlehem, Daw insists that this is a time for celebration:

> Be mery and not sad;
> Of myrth is oure sang:
> Euerlastyng glad
> To mede may we fang. (ll. 963–6)

The Christ child is also given festive attributes. When Coll presents his gift, he notices the child's glee: "Lo, he merys! / Lo, he laghys, my swetyng!" (ll. 1032–3). In addition, the gifts, like those in *Prima Pastorum,* suggest festive motifs. Coll gives a bob of cherries, which imply both festive decoration and

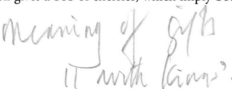

fruitfulness. Gyb gives a bird, or a pet, and Daw gives a ball along with a wish for Christ to play tennis with it (ll. 1059–62). Both of these suggest playfulness and game, perennial festive attributes.

The festive and Christian elements are again spliced carefully together. As with *Prima Pastorum,* the angels' announcement and the nativity follow a particularly festive moment of the play, in this case the overthrow of Mak. The punishment of Mak by tossing him in a blanket invokes several festive themes. It is, along with dunking and riding the hobby-horse, a traditional way to punish offenders during carnival and festival. John Speirs writes of the festive attributes of Mak and his punishment:

> . . . perhaps because he provides merriment, the worst that actually hap-
> pens in the end, when [Mak] is exposed, is that he is tossed in a blanket, as
> if it were a Christmas game—as indeed it is. . . . At the same time, though
> Mak is not actually hanged he is essentially the 'hanged man'; for Mak in
> being tossed in the air undergoes what is essentially a mock death. (342)

Furthermore, tossing in a blanket is also, as scholars have noted, a common medieval practice for inducing labor. Claude Chidamian writes,

> The casting in a canvas, an apparently naïve punishment for Mak, had a
> far richer connotation for the medieval audience than we have ever sus-
> pected. For it is just by this method of tossing that primitive and me-
> dieval peoples hastened delivery in childbirth. (186)

Consequently, the climax of the festive parody, the punishment and over-throw of the false Mak, leads sequentially and causally to the birth of the Christ child. As in *Prima Pastorum,* the two sections, Christian and festive, are structurally correlated. Christ and his redemption becomes the fulfillment of the festive cycle; birth and renewal follow winter hardship and the ritual festive abuse of Mak. Similarly, it is only through the festive cycle crowned by the ritual, labor-inducing overthrow of Mak and all he represents that the birth of Christ and its implied redemption are brought to fruition. The con-nection implies that only through ridding the Church of false and predatory shepherds can the true redemption of mankind become manifest; only by overthrowing corruption can the word become flesh. The two elements are carefully interwoven, even more so than in the first play.[15]

In fact, Christ the child as the lamb of God continues the theme that has run throughout this play and ties all of the puns back together. In the final words of the play, Gyb says of Christ, "Bot he lygys full cold. / Lord, well is me" (ll. 1079–80). The reference to temperature reminds us of the bitter 'weathers' faced by the shepherds at the opening of the play; yet Christ is also the 'wether' of God sent to redeem mankind, even as he is the one true 'child' around which the entire play is focused. These lines also suggest the nature of Christ's redemption. When Christ becomes as cold as the shepherds were, or as the wether /child takes on the hardship and changeability of human existence symbolized by the weather, Gyb becomes well, signifying that the ills of humanity are cured. Christ's incarnation is humanity's redemption, but, again, it is only so within a festive context.

Before ending discussion of this play, it is important to note that *Secunda Pastorum* parodies two villains. It attacks corrupt and predatory shepherds, as symbolized by Mak, within the Church, yet it also attacks the landowners and their agents who make the lives of the peasants miserable for selfish material gain. Notably, the two villains, both elements of authority which the festive instinct would oppose, are often connected in the play. Mak, for example, tries to pass himself off as an agent of the aristocracy, one of the same agents vilified by Coll at the beginning of the play, and Mak's attempt at disguise refers to those abusive tendencies so feared by the shepherds.

Furthermore, if Gyb's drunken and ill-tempered wife can be equated through parody with the aristocratic overseers and agents, then the same comparison can be extended to the surly, hard-drinking Gyll, who like Gyb's wife is a prodigious bearer of children. John Gardner argues that "Mak's Gill, it seems, is a living emblem of all Gyb complained against earlier" (89). Indeed, Mak's false account of a dream, used to lay a foundation for his child/sheep and the fraudulent nativity, recalls many of the puns introduced by Coll and Gyb at the beginning of the play:

> I thoght Gyll began to crok
> And trauell full sad,
> Wel-ner at the fyrst cok,
> Of a yong lad,
> For to mend oure flok—
> Then be I neuer glad;
> I haue tow on my rok
> More then euer I had.
> A, my heed!
> A house full of yong tharmes
> The dewill knok outt thare harnes!
> Wo is hym has many barnes,
> And therto lytyll brede. (ll. 556–68)

Note that Gyll's childbirth consists of croaking, as did "Sely Copyle" the hen, and that Mak uses a reference to the cock, or rooster, two lines later. Notice also that the child adds to the "flok," so that having many children is again compared to shepherding sheep. Finally, notice that Mak places in opposition the possession of many children, or a large flock, and the possession of bread. Certainly this implies that there is never enough food in a large family, but bread also comes from and is semantically aligned with wheat, and wheat is only procured by planting in a field, which landowners prevent by enclosing fields for pasturage of large flocks. Therefore, Mak's continuation of the same puns and images implies that Gyll, like Gyb's wife, can be parodically equated with the landowners and their agents, oppressors who prevent "husbandys" from plowing their fields and instead force them to tend to large flocks.

The continuity of these puns and themes throughout the play, therefore, suggests in the confederation of Mak and Gyll something like complicity between corrupt elements in the Church and the landed classes. Indeed the Church, as a major landowner, is tied to interests which are inseparable from those of the aristocracy. Both the Church and the aristocracy oppress and exploit the peasantry for their own selfish gains. Again, this is a natural festive perspective; both the Church and the aristocracy are authoritarian organizations which the festive instinct seeks to undermine. This indictment of Church and State complicity is nonetheless striking; it is a problem often bemoaned by anti-clerical reformers as the foundation of orthodox persecution and continued corruption. Yet here, in a festive environment hostile to authoritative restrictions, complicity between the two dominant cultural forces is a natural connection, and one made through the parody and pun of festive expression. And this complicity is even more deeply analyzed in the next two plays of the Wakefield Master.

Chapter Seven

Raging Kings and Clergy

In the tradition of ranting Herod, the Wakefield Master chooses to rework another subject that is wholly compatible with festive ideas, patterns, and value systems. On a consistent basis, the story of Herod the Great received the most festive dramatic treatment of all the cycle subjects. Herod acted more like a Summer Lord, King of Fools, or Lord of Misrule than he did a historical and biblical figure. Robert Weimann notes of Herod,

> his grotesque boasting and ranting, which became his proverbial attributes, cannot be derived primarily from the biblical *Herodus iratus;* his association with the spirit of misrule and topsyturvydom was definitely 'popular' and must be considered as part of the genetic background of Herod in the Mystery plays (66).

In fact, the Herod we find as a type throughout medieval drama bears little resemblance to the biblical Herod. Roscoe E. Parker notes the reference in Hamlet to a melodramatic and enraged Herod[1] and writes, "it is obvious that this is not the Herod of the canonical Gospels" (59).

The biblical reference to Herod appears in Matthew 2:16:

> *Tunc Herodes videns quoniam illusus esset a Magis, iratus est valde, et mittens occidit omnes pueros, qui errant in Bethlehem, et in omnibus finibus eius, a bimatu et infra secundum tempus, quod exquisierat a Magis.*
> Then when Herod saw that he had been tricked by the magi, he became very enraged, and sent and slew all the male children who were in Bethlehem and in all its environs, from two years old and under, according to the time which he had ascertained from the magi.

From an orthodox perspective, Herod's wrath is significant as an illustration of the foolishness and impotence of those who defy God. In "The Reputation

of Herod in Early English Literature," Parker traces commentary upon Herod
through orthodox homilies. Parker quotes Chrysostom, for example, who accuses Herod of deliberate madness and folly in the face of God's clear expression of will (64). By the testimony of the magi, Herod perceives the divine will
of God. He consciously chooses to defy that will with his temporal authority,
a choice doomed to inevitable failure. Parker also notes that medieval commentaries often associate Herod with the roaring and wailing of devils (65),
irretrievably condemned and yet foolishly persisting in their defiance of God.[2]
E. K. Chambers writes, "Herod was a heathen; so he was made impotently
comic. He is never much developed, though in the later plays he frequently
rages for more consecutive lines than in the earlier ones" (139).

However, the conventional exegetical interpretation of Herod, which
portrays him as an example of impotent defiance, becomes simply a convenient rationale for festive behavior in a popular dramatic medium. Weimann
concludes that Herod's typical character is the result of "New testament and
apocryphal sources combined with the postritual tradition of the Lord of
Misrule, the *festum stultorum* or similar forms of festive release" (65). In fact,
there is documentation that suggests Herod was often overtly associated with
festive forms. Weimann writes,

> Herod could well be linked with the *rex stultorum* and other forms of in-
> version among the lower clergy, since in the play of the *pastores* at Rouen
> and Autun the *regnum Herodis* was in fact celebrated as a fool's festival
> and the person who performed the role of Herod was presumably none
> other than the king of fools himself. (66) [3]

The degree to which Herod played within a festive tradition and the degree
to which he played the orthodox version varied. Perhaps the most orthodox
ranting Herod of English tradition is the one portrayed in the N-Town version. The writer of the N-Town pageant, presumably aware of the homiletic
interpretation of Herod, makes several significant changes to restore the orthodox significance to the story. In the N-Town *The Slaughter of the Innocents;
The Death of Herod,* Herod's angry defiance is clearly shown to be vain.
Herodes Rex commands Primus and Secundus Miles to kill "every page / of ij
yere age" (ll.45–6), and the Miles respond with enthusiasm. However, as soon
as they are finished promising their slaughter, Angelus appears and warns
Joseph to flee to Egypt:

> For Kynge Herowde with sharp knyff
> His knyghtys he doth sende.
> The fadyr of Hevyn hath to þe sent

> Into Egypt that thu be bent,
> For cruel knyghtys thi childe haue ment
> With swerd to sle and shende. (ll. 75–80)

The N-Town Joseph then arises and declares his intention to flee, and Herod's schemes are thus shown to be completely impotent in the face of God's will. Soon after, the folly of Herod's actions is similarly stressed. As Herod rejoices at the news of the slaughter of the innocents, he displays a foolish sense of self-satisfaction: "I was nevyr meryer herebeforn / Sythe that I was fyrst born" (ll. 164–5). Even as he basks in his assumed success, however, Mors appears to remind the audience of the folly of defying God, comparing Herod with an arrogant page:

> Ow! I herde a page make preysyng of pride!
> All prynces he passyth, he wenyth, of powsté.
> He wenyth to be the wurthyest of all this werde wyde,
> Kynge ovyr all kyngys that page wenyth to be!
> He sent into Bedlem to seke on every syde,
> Cryst for to qwelle yf thei myght hym se.
> But of his wykkyd wyl, lurdeyn, yitt he lyede!
> Goddys sone doth lyve! Ther is no lord but he. (ll. 168–75)

As Herod continues his merriment, Mors stands over him, waiting for the time to strike. Herod's continued boasting further underscores his folly. He emphasizes his mirth, but that mirth is soon to be transferred into the mirth of devils torturing him. Mors swoops in suddenly, kills Herod and his Miles, and delivers them to Diabolus, who says,

> Alle oure! Alle oure! This catel is myn!
> I xall hem brynge onto my celle.
> I xall hem teche pleys fyn,
> And shewe such myrthe as is in helle! (ll. 233–6)

Diabolus finishes the play with an overt recitation of the moral orthodox message to be learned from the story of Herod:

> Off Kynge Herowde all men beware,
> That hath rejoycyd in pompe and pryde.
> For all his boste of blysse ful bare,
> He lyth now dede her on his syde. (ll. 246–9)

Thus, the writer of the N-Town pageant constructs his Herod so as to emphasize the orthodox lesson rather than the festive character.

In the Towneley play, however, the orthodox perspective is almost completely missing. Although Herod rages in a grotesque way, he is not particularly mocked as an object of folly. The tale is shown entirely from his perspective, and the audience cannot see the movement of God's will in opposition to Herod's murderous rage. Perhaps folly can logically be inferred; it is traditional to the role and to the homiletic commentaries. Stevens and Cawley assume this to be the case: "The Towneley Herod becomes an absurd figure rejoicing in a murder which has not been committed" (521). However, while the absurdity of his actions may be proven when cross-referenced with other plays or with biblical and doctrinal interpretation, it is not demonstrated in this dramatic performance.[4] Folly is in no way overtly developed or stressed through the dialogue. In fact, in the absence of clear opposition, Herod's rage seems to gain momentum. With no one stepping forward to contradict him or to indicate his folly, his rages gain a certain authority; they become more threatening and less opposable as the play proceeds.

Indeed, at the end of the play, Herod acts and speaks as if he has been successful, and there is little evidence to the contrary. After the soldiers report their slaughter and are promised rewards, Herod says,

> I lagh that I whese!
> A, Mahowne,
> So light is my saull
> That all of sugar is my gall!
> I may do what I shall,
> And bere vp my crowne.
> I was castyn in care,
> So frightly afrayd;
> Bot I thare not dyspare,
> For low is he layd
> That I most dred are
> So haue I hym flayd (ll. 684–695).

Stevens and Cawley note this change in dramatic tone. They write, "in York, Herod rages because Christ may have escaped; in Towneley, he assumes from what his knights have told him that Christ is dead" (521). At the end of the play, the lesson is given by Herod. Perhaps within traditional exegetical context, Herod indicts himself as a fool with words meant to refer to Christ:

> Thus shall I tech knauys
> Ensampyll to take,
> In thare wyttys that rauys
> Sich mastré to make. (ll. 716–19)

The words frame the type of Herod himself; he is the one who raves as he tries to make himself master. Yet this passage is also consistent with Herod's resistance to a boy usurper, and it is given in a context which does not include the folly of defying God. Without the orthodox context, the statement simply underscores Herod's triumph. Jeffrey Helterman puzzles over this unusual departure from orthodox interpretation:

> If the Wakefield play intends to show the nature and results of Herod's viciousness, why is this the only play of the English cycles extant in which Herod appears to remain in control at the end? The York play ends with Herod's enraged discovery that Christ has escaped his soldiers and in both the *Ludus Coventriae* and Chester versions, Death carries Herod off. The Chester playwright makes the Slaughter of the Innocents itself Herod's punishment by including Herod's son among the victims. . . . These playwrights refuse to allow their audience to contemplate, even briefly, the triumph of evil. Instead they use the instant manifestation of justice to show that evil does not pay. (125–6).

In contrast, the Towneley Herod seems in control of the field at the end of *Magnus Herodes*. Like the other villain we have studied, Cain, his sentence seems suspended until after the dramatic patterns have run their course. Naturally, this changes much of the significance of those patterns.

Furthermore, the festive flavor of the dramatic presentation is much greater in the Towneley play than in the other Herod plays. As I have noted, the rages attributed to Herod's medieval incarnation are characteristic of a festive Lord of Misrule. In *Magnus Herodes*, these rages are particularly grotesque. Herod speaks repeatedly about his "teyn" (anger) and "ire," but at several points in the play his anger boils over into uncontrollable fury. When he begins to realize the magi may not return, he fumes, "What dewill! Me thynk I brast / For anger and for teyn" (ll. 170–1). This reference to bursting from anger is repeated several times, and it suggests something like a fit. When the knights confirm that the magi have indeed left surreptitiously, Herod rages,

> Why, and ar thay past me by?
> We! Outt! For teyn I brast!
> We! Fy!
> Fy on the dewill! Where may I byde,
> Bot fyght for teyn and al to-chyde? (ll. 215–19)

Later, as he chastises his knights for negligence in allowing the magi to escape, he says, "I wote not where I may sytt / For anger and for teyn" (ll. 248–9). When the second Consultus informs Herod that prophecies indicate Christ shall be "Lord myghty" (l. 321), Herod has his most violent rage, claiming he is near death and in danger of bursting his stomach because of his anger:

> Fy! The dewill the spede,
> And me, bot I drynk onys!
> This has thou done indede
> To anger me for the nonys;
> . . .
> War! I say, lett me pant.
> Now thynk I to fyght
> For anger.
> My guttys will outt thryng
> Bot I this lad hyng;
> Withoutt I haue vengyng,
> I may lyf no langer. (ll. 326–9, 345–51).

These rages, considering they are expressed only in Herod's speech and not in any stage directions, are as great as or greater than any displayed by the other Herods.

Furthermore, the Wakefield Master's Herod does not confine himself to rage over the news of the magi's escape. He rages at the supposed audience, at the soldiers, and at the counselors. When he enters the play, he snarls at the crowd,

> Stynt, brodels, youre dyn—
> Yei, euerychon!
> I red that ye harkyn
> To I be gone;
> For if I begyn,
> I breke ilka bone,
> And pull fro the skyn
> The carcas anone—
> Yei, perdé!
> Sesse all this wonder,
> And make vs no blonder,
> For I ryfe you in sonder,
> Be ye so hardy. (ll. 118–30)

When the knights enter and tell him that the magi have escaped, he first rages at the magi. Then he turns his anger at the knights: "Ye ar knyghtys to trast! / Nay, losels ye ar, and thefys!" (ll. 222–3). When the knights protest against such treatment, he becomes even more enraged:

> Fy, losels and lyars,
> Lurdans ilkon!
> Tratoures and well wars!

Knafys, bot knyghtys none!
. . .
If ye byde in these wonys,
I shall dyng you with stonys—
Yei, ditizance doutance! (ll. 235–8, 245–7)

After eventually calming down from this outburst, Herod calls in his counselors, who simply relay to him the prophecies concerning Christ's birth.
Upon hearing the prophecies, Herod turns on the counselors:

Outt, thefys, fro my wonys!
Fy knafys!
Fy dottypols, with youre bookys—
Go kast thaym in the brookys!
With sich wylys and crokys
My wytt away rafys. (ll. 333–8)

Herod's outbursts are particularly appropriate to a festive lord. Furthermore,
since his rage over the magi and Christ is placed here into an overall context
of bad temper, fury, and abusiveness, the orthodox interpretation of the rage
as defiance against God is substantially de-emphasized. Herod seemingly
rages here because it is his very nature. He is, like a Lord of Misrule, a one-di-
mensional caricature.

In addition to his comic rages, so characteristic of misrule and summer
lord figures, Herod repeatedly uses threats of extreme and brutal violence. These
threats are typical of the festive use of violence, especially in their tendency to
make specific anatomical reference. We have seen, for instance, his threats to the
audience to break all their bones, pull their carcasses from their skin, and to tear
them asunder (ll. 123–5, 129). Herod also promises that if anyone is unruly, he
will "brane hym thrugh the hede!" (136). If anyone speaks, he threatens to cut
them up as "small as flesh to pott" (l. 143). Stevens and Cawley note the similarities to festive threats of violence: "Herod's bloodthirsty language is reminiscent here of that used by the ruffler in the mummers' plays" (524).

Herod's threats are also characteristically festive in that he directs them
towards the audience in opening and closing formulas. At the end of the play,
Herod returns to vent his threats upon the audience again:

All wantones wafys—
No langage ye crak!
No sufferan you sauys;
Youre nekkys shall I shak
In sonder.
. . .

> For if I here it spokyn
> When I com agayn,
> Youre branys bese brokyn. (ll. 720–4, 729–31)

As Herod begins speaking of Christ, his threats of violence continue. He promises to break all of Christ's bones with a steel brand (ll. 153–6). He claims to feel no remorse for such violence (ll. 181–2). When he hears the magi have escaped, he threatens them also: "Gett I those land-lepars, / I breke ilka bone" (241–2).

This collection of violent threats, which serve as preface and prologue for the graphic violence of the slaughter of the innocents, is not at all characteristic of a royal figure. Martin Stevens and James Paxson note the disparity between the Towneley Herod's office and his behavior:

> It is Herod's peculiar tendency to promise base violence that belies his office as a supposedly great king. First, he seems to offer (if even in moments of hyperbole) to perform the violent deeds himself. Second, the violence is of specifically ignoble and loutish nature. (71)

Yet if this behavior is not in keeping with a contemporary king, it is nonetheless perfectly appropriate to the actions of a Lord of Misrule. Robert Weimann notes the festive flavor of Herod's violence: "Herod is of course both somber and ridiculous, terrifying and grotesque, but the unique force and dramatic effect of the role are rooted in the tension and interaction of the horrible and the comic" (68). Herod's threats, especially so wildly exaggerated, are part and parcel of a festive lord's office. They serve the purpose of keeping moderation at bay, and they help to maintain the topsyturvy environment of the feast. Stevens and Paxson notice this result in Herods threats:

> Herod is not, as he purports to be, a great king of "ryall" magnificence. His behavior demonstrates that he is simply a street bully, a dockside ruffian given to fits of boxing, grappling, and wrestling. The surrendering of kingly office (administration) and the taking on of the lowest tasks is one kind of folly; it is the inversion of the highest level of state with the lowest. (71)

Herod's Lord of Misrule qualities are further enhanced by other characters drawn from festive culture. He is introduced by Nuncius, who, like Garcio Pikeharnes in *Mactacio Abel,* uses the language and style of a typical festive invocation. Like Pikeharnes, Nuncius is largely an innovation. The York Herod is introduced by a similar figure, Senescallus, in *The Magi* and *The Slaughter of Innocents,* but, as Stevens and Cawley note, "Nuncius of the *Magnus*

Herodes is far better developed as a dramatic character than his parallel in York" (521). Nuncius opens the play with a call for merriment: "Most myghty Mahowne / Meng you with myrth" (ll. 1–2). He then demands silence from everyone in the audience, with the threat of violence for anyone who fails to comply. His words specifically reduce people of varying station and status to one common rank:

> Both of burgh and of towne,
> By fellys and by fyrth,
> Both kyng with crowne
> And barons of brith
> That radly wyll rowne,
> Many greatt grith
> Shall behapp.
> Take tenderly intent
> What sondys ar sent,
> Els harmes shall ye hent,
> And lothes you to lap. (ll. 3–13)

Nuncius next demands fealty from the crowd for his master; again, his words reduce all to one rank:

> Herode, the heynd kyng—
> By grace of Mahowne—
> Of Iury, sourmontyng
> Sternly with crowne
> On lyfe that ar lyfyng
> In towre and in towne,
> Gracyus you gretyng,
> Commaundys you be bowne
> At his bydyng.
> Luf hym with lewté;
> Drede hym, that doughty!
> He chargys you be redy
> Lowly at his lykyng. (ll. 14–26).

Nuncius' introduction of Herod's sovereignty is just that: an introduction. His words make it clear that he initiates a new state of being, a coronation of sorts; he demands the audience pay homage to a new ruler that they are not used to honoring. This is exactly the pattern used to introduce boy kings, kings of fools, summer lords, Lords of Misrule, and all manner of other festive lords. They reign for a brief festive moment, a moment of misrule and topsy-turvy indulgence before conventional order is restored. Furthermore, just as Herod's behavior resembles the actions of a Lord of Misrule, so too his lordship is based, like the Lord of Misrule's, upon violent threats. Nuncius specifically uses threats of Herod's violence to invoke his sovereignty. He begins with vague warnings:

> What man apon mold
> Menys hym agane
> Tytt teyn shall be told,
> Knyght sqwyere, or swayn;
> Be he neuer so bold,
> Byes he that bargan
> Twelf thowsandfold
> More than I sayn,
> May ye trast. (ll. 27–35)

Nuncius soon progresses to more specific threats, however:

> He is the worthyest of all
> Barnes that ar borne;
> Fremen ar his thrall,
> Full teynfully torne.
> Begyn he to brall,
> Many men cach skorne;
> Obey must we all,
> Or else be ye lorne
> At onys.
> Downe dyng of youre knees   + they dont
> All that hym seys;
> Dyspleysed he beys,
> And byrkyn many bonys. (ll. 79–91)

In addition to Nuncius, the knights in *Magnus Herodes* are strikingly clown-like, comic pretenders to courage and dignity who are repeatedly exposed as cowards and scoundrels. When they initially admit the magi have escaped, for example, Herod savages them for dereliction of duty:

> Thefys, I say ye shuld haue spyde,
> And told when thay went by.
> Ye ar knyghtys to trast!
> Nay, losels ye ar, and thefys! (ll. 220–3)

The knights whiningly protest that such treatment is unjust. The third knight insists they should be treated with respect, implying that their status entitles them to a certain deference:

> Why put ye sich reprefys
> Withoutt cause?

Thus shuld ye not threct vs,
Vngaynly to bete us;
Ye shuld not rehett vs
Withoutt outhere sawes. (ll. 229–34)

This response only makes Herod more outraged. He brushes aside their pre-
tensions, calling them "losels and lyars," "Lurdans," Tratoures," and "Knafys"
(ll. 235, 236, 237, 238), all names associated with ruffians and scoundrels.
They have forfeited their rights by their incompetence, he says: "Had ye bene
woth youre eres, / Thus had thay not gone" (ll. 239–40).

The knights quickly change their tune, now claiming with comic bluster that the magi slipped away without notice because they feared the prowess
of the knights:

1 Miles: yr, thay went sodanly
Or any man wyst,
Els had mett we—yei, perdy!—
And may ye tryst.
2 Miles: So bold nor so hardy,
Agans oure lyst,
Was none of that company
Durst mete me with fyst
For ferd.
3 Miles: Ill durst thay abyde,
Bot ran thame to hyde;
Might I thaym have spyde,
I had made thaym a berd. (ll. 261–73)

The threats of the knights seem empty and crude. The first seems to promise
much, but his "yei, perdy!," perhaps played with a nudge and a wink, is deliberately vague and insubstantial. The second knight speaks grandly of their
daunting "lyst," but his weapon of choice, fisticuffs, hardly needs such chivalric apparatus. The third also speaks like a thug and a bully.

Such boasting is typical for the knights, and typical of comic figures.
Robert Weimann writes, "Behind this boasting is an irreverent element of
mimic parody" (70). T. W. Craik argues that these "braggart soldiers" (or *milites
gloriosi*) are used here merely to enhance the comic sense of reversal in the play
(181). In fact, for all their boasting, the knights are hardly eager to back up their
words with action. When Nuncius summons them back to Herod "In armowre
full bright" (l. 405), they are terrified that they will have to fight a battle:

1 Miles: Why shuld we fray?
2 Miles: This is not all right.

> 3 *Miles:* Syrs, withoutten delay
> I drede that we fight. (ll. 408–11)

Rosemary Woolf notes the comic contrast between the chivalric ideal and
these knights, "whose reaction to the message that Herod wants them to appear fully armed is one of cowardly alarm" (205). When Herod instructs them
to slaughter children, however, their courage quickly returns:

> 2 Miles: I wote we make a fray,
> Bot I wyll go before.
> 3 Miles: A! thynk, syrs, I say;
> I mon whett lyke a bore.
> 1 Miles: Sett me before ay,
> Good enogh for a skore. (ll. 458–63)

Stevens and Cawley note the mock-heroic tone of the lines: "The Second Knight
boasts that he will go first. The other two join in a parodic contest of heroic
boasts" (527). Yet even in this cowardly task the bravery of the knights is short-
lived. After they have slaughtered the innocents, they are confronted by outraged
mothers, who humiliatingly beat them. Although they threaten the women, they
are nonetheless cowed by them, and the second knight recommends a timely re-
treat: "Lett vs ryn fote-hote— / Now wold I we hyde" (ll. 575–6).[5] In reversals
such as these, where honor, dignity, and bravery are repeatedly turned topsy-
turvy, the knights play their parts with typical festive attributes.

In addition to using festive characters, *Magnus Herodes* makes use of
clearly festive, cyclical patterns. The struggle between age and youth is particularly manifest in Herod's fear of Christ. Herod, the *senex iratus,* rages against
the coming usurpation of his reign by a mere boy. Speirs writes, "Herod is the
old king who, as in so many folk-tales, is afraid of the newborn child and tries
to do away with him because of prophecies and rumors that the child will
grow up to challenge and overthrow him as a king" (349).[6] Nuncius introduces this theme during the invocation; speaking of Herod, he says,

> He is worthy wonderly,
> Selcouthly sory:
> For a boy that is borne herby
> Standys he abast. (ll. 36–9)

When Herod enters, his wrath keeps returning to this usurper, a mere boy:

> What joy is me to here
> A lad to sesse my stall!
> If I this crowne may bere,

That boy shall by for all. (ll. 161–4)

Herod rages as he remembers the mission of the magi:

> I tell you,
> A boy thay sayd thay soght,
> With offeryng that thay broght;
> It mefys my hart right noght
> To breke his nek in two. (ll. 178–82)

His anger is driven primarily by the notion that this "lad" or "boy" comes to take his place as king:

> Trow ye a kyng as I
> Will suffre thaym to neuen
> Any to haue mastry
> Bot myself full euen?
> Nay, leyfe!—(ll. 187–91)

Herod's fears seem confirmed by the counselers. As he rages at their readings of prophecy, he keeps returning to the fact that a peasant boy seems destined to usurp him:

> Hard I neuer sich a trant
> That a knafe so sleght
> Shuld com lyke a sant
> And refe me my right.
> . . .
> Shuld a carll in a kafe
> Bot of oone yere age
> Thus make me to rafe? (ll. 339–42, 352–4)

It is this outrage, the affrontery of a mere boy trying to usurp his mastery, that drives Herod's anger, and justifies (to his mind) the slaughter of the innocents. He says to his knights,

> The cause now is this
> That I send for you all:
> A lad, a knafe, borne is
> That shuld be kyng ryall;
> Bot I kyll hym and his,
> I wote I brast my gall.
> Therfor, syrs,
> Veniance shall ye take
> All for that lad sake (ll. 432–7)

While the emphasis upon usurpation corresponds generally to festive patterns of overthrowing authority figures, it more specifically reflects the common festive enactment of seasonal change. For life to be renewed, old man winter must give way to the birth of youthful spring. Old characters must be usurped and replaced by young characters.[7] Festive lords were particularly bound by this pattern; they represented temporary, seasonal figures who must be overthrown and give way to change. Herod, in his resistance to usurping youth, corresponds directly to seasonal festive lords. Christ, the boy and the incarnation of new life, is poised to overthrow Herod, the old man and the epitome of ritual festive death.[8]

The inevitable demise of festive lords is perhaps best apparent in the often elaborate tradition of last wills and testaments. Thomas Nashe's "Summer's Last Will and Testament," for example, assumes an audience familiar with the spectacles of Summer Lords bestowing their wealth upon devoted fellow revelers. While Herod resists the usurpation of Christ like any other raging Lord of Misrule, he does indicate the inevitability of his own fall in his distribution of lands and riches. When his knights return from the slaughter, Herod bestows fabulous wealth upon them:

> A hundreth thowsand pownde
> Is good wage for a knyght,
> Of pennys good and rownde,
> Now may ye go light
> With store
> And ye knyghtys of oures
> Shall haue castels and towres,
> Both to you and to toures,
> For now and euermore. (ll. 642–50)

These rewards are a conventional dramatic element of the raging Herod story, but they are developed more elaborately in Towneley than in most cycles. In addition, Herod's munificence is extended to the audience as well, a feature not found in the other cycles. After the knights have left, Herod addresses the audience:

> Now in peasse may I stand—
> I thank the, Mahowne—
> And gyf of my lande
> That longys to my crowne.
> Draw therfor nerehande,
> Both of burgh and of towne:
> Markys, ilkon, a thowsande,
> When I am bowne,
> Shall ye haue. (ll. 664–72)

This final distribution of goods and lands, given unto an audience with whom Herod has no clear feudal relationship and therefore no obligation to reward, makes no sense whatsoever in the standard context of the play; however, it closely resembles the distribution of festive titles and wealth by summer lords to festive participants at the end of their reigns, and it therefore fits Herod's festive role. It is simply one more element that transforms an already festive Herod into a full-fledged Lord of Misrule. The combination of a festive invocation by Nuncius, excessive comic ranting and violence, a squad of foolish *milites gloriosi,* several festive reversals, conflict between the old lord and the usurping boy, and the final festive last will and testament serve to align the scriptural tale with festive tradition.

However, like the other plays, the festive element is not employed here simply as an element of entertainment; it rather creates an environment wherein more risky subjects can be examined, parodied, and satirized. In fact, despite the comic and grotesque emphasis, Herod and his court bear a striking resemblance to contemporary medieval courts. Herod, who calls himself a "lord and king ryall" (l. 160), dispenses his royal prerogative like any good English monarch. After his counselors advise him to slaughter the innocents, for example, Herod says,

> For this nobyll tythand
> Thou shall haue a drope
> Of my good grace:
> Markys, rentys, and powndys,
> Greatt castels and groundys;
> Thrugh all sees and soundys
> I gyf the the chace. (ll. 384–90)

Herod's rewards reflect exactly the medieval English feudal structure. His counselors will receive revenues from rents, as well as castles and grounds, the rights to which were dispensed by the king. Further, Stevens and Cawley note that marks and pounds are "both English monetary units" (527). Finally in giving his counselors "the chace," Herod entitles them to the royal right to hunt. Stevens and Cawley point out that "Such rights were originally a royal prerogative" (527). The king offers similar rewards to his knights after they have completed their grisly task. He initially offers an aristocratic match with a lady, something in which English monarchs were often involved:

> If I bere this crowne
> Ye shall haue a lady
> Ilkon to hym layd
> And wed at his wyll. (ll. 623–6)

Herod then promises to reward them with "pownde" (l. 642) and "pennys" (l. 644), both English currency, and "castels and towres" in perpetuity (ll. 647–50), a promise only an English monarch could fulfill.

Herod's soldiers are even more contemporary. The play repeatedly refers to them as "knyghtys," and whenever Herod wishes to belittle them, he calls their chivalric status into question, as he does when the magi escape: "Knafys, bot knyghtys none!" (l. 238). As I mentioned above, the knights boast of their prowess at jousting: "So bold nor so hardy, / Agans oure lyst, / Was none of that company" (ll. 265–7). Further, when Herod summons the knights, the language is thick with the terms of medieval chivalry. Herod commands, "All the flowre of knyghthede / Call to legeance" (ll. 393–4). When Nuncius summons the knights, he commands them to appear "In armowre full bright; / In youre best aray / Looke that ye be dight" (ll. 404–6), as if they are summoned to a tournament. When they join Herod, Nuncius announces them with similar pomp:

> Kyng Herode all-weldand,
> Well be ye seyn!
> Your knyghtys ar comand
> In armoure full sheyn
> At youre wyll. (ll. 421–5)

The medieval audience would have seen in the *milites* a reflection of contemporary mounted knights.

Certainly, Herod will inevitably resemble a king, and such dramatic presentations tended to incorporate contemporary characteristics so as to enhance realism, but the court of *Magnus Herodes* is particularly evocative of the medieval English court. Stevens and Cawley note the difference, for example, between this Herod and the Herod in *Oblacio Magorum*: "The main difference between the two plays lies in the treatment of Herod and his court. In *Magnus Herodes,* he is more conspicuously used as a vehicle to parody contemporary courtly manners" (522). The Wakefield Master stresses parallels with the contemporary English court throughout the play. During the festive invocation, for example, Nuncius announces Herod in the manner in which medieval monarchs were announced:

> Herode, the heynd kyng—
> By grace of Mahowne—
> Of Iury, sourmontyng
> Sternly with crowne
> On lyfe that ar lyfyng
> In towre and in towne,
> Gracyus you gretyng,
> Commaundys you be bowne

At his bydyng. (ll. 14–22)

Stevens and Cawley note that these lines "echo the opening phrases of a royal letter," and that "Nuncius later tells Herod *thi letters haue I layde*" (522). Similarly, Nuncius' summons of the knights, quoted above, is evocative of a royal summons. Furthermore, when Herod decides to meet with his counselors, he refers to them specifically as his "preuey counsell" (l. 284), a reference to the English king's privy counsel where national policy was decided. Stevens and Cawley write that "Herod grandiosely calls his two counselors a 'privy council' as though he were an English king" (525).

Of even more resonance with middle and lower class ideas of the court is the Wakefield Master's repeated use of French vocabulary in discussions between Herod and court. For example, when Herod speaks with Nuncius about summoning the knights, a courtly occasion , he uses the words "veniance," "legeance," "Bewshere," and "avance," and Nuncius replies with "perchaunce" (ll. 392, 394, 395, 396, 398). The vocabulary shifts to more traditional English vocabulary when Herod is raging or when the scene has shifted from the court. The Wakefield Master highlights this technique in the final two lines of the play when Herod bids the audience "adew" and then says, "I can no more Franch" (ll. 740, 741). This emphasis upon French, still the language of much of the aristocracy and a point of resentment with much of the population, solidly connects Herod, his court, and his courtiers with the contemporary English court.

These parallels with the aristocracy have two effects. They parody and ridicule the monarchy and upper classes, but they also slander contemporary courts and aristocratic practices by equating them with the abusive and murderous actions of Herod, his counselors, and his knights. Herod's selfish and larcenous raging, characteristically exaggerated in the Lord of Misrule tradition, thus becomes a satire of the actions and motivations of the contemporary monarchy. The king is shown to be unconcerned with and scornful of the well-being of the population, as long as his own power is secure. Indeed, the king looks upon the general population with contempt, as "knafys," "brodels," and "losells," put on this earth only to serve his selfish needs.

Beyond general contempt, the monarch is shown to be capable of extreme brutality and cruelty towards his subjects. The emphasis upon parallels with the contemporary court as Herod plans and puts into action his massive infanticide is particularly telling here. The English court, parodied here in comic circumstances, is branded as heartless, scheming, and murderous. Certainly the ravages visited upon the populace by repeated wars of succession would cause this subject to resonate with the audience. As Herod plans his deliberate murders and cruelties to maintain his grip on royal power, he unavoidably mimics the intrigues of the English royalty, and when he does it using the manners and habits of the contemporary court, he suggests a stark condemnation of the monarchy. However, since this satire is constructed within the confines of festive traditions, the power and reach of the monarchy are lowered into the realm of the ridiculous. The legitimacy of royal power is overthrown, but the menace of royal force is rendered laughable.

The knights are the main manifestation of royal force in the play. They wear the trappings of contemporary chivalry, and in this pretense they satirize and undermine the entire code of chivalric values. The heart of the satire lies in the stark contrast between the comically burlesqued courtly manners displayed by the knights in some scenes and the near animalistic brutality shown in others. When they are announced to Herod in their shining armor, they are deferential and dutiful:

> Hayll, dughtyest of all!
> We ar comen at youre call
> For to do what we shall,
> Your lust to fullfyll. (ll. 426–9)

However, these noble manners by characters Herod describes as the "flower of knyghthede" (ll. 393–4) seem incompatible with the nonchalant butchery of innocent children. The first knight's polite comment to the first mother seems almost surreal: "Dame, thynk it not yll, / Thy knafe if I kyll." (ll. 478–9). These manners quickly evaporate as the knights warm to their savagery. The knight changes his address from "Dame" to "hoore" (l. 492). The second knight dispenses with manners entirely: "Com hedyr, thou old stry: / That lad of thyne shall dy" (ll. 504–5). Wolff makes note of this "coarse abuse of the mothers," and writes that it suggests that the knights show "relish in evil" (206). Such characterization seems deliberate. Wolff writes that the Wakefield Master is "aware of the romance ideals of chivalry and of the monstrous inappropriateness of killing babies for knights" (205). The disparity between the values of chivalry and the actions of the knights is part of a consistent pattern of contrasts wherein the knights lay claim to noble status, courtly manners, and courage, only to be identified as brutal, cowardly ruffians.

Here again, the Wakefield Master's portrayal finds significance in the similar contrast between ideal chivalry and realistic brutality among the contemporary aristocracy. The medieval landed classes maintained their status largely through force, but they fostered the myths and legends of chivalric heroes as a justification of their own authority. The knight was supposedly a Christian warrior with refined sentiment, great courage, and an inherent sense of right; such a class of warrior, clearly superior to the mean, lower class peasant or the petty, middle class merchant, was the natural head of the social order. The armed, landed classes bought into this myth wholeheartedly and spent great resources perpetuating it. However, the ideals of chivalry were largely only ideals, and the aristocracy was in fact capable of great cruelty and brutality. In fact, the assumed chivalric superiority attributed to the upper classes often justified extreme abuses of the supposed inferior classes. The knights in *Magnus Herodes* magnify this hypocrisy in their extreme insensitivity towards the innocent children and their desperate mothers. By giving Herod's soldiers the attributes of contemporary knights, the Wakefield Master thus undermines the chivalric ideals which justified an entire class. By connecting contemporary knights with such brutality in the clown-like characters of the Towneley knights, however, the Wakefield Master also lowers chivalry into the realm of comic buffoonery, and the menace posed to the populace by the aristocratic military class is substantially weakened.

Yet perhaps the most damning satire of the medieval English court lies in the portrayal of the counselors. They are the worst villains in the play; for no justifiable reason, they advise a course of action that not only clearly usurps the will of God, but also leads to the wanton murder of thousands of innocents. Herod can perhaps be expected to try to cling to his throne. The knights are, in a sense, only following orders. The counselors, who should know better, however, deliberately devise a plan which seeks to confound God's purpose. In *Magnus Herodes,* the counselors are the ones to advocate the mass slaughter of children.

The roles played by the counselors are much more developed in this play than in the other Herod plays. Stevens and Cawley note that "the episode in which the two counsellors consult their books at Herod's request and find the prophecies of Christ's birth does not occur in York at all" (521). Nor is this an element found in the liturgical plays. The counsellor's knowledge of religious texts leads to two startling implications. First, the counselors are a parody of the high clergy. Herod commands them to abandon their "pystyls and grales;/ Mes, matins" (ll. 297–8), the traditional duties of the priesthood, so they can advice him. In this, they resemble the deans, bishops, and arch-bishops that ran in the same circles and often served as advisors to the English monarch. Indeed, it is precisely these types of advisors, such as the English Chancellor, Archbishop Sudbury, and the English Treasurer, Prior John Hales, who come under attack in the 1381 rebellion. Second, the counselors (parodies of the high clergy) know of God's will and deliberately seek to usurp it for their own worldly advancement. Both implications are confirmed by the reward Herod offers the counselors after hearing their plan:

> If I lyf in land
> Good lyfe, as I hope

> This dar I the warand—
> To make the a pope. (ll. 378–81)

By having Herod offer the papal office as a reward, the Wakefield Master draws an unmistakable connection between the evil counselors and the contemporary high clergy. Further, since the reward is specifically for immoral and mercenary advice to a monarch, it suggests, at the least, inappropriate cooperation by many leaders of the Church. Perhaps it also hints at the unethical relationships common between the high clergy and national monarchs during the great schism.

The parody at least comments upon the extent to which the Church had become invested in the secular medieval state. The Church was guaranteed certain privileges by the secular powers, and in return it did much to legitimize the feudal structure. The play's repeated reference that powers exist "By grace of Mahowne" (l. 15) parodies the medieval religious concept of the divine right of kings, whereby the Church legitimized powers-that-be by attributing them to the will of God. Basing a similar right upon Mahowne in this play equates the doctrine of divine right with the forces of evil. Furthermore, this warped parody of divine right, combined with the reference to papal reward, suggests wholesale complicity between corrupt leaders in the Church and abusive, even brutal, secular powers.

The Wakefield Master enhances his satire upon the secular and ecclesiastical authorities here by echoing significant passages from the book of Micah. The play refers overtly to Micah when the second counselor mentions a passage of prophesy:

> And othere says thus,
> Tryst me ye may:
> Of Bedlem a gracyus
> Lord shall spray,
> That of Iury myghtyus
> Kyng shal be ay, (ll. 315–20).

Stevens and Cawley note that the passage referred to here is Micah 5: 2 (526). The passage reads,

> *Et tu, Bethlehem Ephrata,*
> *Parvulus es in millibus Iuda;*
> *Ex te mihi egredietur qui sit dominator in Israel, . . .*
> But as for you, Bethlehem Ephrathah,
> Too little to be among the clans of Judah,
> From you One will go forth for Me to be ruler in Israel.

Further, the Herod of this play is specifically connected with the prophesies in Micah. Micah 5: 1, the passage preceding the prophesy, reads, "*In virga percutient maxillam iudicis Israel;* With a rod they will smite the judge of Israel on the cheek." Speaking of the child Christ, Herod threatens to beat him, "with this steyll brand" (l. 149).

However, the most significant parallel with Micah lies in the language Herod uses towards the audience as he rants and rages. When he enters, for example, he says he will "breke ilka bone, / And pull fro the skyn / The carcas anone" (ll. 123–5). Further, he tells the audience, "I ryfe you in sonder" (l. 129), and "I clefe / You small as flesh to pott (ll. 142–3). These lines are strikingly similar to a passage in Micah 3: 2–3 which criticizes the unjust rulers of Israel. The passage reads,

> *Qui odio habetis bonum, et diligitis malum;*
> *Qui violenter tollitis pelles eorum desuper eis,*
> *Et carnum eorum desuper ossibus eorum?*
> *Qui comerderunt carnum populi mei,*
> *Et pellem eorum desuper excoriaverunt,*
> *Et ossa eorum confregerunt,*
> *Et conciderunt sicut in lebete,*
> *Et quasi carnem in medio ollae.*
> You who hate good and love evil,
> Who tear off their skin from them
> And their flesh from their bones,
> And who eat the flesh of my people,
> Strip off their skin from them,
> Break their bones,
> And chop them up as for the pot
> And as meat in a kettle.

The immediate parallels are obvious. Both passages involve rulers breaking the bones of their subjects, tearing their flesh, tearing skin from their bodies, and chopping them up like meat for the pot. On one level, these echoes characterize Herod as an evil ruler of Israel but they also turn Herod into a type of any unjust and abusive ruler. And considering that Herod is also painted as a contemporary king, this second meaning suggests profound injustice by English monarchs.

Even more significant is the entire context of Micah, evoked in this play by the numerous scriptural parallels. Micah is repeatedly concerned with unjust and oppressive rulers who abuse their power over their subjects and cause pain and hardship for their own selfish gain. For example, Micah 2: 1–2 says,

> *Vae qui cogitates inutile,*
> *Et operamini malum in cubilibus vestries!*

In luce matutina faciunt illud,
Quoniam contra Deum est manus eorum.
Et concupierunt agros, et violenter tulerunt;
Et rapuerunt domos;
Et calumniabantur virum, et domum eius;
Virum, et haereditatem eius.
Woe to those who scheme iniquity,
Who work out evil on their beds!
When morning comes, they do it,
For it is in the power of their hands.
They covet fields and then seize them,
And houses, and take them away.
They rob a man and his house,
A man and his inheritance.

Along with the abuses of secular authorities, Micah is also concerned with the corruption of spiritual leaders. Micah 3:11 says,

Principes eius in muneribus iudicabant,
Et sacerdotes eius in mercede docebant
Et prophetae eius in pecunia divinabant; . . .
Her leaders pronounce judgements for a bribe,
Her priests instruct for a price,
And her prophets divine for money.

These echoes of passages from Micah link the context of brutal and corrupt abuse with the themes and parodies of this play. By extension, the thick contemporary coloring of the characters and manners in the play connects Micah's portrayal of cruel rulers and corrupt spiritual leaders with England's own monarchy, aristocracy, and Church.

These concerns echo the social commentary of the Wakefield Master in other plays, and Micah is a powerful statement for anyone concerned with the corruption or abusiveness of secular and ecclesiastical authorities. Herod's evocation of Micah, along with the corruption and brutality of his court, aligns *Magnus Herodes* with the social commentary of the other plays, especially the two shepherds' plays. The reference in Micah 2: 2 to the powerful taking away the fields and property of their subjects must have had a special relevance to the Wakefield Master, who is openly critical of enclosure practices in both *Prima Pastorum* and *Secunda Pastorum*.[9] Beyond these and other scriptural parallels, the shepherds' plays and *Magnus Herodes* are linked both by subject and theme. The story of the shepherds and the story of Herod's rage pivot upon the same subject, the birth of Christ, but each approaches the nativity from a different perspective. In this sense, they are simply different facets of the same historical and scriptural event. The plays are also connected by symbol and theme. In *Secunda Pastorum*, for example, the Wakefield Master emphasizes children and the childbearing of shrewish women; in *Magnus Herodes*, Herod's soldiers slaughter children recently born around Bethlehem to shrewish women. (It is not unreasonable to imagine that the same actress or actor who played Gyll, for example, could have also played the role of one of the irate mothers; the roles certainly fit the same type.)

The primary connection between the two subjects, however, lies in the alternate perspectives upon abuse of power. In both *Prima Pastorum* and *Secunda Pastorum*, for example, the shepherds complain of the abuse visited *upon* the lower classes. The sufferings of medieval English peasants are inserted into the portrayal of biblical shepherds, and the plays focus upon the effect aristocratic actions have on the working classes. The aristocracy is never scrutinized, however, and for good reason. Open criticism of the upper classes could be dangerous in medieval England. In *Magnus Herodes*, the audience is treated to a different facet of the same subject. Herod and his court act out the initiation of a similar abuse of the populace, but here the play is primarily concerned with motivations of the aristocratic abusers. Within the tradition of a festive lord, Herod's actions are extreme and violent, and the actions of his court seem excessively cowardly and corrupt, good fodder for a comic celebration. However, although the subject is traditional and the characters are comic, the audience would surely not forget that this apparently English king and his court are the same rulers that the notably English shepherds complained about in *Prima Pastorum* and *Secunda Pastorum*. The aristocratic authorities portrayed in this play, callous, corrupt, and brutally self-interested, are the same as those that make life miserable for the Yorkshire shepherds complaining on the moors before Christ's birth. The contemporary attributes of Herod and his court solidify this connection, and the references to Micah confirm that the Wakefield Master is concerned with aristocratic abuse and Church corruption.

Perhaps this concern is why Herod remains unpunished at the end of the play. Perhaps the Wakefield Master attempts with this play to create a realistic environment that matches that of the audience. The message of *Magnus Herodes* is that evil can indeed triumph in this world, as the audience could see in their own lives. Jeffrey Helterman writes of the play that

> the audience experiences the lack of satisfaction that comes when evil is unpunished and virtue is unrewarded. This experience comes even to the faithful who know the ultimate rightness of things. The other playwrights, who "solve" the problem of injustice by the immediate punishment of Herod, do not provide their audience with a way to deal with the injustices common in their daily life. (137)

The Wakefield Master, by contrast, does provide a way for the audience to deal with injustice, and he does so by using elements of festive culture. He converts contemporary oppression into the form of festive characters. The festive rogue is tolerable because his rule is cyclical, just like the seasonal forces of nature he represents. Winter is a brutal, life-destroying force, but it passes away into Spring; those who understand Winter's temporary nature can maintain hope even on the darkest and coldest of days. Those used to the pattern of a Lord of Misrule can expect his demise. Therefore, by giving oppressive contemporary forces the characteristics of festive types, the Wakefield Master provides a pattern of regeneration and, consequently, hope for his audience. Herod is a temporary, seasonal Lord of Misrule; the powerful may be corrupt, and oppression may go unpunished, but Spring and renewal is always around the corner, so there is a reason for hope.

The play also continues to implicate the Church in the oppression of the populace. In the shepherds' plays, the abuse of the people is at the hands of agents of shadowy landowners. In *Magnus Herodes,* the aristocracy and monarchy are clearly identified as responsible parties. In the shepherds' plays, Church corruption is symbolically implied through the actions of corrupt of predatory shepherds; here, the leaders of the Church are clearly identified as corrupt and complicit in the miseries of the people. What the shepherds' plays imply through innuendo, *Magnus Herodes* confirms with explicit characterization. In fact, by connecting contemporary secular and ecclesiastical authorities with Herod and his court, *Magnus Herodes* implies that the English court and Church are partners in their oppression of their subjects, and that these supposedly Christian princes and clerics are actually the enemies of Christ. This implication is developed further in the Wakefield Master's next play, *Coliphizacio.*

Chapter Eight
Christ as a Comic Figure

In the subject of Christ's buffeting, the Wakefield Master again chooses a subject that shares much with the festive impulse. The beating of a god, especially in preparation for a sacrifice, and particularly a sacrifice which will lead to the victim regenerating and returning to life, is bound to be an attractive subject to devotees of festive culture. Indeed, there is stanzaic evidence that the other plays dealing with the beating and killing of Christ were also attractive to the Wakefield Master.[1] The *Flagellacio,* or *Scourging,* is particularly dominated by the Wakefield Master's thirteener stanza, from the opening of the play through line 351, and several of the other stanzas reflect some patterns of the thirteener. The *Processus Crucis,* or *Crucifixion,* contains the following thirteener spoken by Pilate to the audience, a speech reminiscent of Herod's furious boasting:

> What! Peasse in the dwillys name,
> Harlottys and dustardys all bedene!
> On galus ye be maide full tame,
> Thefys and mychers keyn.
> Will ye not peasse when I bid you?
> By Mahownys bloode, if ye me teyn,
> I shall ordan sone for you
> Paynes that neuer ere was seyn,
> And that anone!
> Be ye so bold, beggars, I warn you,
> Full boldly shall I bett you;
> To hell the dwill shall draw yow,
> Body, bak and bone. (ll. 9–21)

The *Conspiracio* (*Conspiracy*) and *Processus Talorum* (*Play of the Dice*) also have Wakefield thirteeners in them. In all of these cases, the stanzas reflect a distinctly festive interpretation of Christ's passion. Characters rant, bluster, threaten, and make game references. However, for reasons about which we can only speculate, the Wakefield Master chooses to spend most of his artistic effort on the buffeting of Christ before Annas and Caiphas.[2] In *Coliphizacio,* the festive elements recast Christ into the image of a festive lord, and they recast part of the Passion into a ritual festive game.

In several significant ways, this frivolity runs counter to Catholic doctrine; the orthodox interpretation of Christ's passion is clearly antithetical to festive traditions. Christ's suffering is a sacred event which must not be parodied, especially with games and play. The Passion is represented in two common ways by orthodox sources: it is treated as a subject of deep reverence and seriousness, or it is treated in a way which evokes intense emotional empathy for Christ's suffering. V. A. Kolve writes of the seriousness of the two surviving continental liturgical plays that deal with the passion

> Both plays crucify Jesus, but they do so without violence, never going beyond the scorn of the crowd specifically recorded in Scripture, as when the Jews cry '*Si filius Dei es, descende de cruce*' and '*Alios saluos fecit, seipsum non potest saluum facere.*' The mood is grave and decorous. . . . (176).

Kolve also notes that medieval narrative poems were also reticent to elaborate upon the scriptural version of the Passion:

> The *Northern Passion* describes at unusual length the putting of Christ on the cross, but 58 lines of verse suffice for the whole. The *Cursor Mundi,* a liesurely poem of nearly 30,000 lines, devotes only 10 of these to a description of this action and the raising of the cross. (177)

The other tradition tends towards an emphasis upon Christ's suffering. G. R. Owst notes, for example, that medieval sermons tended to stress and even exaggerate the details of Christ's pain to heighten the awareness, compassion, and appreciation of the audience. He gives this example from an anonymous preacher:

> He was betun and buffetid, scorned and scourgid, that unnethis was ther left ony hoole platte of his skyn, fro the top to the too, that a man mygte have sette in the point of a nedil. But al his bodi rane out as a strem of blood. He was crowned with a crowne of thornes for dispite. And whanne the crowne, as clerkis seien, wolde not stik fast and iust doun on his heed for the longethornes and stronge, thei toke staves and betun it down, til the thornes thrilliden the brayne panne. He was naylyd hond and foot with scharp nailis and ruggid, for his peyne shulde be the more; and so, at the last, he sufferid moost peynful deeth, hanging ful schamefulli on the cros. (508)

This treatment of the passion shares much with the mystical visions of Margery Kempe and others in the late medieval period. Christ's suffering evokes emotional agony which then purifies the one who contemplates the event. In neither of these orthodox interpretations of the Passion do we find games, parodies, or festive lords. T. W. Craik writes, "Christ, in the Passion plays, . . . is the victim of worldly authority: helpless, passive, resigned, his plight excites nothing but pity, which is increased by the thoughtful spectator by the paradox of his omnipotence" (193).

In the Wakefield Master's *Coliphizacio,* however, the orthodox Catholic tradition of Christ's passion is enhanced by festive characters and details which turn the buffeting into a raucous game and a ritualistic festive reversal. Indeed, there is something of a double reversal here; the scene in which Christ is beaten is treated as a festive game, and Christ's passion becomes an overt ritualistic overthrow of a festive lord. However, as Shearle Furnish points out, this scene is a play-within-the-play (62–3), and this festive game is only part of a much larger festive environment. The men who overthrow Christ are themselves festive characters, Lords of Misrule who reign in an atmosphere of chaos and injustice. As in *Magnus Herodes,* the authorities who attempt to restore order are in fact the true Lords of Misrule, the blustering, comic pretenders whose very authority usurps natural, divine order. To a degree, such a portrayal is orthodox, yet these pretenders, like Herod and his court, are closely linked with contemporary medieval authorities, namely the aristocracy and the high clergy. The effect is to undermine both the Church and the corrupt judicial structures of the day.

Critics have repeatedly noted and argued over the relationship between the *Coliphizacio* Christ and the tradition of festive lords. Stevens notes the references to "King Copyn" (l. 241) and the "new play of Yoyll" (l. 498) in the script and argues that Christ plays the role of a "Carnival King" in the Bakhtinian sense ("King Carnival" 43–66). Diller argues that such references characterize the perceptions of the evil characters only, and that festive attributes are themselves thus denounced ("Laughter" 8–9). Certainly the references are there, and they combine to create an unorthodox and festive portrayal of Christ that we should not underestimate. Christ, the true ideal and center of Christianity, becomes a festive character, a mock lord who reverses conventional order. For example, the torturers repeatedly refer to him as a mock or pretend king, a usurper of the normal order and hierarchy. The first torturer tells Cayphas, "Men cal hym a kyng" (l. 131) and notes the approval of the populace: "All men hym prase; / Both master and knaue" (ll. 148–9). The torturer's reference to acclaim from across the social spectrum is particularly festive. As noted in Chapter Two, elimination of hierarchical rank was fundamental to festival and carnival celebrations. By placing Christ's followers outside of class divisions and barriers, the first torturer attributes to Christ's mock reign the same qualities as those attributed to festive lords.

Cayphas' subsequent examination of Christ also emphasizes his mock king status: "How durst thou the call / Aythere emperoure or kyng? / I do fy the!" (ll. 189–91). Cayphas is particularly incensed by the unseemliness of an apparent peasant pretending to be a king. He questions Christ about his ancestry and pedigree, and he mocks him for supposedly being a lord and yet not having the dress (boots and spurs) of the aristocracy:

> Speke on oone word,
> Right in the dwyllys name!
> Where was thi syre at bord
> When he met with thi dame?
> What, nawder bowted ne spurd,
> And a lord of name? (ll. 209–14)

To Cayphas, the prospect of a lowly peasant being made king is both preposterous and insulting. He tells Christ, "Perdé if thou were a kyng, Yit myght thou be ridyng / Fy on the, fundlyng!" (ll. 218–19). To be mounted was one sign of being aristocratic, as indeed the aristocracy's power was based upon the status of the mounted warrior class. Yet aristocracy is not an essential part of festive lords and kings. Indeed, the lower the station, the more suitable a candidate for the position of mock king. The entire idea of choosing a festival or carnival king is grounded in the notion of choosing the least likely: the youngest boy, the lowest sub-deacon, and the crudest peasant. The play's emphasis upon Christ's lack of aristocratic credentials therefore implies that worldly hierarchical office is unsuited for Christ, while the temporary role of festive mock king is a natural fit. To his abusers, Christ is a foundling lord, replacing temporal authority for a short period of time, before being deposed by the conventional hierarchy. Cayphas tells Anna, "He has renyd ouer-lang / With his fals lyys" (ll. 326–7). He implies that Christ's kingship has been wrongly stolen from the proper authorities: "Say, thefe, where is thi crowne?" (l. 372).

In addition to these portrayals of Christ as a mock king and usurper of authority, Christ's persecutors associate him with disorder by arraying him against the traditional structure of laws. The torturers' first accusation against Christ is that he encourages the people to abandon their laws. The second torturer tells Christ,

> Sich wyles can thou make,
> Gar the people forsake
> Oure lawes, and thyne take;
> Thus art thou broght in blonder. (ll. 23–6)

The first torturer reiterates this charge, adding the concept of liege law: "Fare wordys can thou paynt, / And lege lawes new" (ll. 31–2). By mentioning "lege lawes new," the torturer pits Christ against the formalized medieval structure of allegiance a subject was bound to show his lord. The torturers repeat their charges of Christ's lawlessness before Cayphas and Anna. The second torturer says,

> He has bene for to preche
> Full many long yeris,
> And the people he teche
> A new law. (ll. 95–8)

The first torturer agrees with the second; he tells Cayphas, "He wold fayn downe bryng / Oure lawes bi his steuen" (ll. 133–4). The second torturer specifically connects Christ's status as a pretend king with his usurpation of the law: "If he reyne any more / Oure lawes ar myscaryd" (ll. 172–3). Cayphas uses this charge to justify his order to the torturers to buffet Christ:

> For sen he has trespast,
> And broken oure law,
> Let vs make hym agast
> And set hym in awe. (ll. 456–9)

Beyond vague references to upsetting the conventional laws, the play also associates Christ with direct opposition to Caesar, the secular authority of the day. The second torturer says of Christ, "He settys not a fle-wyng / Bi Syr Cesar full euen" (ll. 137–8). Cayphas later repeats the charge during one of his rages: "Sir Cesar he defyes; / Therfor shall I hym hang" (ll. 329–30). Christ's apparent opposition to the law and established hierarchy again ties him to the festive impulses in the play. As noted in Chapter Two, festive celebration is almost inherently lawless, seeking to usurp conventional order and replace it with festive norms and behaviors. Such usurpation can also be seen in the accusation that Christ ignores the strict customs of the Sabbath (l. 125). Mikhail Bakhtin notes that medieval carnivals and festivals were marked by a suspension of many everyday laws and customs; license replaced restriction until the festive moment was completed (*Rabelais* 71–82). Therefore, in bringing new laws that upset the established order, Christ engages in profoundly festive behavior.

The play also associates Christ with reversal and topsy-turvy patterns in the manner it uses to relate his miracles. The torturers tell Cayphas how Christ reverses the natural order by healing the lame and the blind and by raising men from the dead:

> *2 Tortor:* The halt rynes, the blynd sees,
> Thrugh his fals wyles;
> Thus he gettys many fees
> Of thym he begyles.
> *1 Tortor:* He rases men that dees—
> Thay seke hym be myles—(ll. 118–23)

Indeed, the torturers use Christ's healing of others as evidence for their indictment. The second torturer relates Christ's healing to Cayphas in the manner
of a witness giving evidence in a criminal trial:

> This is his vse and his custom:
> To heyll the defe and the dom,
> Wheresoeuer he com;
> I tell you before, syr. (ll. 127–30)

Such practices are evidence against Christ because they defy the natural order
as the torturers see it, and, as such, are seditious and dangerous. The second
torturer says to Cayphas,

> If he abowte waue
> Any langere,
> His warkys may we ban;
> For he has turned many man
> Sen the tyme he began,
> And done vs great hangere. (ll. 151–6)

In addition to associating Christ with disorder and reversal, the play also associates him with cyclic regeneration. Clearly, Christ's death and resurrection are cyclical in nature, but other cyclical patterns are also emphasized. The second torturer
relates Christ's comments about the destruction and rebuilding of the temple:

> Sir, I hard hym say he cowthe dystroew
> Oure tempyll so gay,
> And sithen beld a new
> On the thrid day. (ll. 105–8)

Christ's healing of the dead is also related with cyclic emphasis. The first torturer tells Cayphas how Christ brought Lazarus back to life:

> Sir, Lazare can he rase—
> That men may persaue—
> When he had lyne iiii dayes
> Ded in his graue. (ll. 144–7)

Thus, Christ is portrayed as a mock king associated with disorder, usurpation, reversal, and cyclical regeneration. Clearly, the festive elements of the play have appropriated Christ into their own world-view. This becomes particularly clear when Christ's buffeting, traditionally a sacred part of his passion, is turned into a festive game of ritual violence.

As Cayphas examines Christ and becomes increasingly angry, he begins to speak of punishing Christ in terms which are unmistakably festive. Cayphas says,

> Therfor I shall the name—
> That euer shall rew the—
> King Copyn in oure game;
> Thus shall I indew the
> For a fatur (ll. 239–43)

Cayphas's reference to "King Copyn" is an overt evocation of festive tradition. Stevens and Cawley argue that the name means something like "coxcomb," and that a King Coxcomb is a festive lord: "If such is the meaning, there may be an allusion here to the King of Fools, the *dominus festi* of the Feast of Fools" (558). Certainly, Christ is called a "foyll" (l. 496) or "fool" by the torturers as they prepare to beat him, and Froward says they shall soon "fon" him (make him a fool) in the buffeting (520). Further, Cayphas has said he will prove Christ is a "fatur" or fool through making him King Copyn. As the torturers prepare for their beating of Christ, they also make overt reference to festive tradition:

> We shall teche hym, I wote,
> A new play of Yoyll,
> And hold hym full hote.
> Froward, a stoyll
> Go fetch vs. (ll. 497–501)

By describing the proposed beating as a Yule-tide game, the torturers make clear that the buffeting is played like ritual festive violence.[3] Stevens and Paxson note the specific festive import that the Yule reference would have had to the audience at Wakefield. They write that

> York . . . maintained a popular fool's festival known as the "feast of Youle" which took place on St Thomas Day (December 21) at least up to 1572. . . . It was in this latter year that the Ecclesiastical Commission sent a letter to the City Council in an effort to suppress the revelling which featured "two disguised persons called yule and yules wife" who rode "thorow the cite verey vndecentlie and vncomely." . . . (54)

This tradition of the festive Yule figure who is also a king of fools would thus have been well known to the nearby inhabitants of Wakefield. Stevens and Paxson write,

> It is, of course, a Northern matrix, including no doubt popular festivals, out of which the Wakefield plays were born. And thus, when Secundus Tortor in the Wakefield "Buffeting" treats Christ as a "fond foyl" to learn a "a new play of yoyll" [sic] he might well have brought to mind for the audience the York St. Thomas festival. (55)

Cayphas' naming Christ "King Copyn" and the torturers' determination to teach him a new game of Yule, therefore, suggest that Christ's buffeting has taken on festive significance here.

The ritual festive nature of the buffeting is further enhanced by the degrading language used towards Christ. Cayphas says to Christ, "Speke on in a torde" (l. 215) and "the dwillys durt in thi berd" (l. 246). Both references connect Christ's mouth, head, or speech with defecation. As noted in Chapter Two, the tendency to degrade the upper stratum through contact with the lower stratum (as has been done here) is particularly festive and is usually connected with ritual violence or sacrifice. These references echo Cain's abuse of Abel in *Mactacio Abel*. In both cases, the degrading references are used within the framework of festive ritual violence and usurpation.

In addition to the use of festive titles, games, and insults, Christ's buffeting is clearly connected with festive ritual by the actions of the Torturers during the beating. Christ is mocked like a king, and the mockery is specifically tied to his beating. Anna sets the tone of this teasing when he tells the torturers,

> Com and make redy fast,
> Ye knyghtys on a raw,
> Youre arament;
> And that kyng to you take,
> And with knokys make hym wake. (ll. 462–6)

As the torturers situate and prepare Christ for the beating, they mock Christ to his face with over-exaggerated politeness and courtesy:

> *2 Tortor:* Com, syr, and syt downe.
> Must ye be prayde?
> Lyke a lord of renowne,
> Youre sete is arayde.
> *1 Tortor:* We shall preue on his crowne
> The wordys he has sayde. (ll. 521–6)

As they beat Christ, however, the torturers perform a specifically festive game. After blindfolding him, they hit him vigorously:

> *Froward:* Yei, that was well gone to;
> Ther start vp a cowll.
> *1 Tortor:*Thus shall we hym refe
> All his fonde talys.
> *2 Tortor:* Ther is noght in thi nefe,
> Or els thi hart falys
> *Froward.*: I can my hand vphefe
> And knop out the skalys. (ll. 584–91)

Having beaten Christ severely, with typical festive reference to anatomical parts (knocking out his teeth, etc.), the torturers tease Christ by asking him to identify the assailant:

> *1 Tortor:* Godys forbot ye lefe,
> Bot set in youre nalys
> On raw.
> Sit vp and prophecy-
> *Froward:* Bot make vs no ly-
> *2 Tortor:* Who smote the last?
> *1 Tortor:* Was it I?
> *Froward:* He wote not, I traw. (ll. 592–8)

Martin Stevens and A. C. Cawley note that "the game which the torturers play at Christ's expense is, in fact, an ancient game known as Hot Cockles, 'in which one player . . . knelt down with his eyes covered, and being struck on the back by the others in turn, guessed who struck him' (OED)" (561). The game parallels the ritual violence typical of festive expression; the victim is blindfolded and then beaten and teased.[4] John Speirs notes the similarities between Christ's buffeting in *Coliphizacio* and rituals of pretend sacrifice:

> Christ has something of the mysterious impersonal or non-human quality of the sacrificial victim, something even of the passivity or immobility of a masked figure or of a sacred doll or puppet, image of a god. Thus, the *Buffeting* is, it seems, essentially a rite. Christ is placed on a stool blindfolded and mockingly required to say who struck him last. (353)

As the torturers finish their beating, they revel in the fact that Christ has been knocked into a stupor and is apparently so disoriented from the beating that he can hardly walk:

Froward: It semys by his pace
He groches to go thyder.
1 Tortor: We haue gyfen hym a glase,
Ye may consyder,
To kepe.
2 Tortor.: Sir, for his great boost,
With knokys he is indoost.
Froward: In fayth, syr, we had almost
Knokyd hym on slepe. (ll. 603–11)

As noted in Chapter Two, this enjoyment of exaggerated physical abuse is typ-ical of festive violence and symbolic of the seasonal cycle of death and regen-eration. Christ has become the king of fools; he is mocked and reviled and then overthrown in a ritualistic, violent manner.[5]

However, Christ is by no means the only festive character in *Coliphizacio;* nor is he even the most festive. Indeed, the actions of Christ, sit-ting patiently and quietly throughout his ordeal, belie the title of fool given him by his persecutors, who are far more foolish than he. Moreover, his role is only one part of a larger pattern of chaos and misrule that pervades the play. For example, the play begins in an environment dominated by topsy-turvy festive sensations. As the torturers convey Christ to Cayphas and Annas, for example, they sound like Cain driving his team of plough animals: "Do io furth, io! / And trott on apase" (ll. 1–2). Stevens and Cawley note that the tor-turers use "language used in driving animals," and that the same language is used again at the end of the play (555). This fundamental reversal, wherein Christ, the master of creation, is treated like a common plough animal, sets the stage for a series of unusual and inappropriate scenes. Indeed, the tortur-ers are aware that all is not right. As they drive Christ, for example, they note the bizarre difficulty they have had getting him to Cayphas and Annas:

It is wonder to dre,
Thus to be gangyng.
We haue had for the
Mekill hart-stangyng. (ll. 14–17)

The cause of their trouble is not clear. The second torturer blames Christ for their struggles and curses him for it, although without any clear explanation of how Christ has hindered them:

He has done vs greuance;
Therfor shall he drynk.
Haue he mekill myschaunsce
That has gart vs swynke

In walkyng,
That vnneth may I more. (ll. 57–62)

When they reach Cayphas and Anna, the torturers try to explain why they
have taken so long, again without success:

Sir, we wold fayn witt.
All wery ar oure bonys;
We haue had a fytt
Right yll for the nonys,
So tarid. (ll. 70–4)

Cayphas and Anna question the torturers about their inexplicable tardiness,
seeking to find the root of the problem in understandable complications, such
as fear, bad directions, hindrance by others, or bad light:

Cayphas: Say, were ye oght adred?
Were ye oght wrang led,
Or in any strate sted?
Syrs, who was mys caryd?
Anna: Say, were ye oght in dowte
For fawte of light,
As ye watched therowte? (ll. 75–81)

None of these is the cause, however. The first torturer explains that everything
just seems wrong and that he can't even see straight:

Sir, as I am true knyght,
Of my dame syn I sowked
Had I neuer sich a nyght;
Myn een were not lowked
Togeder right
Sen morowe; (ll. 82–7)

In other words, the world within the play, the world of those authorities overthrowing Christ, is out of joint, disordered, and not working properly.[6]
   This sense of universal disruption occurs again when the torturers begin
to buffet Christ. Although they eventually beat him severely, the two torturers
seem disoriented at first, as both of them miss him with their attempted blows:

1 Tortor: Now sen he is blynfeld,
I fall to begyn;
And thus was I counseld

The mastry to wyn.
2 Tortor: Nay, wrang has thou teld;
Thus shuld thou com in.
Froward: I stode and beheld—
Thou towchid not the skyn
Bot fowll. (ll. 573–81)

In an environment where everything seems out of joint, the torturers find themselves struggling to do even the simplest of tasks.

Within this environment of chaos, Christ's accusers become the true representatives of misrule. If Christ is a typical victim of festive violence, Cayphas and the torturers are typical initiators of it and possess qualities that are typical of festive characters. The torturers act as foolishly as the shepherds in *Prima Pastorum*. I have already noted their difficulty in conveying Christ to Cayphas and Anna and their initial difficulty in beating Christ. They also argue with Froward about getting a stool for Christ to sit on. Froward thinks such comforts unnecessary, but the first torturer points out that Christ must be sitting so they can reach his head:

Sir, we do it for a skawnce.
If he stode vpon loft,
We must hop and dawnse
As cokys in a croft. (ll. 511–4)

Aside from comparing them to cocks (the coxcomb was a conventional symbol of the medieval fool), the reference suggests comic behavior in the image of the (apparently short) torturers hopping and dancing as they try to beat Christ (who is apparently tall). In addition, the simile may be a direct reference to a real festive practice. Stevens and Cawley suggest that the comparison perhaps refers "to the Shrove-tide game of throwing sticks at a cock, which was trained to hop aside in an effort to avoid the fatal blow" (561). Froward also fills a typically festive role as the cheeky servant boy who defies his master. When cursed by the first torturer, he responds with a rebuke reminiscent of Jack Finney (or, for that matter, Iak Garcio or Garcio Pikeharnes):

Syr, I myght say the same
To you, if I durst.
Yit my hyer may I clame;
No penny I purst.
I haue had mekyll shame,
Hunger and thrust
In youre seruyce. (ll. 549–55)

Cayphas is also a festive character. He uses vile and specifically festive language. In this respect he is closer to a true Lord of Misrule than any other character in the play. Indeed, he shares much with the Wakefield Master's other two Lords of Misrule, Cain and Herod. Rosemary Woolf notes the numerous characteristics shared among the Towneley Cain and Cayphas. She writes that Cayphas

> is reminiscent of the Towneley Cain in the violent breaches of decorum in his speech. Excremental imagery recurs, as when he says to Christ, 'weme! The willys durt in thi berd, / vyle fals tratur.' His insults include distastefully oblique accusations against Christ's mother, . . . this being followed by the more blunt corollary that Christ is a bastard (fundlyng). (251)

Cayphas also shares festive characteristics with Herod. He struts about the stage boasting of his power and bragging about his station (ll. 222–34). He makes exaggerated and ridiculous threats. Indeed, like Herod in *Magnus Herodes,* he displays the same uncontrollable fury as the festive Lord of Misrule.[7] As he tries to question Christ and yet receives no answer, he becomes increasingly angry and agitated:

> Great wordys has thou spokyn
> Then was thou not dom.
> Be it hole worde or brokyn,
> Com owt with som,
> Els on the I shall be wrokyn
> Or thi ded com
> All outt.
> Aythere has thou no wytt
> Or els ar thyn eres dytt.
> Why, bot herd thou not yit?
> So, I cry and I showte! (ll. 250–60)

Anna tries to calm Cayphas down, but Cayphas only loses more control over his temper. As Anna reasons that they should examine him, Cayphas exclaims, "Bot I gif hym a blaw / My hart will brist" (ll. 276–7). Anna again asks him to wait, but Cayphas fumes, "Nay, bot I shall out-thrist / Both his een on a raw" (ll. 279–80). We may imagine Cayphas' actions as he gives these lines, face contorted, frothing at the lips, barely able to control his fury. As he recalls Christ's claim to kingship, he rants, "War! Let me gyrd of his hede!" (l. 289). Anna advises that they act only within the law, but this suggestion only makes Cayphas more furious: "Nay, I myself shall hym kyll, / And murder with knokys" (ll. 298–9). When Anna reminds him that he is a priest and again suggests lawful due process, Cayphas loses control again: "War! Let me bett hym!" (l. 317).

Cayphas' threats are exaggerated and stylized. They emphasize physical fist-beating and are anatomically graphic, just like the comments of the guards as they later buffet Christ. Again, the pattern is reminiscent of ritual festive violence. The need to punch, knock and beat Christ recalls the ritual overthrow of the mock king or king of fools, as do the references to thrusting out his eyes and striking off his head. Other threats directly refer to medieval forms of execution. Cayphas says, "Therfor shall I hym hang," (l.330) and "I shall gyf hym a wryng / That his nek shall crak" (ll. 343–4). This type of wild ranting and exaggerated threatening is characteristic of Lords of Misrule, and Cayphas plays this role on several levels. He emphasizes his uncontrollable fury throughout the middle third of the play. Like Herod, he is physically affected by his rage, sweating, bulging, and panting in the throes of his fury. He says, for example,

> My hart is full cold,
> Nerehand that I swelt.
> For talys that ar told
> I bolne at my belt—
> Vnethes may it hold
> My body, and ye it felt!
> Yit wold I gif of my gold,
> Yond tratoure to pelt
> For euer. (ll. 404–12)

In addition, like Herod and other Lords of Misrule, Cayphas's rage is inextricably bound to his fear that this mock king has come to replace his own order. As Anna reasons with him and advocates a legal approach, Cayphas desperately tries to make him understand this threat:

> Nay, syr, bot I shall hym styk
> Euen with my awne hend;
> For if he rene and be whyk,
> We ar at an end,
> All sam.
> Therfor, whils I am in this brethe,
> Let me put hym to deth. (ll. 382–8)

Christ represents to Cayphas the usurper king; it is this fact that drives Cayphas, like Herod, to murderous rage. Yet this pattern is also clearly festive. The representative of one phase in the cycle (e.g. old man winter) bitterly resists his replacement by the next phase in the seasonal cycle of regeneration.

With the intrusion into the play of these many festive elements, Christ's passion is appropriated into a festive context. However, it does not necessarily follow that reverence for Christ's suffering is eliminated. A. P. Rossiter

writes, "The very values of martyrdom—of *any* suffering as significant—are
implicitly denied by thus making game of it" (69). Rossiter's conclusion is a
tempting one, but one that ultimately misreads the context of the games performed at Christ's expense. It is true that rather than undergoing a serene and
dignified suffering, Christ is proclaimed a mock king and overthrown in a festive manner. His indictment brands him as an advocate of festive license; his
appearance is associated with the removal of hierarchical order and the advent
of festive rebellion. To a degree, Christ is a type of carnival king; the particulars of festive culture which he represents would have resonated deeply with
the audience, creating, if anything, more sympathy for him. His abusers, on
the other hand, who represent established order and established law, are
shown to be the real fools, the true Lords of Misrule. Their raging attempts to
deny the new law are cast in festive terms; they are in fact the usurpers, and
their fury is driven by a sense of their own inevitable festive demise. Moreover,
as with the other plays, the festive reinvention of the buffeting is more than
simply entertaining. It brands as villainous the very orthodox structures that
claim to be the true guardians and interpreters of Christ's passion. Specifically,
the Wakefield Master's reinterpretation of the buffeting parodies and satirizes
legal abuse and ecclesiastical corruption, and, like *Magnus Herodes,* it highlights the complicity of the Church in the evil of the State.

This parody is best seen in the corruption and worldliness of Cayphas
and Anna. Both men are overtly associated with medieval priests, especially
with the higher ranks of the clergy. Cayphas speaks of singing mass (l. 231),
and Anna reminds him that he is "A man of holy kyrk" (l.301). Cayphas calls
himself a prelate (l. 222), and while restraining Cayphas from violence, Anna
repeats this: "Sir, ye ar a prelate" (417). In the insistence that they should turn
the buffeting of Christ over to "Men of temperall laws" (l. 401), rather than
carrying out the punishment themselves, Anna again implies that they are medieval clerics. When he tells Cayphas, "Sir, ye wote better then I / We shuld
slo no man" (ll. 391–2), Cayphas curses his own ordination as a priest:

> He that first made me clerk
> And taght me my lare
> On bookys for to barke—
> The dwill gyf hym care! (ll. 443–6)

These anachronistic ecclesiastical references continue throughout the play. As
the torturers prepare to beat Christ, for example, they ask Cayphas, "Sayn vs,
lord, with thy ryng" (l. 492). Cayphas responds by promising his blessing to
whomever "knokys hym the best" (l. 494). Rosemary Woolf writes about
these characters,

> Annas and Caiaphas as bishops are forbidden by canon law to sentence
> a man to death: this can only be done by Pilate as a judge in the civil
> courts. This anachronism is of course of the same order as the under-
> standing of Cain's sacrificial offerings as tithes, and like many of the
> anachronisms dispels any tendency to think of the action happening in
> a strange country long ago; . . . (252)

This anachronism in effect brings the contemporary ecclesiastical structure
into the play, notably associating it with fools and Lords of Misrule. Jeffrey
Helterman writes, "the Wakefield Master puts current legal language into the
mouths of Christ's oppressors and makes the court ecclesiastical rather than
Jewish" (140). Significantly, however, he specifically places contemporary figures in the roles towards which the audience will naturally direct its hostility.
G. R. Owst writes, "Caiaphas and Annas stand for the evil Ecclesiastical
Lawyer, dressed as 'Bishops of the Old Law' in mitre and rochet, hood and
tabard. . . . Their presence here in the Play offers our dramatist his sole chance
to pillory the sins of churchmen" (496).

Rendered as contemporary prelates, Cayphas and Anna are indeed
shocking indictments of the governing ecclesiastical structure. John Gardner
writes that their characters "are designed to provoke much darker laughter—
that of rage" (105). Cayphas in particular seems to disregard the ethical and
moral responsibilities of priesthood. As noted above, he displays vicious fury,
wanting to beat, blind, and murder Christ. Such violence is a perversion of
the role of the priest, particularly a bishop such as Cayphas represents.

In addition, Cayphas seems shockingly corrupt in his use of the law. As
he addresses Christ, for example, he suggests that Christ's only hope for escape lies in bribery: "Fy on the, fundlyng! / Thou lyfys bot bi brybré" (ll.
220–1). He then describes how influential he is, suggesting that he can clear
Christ if Christ pays him, and that, as a man of law, he is entitled to the income generated by such bribery:

> Lad, I am a prelate,
> A lord in degré:
> Syttys in myn astate,
> As thou may se,
> Knyghtys on me to wate
> In dyuerse degre.
> I might thole the abate,
> And knele on thi kne
> In my present.
> As euer syng I mes,
> Whoso kepis the law, I gess,

He gettys more by purches
Then bi his fre rent. (ll. 222–34)

Christ's failure to offer a bribe is, in fact, the event that sends Cayphas into a murderous rage. This flagrant corruption in Cayphas, portrayed here as an important ecclesiastical figure, suggests corruption among members of the contemporary high clergy, and it echoes contemporary portrayals in medieval anti-clerical literature. The author of *Of Prelates,* for example, writes,

> Prelatis also robben the pore lige men of the king bi fals extorisions taken
> bi colour of holy correccion, & geuen men leue to dwellen in synne fro
> yer to yer, fro seuene yer to seuene yer, & comunly al here lif, yif thei
> paien bi yere twenti shillyngis or more or lesse, and thus by sutilte of
> sathanas thei han founde newe peynes orible & schameful to make men
> paye a gret raunson, to geue gold & bathe hem in lustis of synne as swyn
> in feen. And men seyn that summe bischopis getith in o yer two thou-
> sand mark or poundis; . . . (Matthew 62–3)

Although he is a priest, Cayphas fails to observe the most basic behavioral standards of the priesthood; he is willing and even eager to betray his most sacred ethical responsibilities to reap financial gain. Cayphas' boasts also reveal a deep arrogance in his possessions, another flaw of prelates bemoaned by anti-ecclesiastical writers. For example, a Lollard sermon for the second Sunday in Advent says, "Pride thanne schal be ful hig in prelatis, for hir pride schal passe alle temporalle lordes in alle thyngis that longeth to lordes astaat, as in stronge castellis and ryall maneris, proudeli aparaylit withinne, in halles, chaumbres, and alle othere houses of office" (Cigman 23).

Equally disturbing is Cayphas's perversion of his aristocratic station. He and the other tormentors of Christ are all part of the upper classes and represent liege law, a secular authority, as well as ecclesiastical authority.[8] Cayphas claims to be a lord with knights waiting upon him. Like the Miles in *Magnus Herodes,* the torturers are repeatedly called knights (ll. 82, 226, 434, 463). Cayphas is a wealthy, privileged man. He need not solicit bribes; they are merely supplemental to his land rents. Yet he is quick to use his aristocratic station to acquire even more wealth. His requests for bribery are surrounded by references to his power, his station, and his status as a priest. He uses his station to corrupt the system, and he displays contempt for the law in his desire to murder Christ, regardless of the proper legal procedures. As I noted above, much of his fury is class-based. He is outraged that a peasant such as Christ should presume to take a royal position; therefore, he determines to punish Christ, regardless of whether or not such actions are legal. He respects the law only so long as it serves his needs and is convenient. When he is angered, he is quick to abandon it, at least in his language. In his brutal and selective application of the law, Cayphas, who is portrayed as a contemporary aristocrat, indicts the aristocracy and suggests that aristocratic application of the legal process is unjust and self serving.

However, while Cayphas's corruption and anger are disturbing, they are equaled by Anna's colder, more calculating perversion of the law. Cayphas clearly indulges in activities that are sanctioned by neither the Church nor the law. Anna, however, is a model of priestly conduct, and he works within the letter, if not the spirit, of ecclesiastical law.[9] Nonetheless, his application of the law deliberately achieves an end equally evil as the end Cayphas would like to achieve with his brash, corrupt, and illicit sense of justice.[10] This careful use of the law to achieve deliberate injustice impeaches contemporary law, and Anna's willing role in the play's legal injustice suggests that the ruling ecclesiastical bodies of the church are complicit in wide-scale legal abuses. Christ is not just portrayed in opposition to a few corrupt individuals; he is opposed to an entire legal and ecclesiastical system. Indeed, as noted above, Christ is placed in opposition to the law from the very beginning.[11]

While Christ seems to oppose liege law, however, he is clearly judged by a form of ecclesiastical law. When he is brought before Cayphas and Anna, it is for preaching (l. 94) and for teaching "A new law" (l. 97). Christ's "new law," is his new covenant, that which replaces the "old law," or old covenant of Abraham and Moses, and is thus specifically doctrinal. The first torturer makes it plain they bring Christ to Cayphas and Anna because they as priests are defenders of the old law:

> Bot wold ye two, as ye sytt,
> Make it ferme and stabyll
> Togeder?
> For ye two, as I traw,
> May defend all oure law;
> That mayde vs to you draw
> And bryng this losell heder. (ll. 163–9)

Indeed, the law of Cayphas and Anna corresponds closely to the proceedings of medieval ecclesiastical courts. Upon hearing the charge of preaching a new law, Cayphas declares he will examine Christ:

> Now fare myght you fall
> For your talkyng!
> For, certys, I myself shall
> Make examynyng.
> Harstow, harlott, of all? (ll. 183–7)

This examination of Christ is anachronistically portrayed as the typical examination given by the high clergy of those suspected of unorthodox beliefs. The
contemporary nature of these ecclesiastical proceedings is most obvious in
Anna's restraint of Cayphas. Cayphas is not allowed to harm the prisoner, just
as medieval priests were not allowed to torture or coerce suspected heretics.
However, this restriction was easily bypassed by medieval examiners, who
could use the civil authorities to arrest suspects and to apply torture. Indeed,
surviving documents show a great deal of cooperation between Church and
State authorities in the "examination" of suspected heretics. John A. F.
Thomson writes that in fifteenth century England, "the officials of the secular government played a more active role in it [persecution], not only acting
as executioners but also taking an active part in hunting down offenders" (5).
In his introduction to the Norwich heresy trials, Norman P. Tanner writes,

> The secular authorities are shown to have cooperated with the Church and
> to have taken the initiative; they arrested and imprisoned at least some of
> the suspects; they conducted a preliminary inquiry into their heretical be-
> liefs and activities; and they handed them over to the bishop. (10)

Cayphas and Anna also use the secular "knyghtys." The knights bring Christ to
the examination and provide Cayphas and Anna with preliminary accusations
about Christ's heretical practices. They are also used to do the dirty work, but before this is possible, Cayphas and Anna must examine him and find reason for
punishment. Anna understands this, and this need for prior examination seems
to be his only motivation for restraining Cayphas. He tells his angry colleague,

> Sir, ye ar vexed at all,
> And perauentur he shall
> Hereafter pleas you.
> We may bi oure law
> Examyn hym fyrst. (ll. 271–5)

Anna does not wish to fairly evaluate Christ; he only wishes to condemn him in
a legal process. When Cayphas wishes to beat Christ, Anna says "Abyde to ye his
purpose knaw" (l. 278). Later, when Cayphas wants to kill Christ, Anna says
"Sir, we may not lose hym / Bot we were dampnabill" (ll. 285–6), indicating
that his only hesitation is that he doesn't wish to violate the process of the law.
Concerning this quote, Stevens and Cawley write,

> Annas throughout argues for a legal interrogation prior to the use of
> physical torture or punishment. He is not set on fair treatment as such,

rather he wants the permission of the law to carry his foregone conclusion into execution. In this sense he is the direct embodiment of the crooked administration of the law against which the Wakefield author inveighs elsewhere. (559)

Anna restrains Cayphas because without a proper examination, Christ cannot be found guilty of unorthodoxy, and without guilt, Anna and Cayphas cannot legally harm Christ. After another wild threat, Anna tells Cayphas,

> Syr, do away!
> For if ye thus thrett hym,
> He spekys not this day.
> Bot herys:
> Wold ye sesse and abyde,
> I shuld take hym on syde,
> And inquere of his pryde
> How he oure folke lerys. (ll. 318–25)

Anna wishes to show restraint only because he wishes to bring the full force of legal punishment to bear upon Christ.

In his manipulation, Anna represents the evil of the medieval legal system. He does that which abides by the letter of the law, but in doing so he deliberately violates his ethical responsibilities as a lawyer and as a priest. Helterman notes that Anna "by his devotion to the letter of the law destroys its spirit" (150). This intention is clear in Anna's own commentary on the use of law:

> All soft may men go far;
> Oure lawes ar not myrk,
> I weyn.
> Youre wordys ar bustus;
> *Et hoc nos volumus,*
> *Quod de iure possumus.*
> Ye wote what I meyn (ll. 306–12).

Anna's Latin, which Stevens and Cawley interpret, "And we wish to do that because we can by law" (559), betray a callous disregard for right or wrong. Because they are done within the legal system, Anna's actions imply that the system itself is inherently perverted and unjust.

The depiction of Anna's abuse of the law recalls contemporary resentment of the legal system by the general English populace, as is most apparent in the peasant rebellions. Indeed, the abolition of the current legal system, perceived as corrupt and mercenary, is one of the most persistent demands of such movements. In his analysis of the 1381 uprising, Rodney Hilton writes,

"[John] Ball, according to Walsingham, wanted to kill all the lawyers, justices, and jurors; the same chronicler says that [Wat] Tyler, above all things, wanted the king's commission to execute lawyers and all concerned in the operation of the law, so that 'all things would henceforward be regulated by the decrees of the common people.' (226)

Indeed, the majority of those killed in the rebellion were lawyers (223). Interestingly, the charges made repeatedly against Christ in the *Coliphizacio,* namely that he wishes to destroy the old law and replace it with his own, are exactly the same as those made against Ball and Tyler.

Beyond legal corruption, Cayphas and Anna represent the complicity of Church and State in wide-scale injustice. The liege law of the knights is defended by ecclesiastical lawyers who themselves are representative of the ruling aristocracy. Cayphas, a "man of holy kyrk" (301), is a "lord in degré" (l. 223) with estates and knights in waiting. Christ's usurpation of liege law is condemned in the ecclesiastical courts by proceedings which smack of the examination of heretics. And while Cayphas and Anna cannot punish heresy, they can, for all practical purposes, have secular authorities dispense punishment (both the beating and Christ's execution) once guilt has been established within an ecclesiastical court. Anna reveals this strategy to Cayphas after another of Cayphas's violent outbursts:

> Nay, on oder wyse than,
> And do it lawfully.
> . . .
> Sir, take tent to my sawes:
> Men of temperall lawes,
> Thay may deme sich cause;
> And so may not we. (ll. 396–7, 400–3)

As if the Wakefield Master wants this point emphasized, Cayphas is slow to accept this strategy, and Anna repeats it. He points out explicitly that as prelates, they cannot engage in violence, but they can get secular authorites to do it for them:

> Be not to breme!
> Sich men of astate
> Shuld no man deme,
> Bot send them to Pilate.
> The temporal law to yeme
> Has he;
> He may best threte hym,
> And all to rehete hym. (ll. 420–7)

Convinced at last, Cayphas determines to adjudge a little physical punishment before Christ is sent to Pilate. He says,

> No, bot I haue knyghtys that dar
> Rap hym on the pate.
> . . .
> Bot certys, or he hens yode,
> It wold do me som good
> To se knyghtys knok his hoode
> With knokys two or thre. (ll. 434–5, 452–5)

At this point, Cayphas's violence and Anna's subtle machinations merge. Anna agrees that Cayphas is finally showing good sense, and he gives the command to the knights:

> Syr, as ye haue hast,
> It shal be, I traw.
> Com and make redy fast,
> Ye knyghtys on a raw,
> Youre armament;
> And that kyng to you take,
> And with knokys make hym wake. (ll. 460–6)

Again, this blending of ecclesiastical and secular abuse is developed with a particular emphasis upon contemporary secular and religious imagery. Because he cannot participate in the buffeting, Cayphas curses those who ordained him and taught him the priesthood (ll. 443–6). Both men call the torturers "knyghtys," and Anna emphasizes the preparation of their armor.

Furthermore, these contemporary characters engage in patterns of action typical of contemporary cooperation between Church and State. The entire proceeding is reminiscent of joint Church and State prosecution of accused heretics, be they Lollards, Waldensians, or simple wailers like Margery Kempe. In fact, the testimony of some Lollards indicates that such inquisitorial examinations were already associated with Caiaphas in popular thought. In the Norwich trials, for example, John Skylan admitted believing

> that the cursed cayfaces, bisshopes, and here proude prestes every yer make
> new lawes and newe ordinances to kille and brenne alle trewe Cristis puple
> whiche wolde teche or preche the trewe lawe of Crist, whiche they hede and
> kepe cloos from knowyng of Goddis puple. (Tanner 147)

Skylan's belief is echoed by Margerie Baxter and others (43–47). These connections suggest that the abuse of ecclesiastical law by secular and religious authorities was a common topic, and that this topic was specifically associated with Christ's appearance before Caiaphas and Anna. The Wakefield Master stresses the contemporary qualities of this secular and ecclesiastical complicity by having the first torturer ask to be signed by the bishop's ring:

> Sir, sytt ye and see it,
> How that we hym knap
> Oone feste!
> Bot or we go to this thyng,
> Sayn vs, lord, with thy ryng. (ll. 488–92)

Cayphas is quick to oblige: "Now he shall haue my blyssyng / That knokys hym the best" (ll. 493–4). The secular knights beat Christ to satisfy ecclesiastical leaders, while priests justify and sanctify the violence of the knights. The Church and the State have joined forces to perpetrate a massive injustice.

Coliphizacio, therefore, is far from an orthodox presentation of Christ's passion. It is a raucous festive ritual loaded with parody and symbolism which in fact undermines the established order by setting it in festive opposition to its very foundation. Through festive elements, Christ himself is appropriated into a festive, anti-authoritarian, anti-hierarchical role. He is beaten for a perceived opposition to liege law and ecclesiastical authority. His persecutors brand him as a king of fools and ritually depose him through festive violence. Yet in the process, Christ becomes the foe and victim of both the secular authority and the orthodox religious establishment. He defies and is betrayed by men who represent the leadership of his own church; he defies and is beaten by men who represent Christian secular law. The leaders of the orthodox Church are portrayed within a festive context as corrupt, murderous, and schemingly vicious. Their complicity in the abuses of the aristocratic, secular authority is portrayed as intentional and self-serving. In their corrupt minds, they see Christ's new law as folly and usurpation, yet the play reveals them as the true usurpers and their order as the true folly and misrule. In their actions, the Wakefield Master creates his most stunning festive reversal. In the topsy-turvy world of *Coliphizacio,* the corruption and worldliness of the Church causes it to betray, inflict violence upon, and condemn to death the very incarnation of God whom it exists to serve.

Conclusion
A Festive Flavor

Our limited store of specific knowledge about the Wakefield Master prevents a completely satisfying conclusion to this analysis. We can assume he was at least moderately educated in the Church. We can assume knowledge of music and of scripture.[1] The specifics are, however, elusive. In what order was he trained? What was the nature of his education? What personal circumstances formed his view of society, of morality, and of the human condition? All traces of his identity have been scoured away by the very inexorable cycles of time and change which his characters so eloquently regret. Yet if the man cannot tell us more about the plays, the plays can at least tell us something about the man. No warmly dressed burgher could write with such passion and empathy about the miseries faced by shepherds on wind-blown fields in the heart of winter. No well-fed prelate could write such biting criticism of Church and State complicity. No pious parson could relish in the scatological degradation of a pompous, priest-like Abel. The plays of the Wakefield Master are unique among medieval cycle plays, and their unusual qualities have much to say about their author.

As I have noted throughout this study, one of the most telling marks of the plays is that they are consistently built around topics friendly to or resonant with festive topics. The murder of Abel involves sacrifice of both animals and wheat, along with a bonfire and the overthrow and death of an authority figure. The story of Noah presents the regenerative cleansing of the world through the agency of a cyclic inundation of water. The shepherds' story is set around the time of Yule and New Year's Day and climaxes with the birth of a god who will renew the world. The account of raging Herod inevitably contains a festive, raging lord who is furious over the birth of a new king who will replace him. The story of the buffeting includes the ritual beating and overthrow of a god before his sacrifice and resurrection.

Yet while these stories naturally deal with subjects and forms sympathetic to the festive worldview, the Wakefield Master does much to enrich the
festive feel of the plays. As this analysis has shown, the plays include festive
patterns, characters, and behaviors not commonly found in the orthodox
treatment of these subjects. Plays such as *Mactacio Abel* and *Magnus Herodes*
open with the traditional invocation of festive celebrations. *Prima Pastorum*
prefaces the redemptive (and hence regenerative) birth of Christ with a festive
feast, while *Secunda Pastorum* prefaces it with the ritual festive overthrow
(being cast in the blanket) of the scoundrel Mak. Festive characters are also
common. Fools, such as Garcio Pikharnes, Iak Garcio, Nuncius, and Froward
people the plays, often inserted in roles unique to the Towneley versions of the
plays. Characters such as Mak and Gyll insert fraud and conflict. Other, more
traditional characters, such as the shepherds in *Prima Pastorum,* the knights
in *Magnus Herodes,* and the torturers in *Coliphizacio* play their roles with zest-
ful, festive folly. Herod, Cain, and Cayphas each adopt characteristics of festive summer lords or Lords of Misrule, raging and cursing around the stage in
a comic manner. Festive behavior is even more frequent. Beatings such as
those in *Mactacio Abel, Processus Noe,* and *Coliphizacio* are performed with exaggeration and enthusiasm normally only found in ritual, festive violence.
Characters subject each other to verbal abuse that connects the upper zone of
the mouth and head with the lower zone of feces and the buttocks. Serious
subjects such as the Mass, the enclosure of common fields, and heretical inquisition are subjected to parody and ridicule. This propensity towards the
festive world is far stronger than scholars have hitherto recognized. It promises to be a valuable tool both in identifying other plays, or sections of plays,
by this author and in learning more about the personality and preferences of
this otherwise anonymous writer.

As a means of identification, it may well be as effective as the recogni-
tion of the famous Wakefield Master's stanza. Indeed, if it is organized in the
thirteener form, as Martin Stevens and A. C. Cawley do in the 1994 EETS
edition of the plays, the stanza is not very rare. In the introduction to the
plays, Stevens notes that such stanzas, or pieces of such stanzas, appear in nine
other Towneley plays, and he suggests that these too are therefore the work of
the Wakefield Master (xxix-xxxi). Yet several of these, such as the *Ascencio
Domini,* possess absolutely no stylistic or thematic similarities with the six
plays traditionally attributed to the Wakefield Master. Are we to assume they
are the work of the Master simply because they share stanzaic form with his
other plays? Indeed, the thirteener is common to other mystery cycles as well.
The N-Town play, *The Shepherds,* is also written in the thirteener form, but
this means neither that the Wakefield Master wrote the play nor that he was

influenced by it (it is far different from the Towneley shepherds' plays). Therefore, the use of the stanza as a means of identification is extremely limited. For all practical purposes, scholars dispensed with it long ago. *Mactacio Abel,* for example, long accepted as the Master's work, contains only one full Wakefield stanza at the very end of the play.

The thematic fingerprint of the Wakefield Master is, therefore, an equally important indicator of authorial identity. *Mactacio Abel* is attributed to the Master almost entirely because of its comic flavor. However, while *Mactacio Abel* clearly shares attributes with plays such as *Magnus Herodus,* it seems from the modern perspective to have little in common with *Prima Pastorum.* And herein lies the importance of recognizing the anonymous author's propensity towards the festive. Festive forms, characters, and traditions provide a consistent common denominator for these plays, as well as for *Iudicium, Flagellacio,* and perhaps other plays in the Towneley cycle. Festive elements, which are rare in the mystery plays, can provide an excellent criterion for determining whether or not a play is likely to have been revised by the Wakefield Master. If he wrote a play with only one of his signature stanzas in it (Mactacio Abel), he might have written others without any such stanzas at all. The analysis of festive characteristics to attribute authorship is therefore potentially useful.

In addition to indicating which plays might be his, the festive qualities of the plays might also help flesh out the otherwise sketchy information we have about the author. It is reasonable to suggest, for example, that the Wakefield Master's repeated use of festive forms indicates a close familiarity with festive celebrations. The zeal with which he uses festive language and with which he utilizes parody and usurpation also suggests that he was fond of the type of behavior common in festive celebrations. This familiarity with and fondness for things festive might also suggest a third conclusion: that the author came from the lower echelons of society. If he was in the Church, his propensity towards the festive construct indicates that he was a lower member of the clergy.

Another unique characteristic of the plays lies in how the festive elements are applied. I note from the beginning of the study that this author attacks abuses (both perceived and real) common in medieval English society, and he uses the festive construct to do so. Festive patterns and forms are used to reduce the official world to the comic, in which state it is overthrown and rendered non-threatening. Corrupt priests become foolish shepherds, and in this form they can be mocked and degraded. A violent, militant aristocracy becomes a group of bumbling, cowardly *milites gloriosi;* in this form they can be chased and humiliated by angry housewives. These attacks are more than comic relief, however; by highlighting unethical abuses, they are reform-minded and satirical.

The Church *is* materialistic and corrupt. Predatory clergy *do* exist. The landed class *does* enforce its will by force. The parody and satire in the plays refer to real abuses and suggest a genuine desire for reform. This tendency towards parody and satire of the official world, consistent in all of the plays examined by this study, thus provides another useful characteristic for identifying additional plays by this author. Scholars have long noticed the author's criticism of social abuses (Cawley xx), but this analysis reveals a reform agenda on a much wider scale, particularly towards the Church. The Church is satirized both as a body and in the actions of its members. The plays identify abuses throughout the Church, from the minor clergy through the papacy. Such reform-minded parody or satire is found in all the plays, and thus it should be used as a criterion for attributing other work to the Wakefield Master.

This consistent tendency can also suggest more information about the author. It suggests that the Wakefield Master was a man sympathetic to the various medieval reform movements. Since his satire seems particularly well focused upon the abuses of the upper classes, the analysis implies a strong sympathy with the lower classes. Similarly, the parody and satire of the Church suggests that the Wakefield Master was influenced by at least some of the many anti-ecclesiastical currents of the day. This analysis has indicated that many themes in the plays parallel mainstream Lollard beliefs. This is not to say that the author was a Lollard,[2] but he certainly shares many of their concerns about the orthodox Catholic Church.

Yet in identifying common and dominant strains in the play, I do not propose that we forget the obvious complexity of the Wakefield Master. His use of the festive suggests he is drawn to festive forms, and he seems burdened by social and religious abuses, but this playwright is also capable of extreme devotion and civic pride, and it is this ability to mix seemingly irreconcilable elements in ongoing dialogue that makes his work so intriguing. In large part, he is a "Master" because he is able to blend Christian with festive and devotion with parody in such a way as to make us laugh, weep, despise, respect, pity and abhor as we experience his dramatic vision. As Gyb tells us in Prima Pastorum, life is change and variability:

> Thus this warld, as I say,
> Farys on ylk syde,
> For after oure play
> Com sorows vnryde (ll. 14–17)

It is his ability to adapt his "play" to the multi-faceted nature of his world that gives the Wakefield Master his depth and reach; paradoxically, it is also his most enduring quality.

Notes

NOTES TO CHAPTER ONE

1. I use throughout the 1994 EETS edition of the play as edited by Martin Stevens and A. C. Cawley. This edition prints the Wakefield Master's stanza as a thirteen-line stanza rather than the more traditional nine-line version. Thus, the numbering of the lines varies from previous editions of the play.

2. By orthodox, I mean here the standard and accepted tradition of Christian doctrine as laid out by the official culture of the Roman Catholic Church, and not by any of the Eastern churches. While "orthodoxy" certainly encompasses both traditions, and while common usage usually assigns the term to the Eastern churches, "orthodoxy," or "right belief," is simply that doctrine, stated by the hierarchy of church leaders, to which members of the church must subscribe. It is this dynamic, namely Christianity as solely and exclusively defined by the Church hierarchy, that I wish to capture with the term.

3. There is much evidence to refute this long accepted and deeply treasured assumption. Lawrence Clopper writes that "at the present state of our studies, we lack the substantive and documentary evidence that would establish much of a clerical presence in civic Biblical drama. And we cannot, I think, attribute the absence of references to the clergy in the dramatic records solely to the loss of documents because, in those cities where records are extant, the clergy still do not seem to play a very significant role" (117). Indeed, Clopper says, "we have no names of playwrights before the sixteenth century and those who sign their work, like Robert Croo at Coventry, are not clerics" (116). Clopper points out that source materials which would have enabled any literate man to construct a cycle of plays, such as "the *Stanzaic Life of Christ,* the *Northern Passion,* the *Cursor Mundi,*" etc., "were available in English" by the "late fourteenth and early fifteenth centuries" (116). After reviewing the documentary evidence, Clopper concludes, "The evidence suggests a divorcement between the ecclesiastical and secular establishments with regard to plays" (125).

4. This interpretation, at one time taken as bedrock fact, seems to have been a projection of the model of development of Greek drama upon the English variety. Such a model of development is an attractive one, and, despite the evidence, difficult to eradicate. In his book, *The Middle English Mystery Play,* Hans-Jürgen Diller, while acknowledging the discovery of multiple sources, noting the improbability of recognizable strata in the plays, and discounting the practice of "evolutionary" criticism,

nonetheless proceeds to trace the development of medieval plays through various strata from 'liturgy to drama," arguing that to go back and revise would mean writing 'an entirely new book" (5). Diller's book is quite good, of course, but his failure to revise means continued perpetuation of this noxious myth.

5. Richard Axton writes, "the traditional idea that the early Middle Ages saw a 'gradual secularization' of liturgical drama, in preparation, as it were, for the coming of the cycle plays, is clearly inadequate" (13). Robert Weimann points out that classical modes of dramatic performance survived well into the late Middle Ages (1–14) in Europe, and that folk plays and dramas were a consistent part of European culture from long before we have written records. Weimann concludes that "the evolutionary idea of a gradual secularization of liturgical drama has as a matter of course led scholars to underestimate and, in fact, neglect the secular elements in the early, precycle traditions, and it has severely oversimplified, if not distorted, the complex relationship between the cycles and the popular elements in the early European dramatic tradition" (50).

6. I use the term "festive" here as do C. L. Barber and other scholars before me in reference to those elements associated with the popular, agrarian, and perhaps neo-pagan festivals that dominated medieval England. Although they often (but not always) occurred in proximity to each another, the folk festive celebrations should not be confused with the official feasts of the Roman Catholic Church, which often imposed its own calendar over pre-existing pagan calendars in an attempt to appropriate and hence control these very powerful and deeply-rooted traditions. The word calendar even comes from the Roman "calends," a specific time of festive, pagan celebration that, as did all such celebrations, marked the cyclical passage of time. The folk festival should also not be confused with the celebration of the Eucharist, the center of the Catholic service. Although the two perhaps share at some level a common theoretical basis, observance of the Mass was always a solemn, quiet, and introspective occasion, whereas folk feasts and festivals were times of raucous excess and irreverent parody.

7. Stevens looks specifically at the role of Herod("Herod as Carnival King in the Medieval English Drama" 43–66), while Gash examines the possibility of an author specifically manipulating an audience's reactions against the orthodox (74–98).

8. Alexandra F. Johnston notes how common and popular such activities were: "The popularity of Robin Hood in the south and west of England and in Scotland is truly astounding. Exactly what is meant by a Robin Hood play or game is again unclear. They were largely parish-based, associated with May Ales and other May day activities such as morris dancing. There is some evidence that they represented a secular manifestation of the boy/bishop role reversal. In Wing, Buckinghamshire, for a few years in the sixteenth century, we have evidence that the Lord and Lady of the May, elsewhere identified as Robin Hood and Marian, were servants of a local landowner who explicitly granted permission allowing them to become the rulers of the festival. On the other hand, Robin Hood, with his traditional cronies Little John and Maid Marian, may more normally have performed formulaic farces, versions of which have survived. Hard evidence for Robin Hood activities is now available from over fifty locations (from such counties as Berkshire, Buckinghamshire, Cambridgeshire, Devon, Dorset, Herefordshire, Shropshire, Surrey, Wiltshire, and Worcestershire), and more is being found each year as we cull through the surviving church warden's accounts" ("What if No Texts Survived?" 7–8).

NOTES TO CHAPTER TWO

1. In the analysis which follows, I will necessarily repeat some quotations as I move from pattern to pattern. This is for the sake of clarifying each element of festive formula.

2. See Chapter Three for the details of this mock Mass.

3. Chambers hypothesizes that the peaked cowl of the fools comes from distinguishable and traditional parts of sacrificed animal heads. He writes, "there can be little doubt as to the nature of the traditional 'habit des fous' from the fourteenth century onwards. Its most characteristic feature was that hood garnished with ears. . . . A similar hood, fitting closely over the head and cut in scollops upon the shoulders, reappears in the *baton,* dated 1482, of the fools in the ducal chapel of Dijon. Besides two large asses' ears, it also bears a central peak or crest. The eared hood became the regular badge of the sociétés joyeuses." (384). After giving further examples of such headdresses, including those with bells attached to the ears, Chambers continues: "Such a close-fitting hood was of course common wear in the fourteenth century. It is said to be of Gaulish origin, and to be retained in the religious cowl. The *differentiae* of the hood of a 'fool' from another must be sought in the grotesque appendages of ears, crests and bells. . . . [I]t is not, I think, unfair to assume that it was originally a sophistication of a more primitive headdress, namely the actual head of a sacrificial animal worn by the worshipper at the New Year festival. That the ears are asses' ears explains itself in view of the prominence of that animal at the Feast of Fools" (385).

4. Pikeharnes' name, as I will discuss in Chapter Three, specifically refers to apparel. Stevens and Cawley interpret the name as meaning "thief," because "pick" means steal and "harness" often means armour. However, this interpretation is problematic. Garcio is not a thief, and when confronted with Cain's crime, he reacts with fear of and respect for the law. In fact, "pike" is not "pick," and it could refer to a number of concepts. Also, "harnes" is not exclusively "armor"; it is often used to refer to a variety of garments and specialized clothing. In the *Processus Talorum,* for example, as the soldiers argue over Christ's garment, Secundus Tortor says "The hole of this harnes is holdyn to you, / And I am leuerd a lap is lyke to no lede, / ffor-tatyrd and torne" (l. 282). Therefore, Garcio's name could refer to a number of qualities having to do with clothing, and I feel certain that the name refers to his own clothing. Medieval fools typically wore tattered clothing and peaked hoods; given the foolish pranks, parodies, and inversions of the boy, "Pikeharnes" probably refers to a "peaked harness," a traditional fool's cap. If not, the name could also refer to a "picked" or tattered garment. This type of dress on Pikeharnes' character could also help to explain one of his more cryptic comments. When he reenters the play after Abel's murder, he says, apparently to Cain, "I shrew thi ball vnder thi hode" (l. 390). If Pikeharnes is dressed as a fool, however, the phrases could be directed towards a marotte, an extremely common accessory to the fool character which Chambers describes as "a kind of a doll carried by the 'fool,' and representing a replica of his own head and shoulders upon the end of a short staff" (385).

5. The glossary is admittedly not a complete or accurate terminology of all the words in the Towneley cycle. For example, *Prima Pastorum* uses "fool" six times, only three of which are mentioned in the glossary. However, the fact that most references to fool in the glossary come from a few of the Wakefield Master's plays generally indicates the increased importance of fools and folly in these plays compared with other plays.

6. In his excellent examination of Rabelais, Mikhail Bakhtin examines the excess and variety of feasting and references to feasting in festive culture. Bakhtin writes, "The mighty aspiration to abundance and to a universal spirit is evident in each of these images. It determines their forms, their positive hyperbolism, their gay and triumphant tone. This aspiration is like yeast added to the images. They rise, grow, swell with this leaven until they reach exaggerated dimensions. They resemble the gigantic sausages and buns that were solemnly carried in carnival processions" (278).

NOTES TO CHAPTER THREE

1. In their notes to the play, Stevens and Cawley note that the play is "an amalgam of a wide variety of stanza forms" (441). While this could indicate the hand of many different authors, it could also indicate wide experimentation of one author seeking to find an acceptable stanza. Notably, while the play contains only "two irregular stanzas of the Wakefield author," it nonetheless is regarded by most scholars to be the Wakefield Master's work. Cawley and Stevens, for example, write, "It is reasonable to conclude that the play in its extant form is . . . on stylistic though basically not on metrical grounds . . . attributable to the Wakefield author" (441).
2. In this and other period quotes, I have standardized the text according to modern orthography. Thus, "techith" is spelled with a final thorn, which I have replaced with "th," and "gave" is spelled with an initial yogh, which I have replaced with a "g."
3. Related to "Caym's Castels" was the common acrostic, likely popularized by the Lollards, of CAIM as representative of the four mendicant orders: Carmelites, Austins, Iacobites (Dominicans), and Minorites (Aston 98).
4. Stevens and Cawley note that "the presence of a third character, Pikeharnes the servant, is of course an historical anomaly" (441). They add, however, that the character is "not unique to Wakefield" (441). They point out that the Brewbarret character from the York *Sacrificium Cayme et Abell,* while "a more compliant character than Pikeharnes," has much in common with the Towneley character (441). They conclude that the fragmentary nature of the York play prevents clear analysis, but they speculate that enough character and verse similarities exist between the two plays to hypothesize an influence (441). Certainly, the York play evinces some of the same festive impulses studied here.
5. See Hanks (50) and Prosser (78).
6. I explore the traditional typological connection between the shepherd and the priest in more detail in Chapter Five.
7. Herein we most likely find the root of the so-called "scarecrow" figure that watches over fields through the summer growing season. Such figures are rarely successful in driving away birds, but their overall duty of protecting the crop fits the role of the more ancient "spirit of the corn" figures.
8. John Barleycorn derives from just such a figure.
9. I am particularly reliant upon Chambers' text here because it is the classic work on the subject.
10. Interestingly, herein lies the significance of the child's rhyme, "Jack be nimble, Jack be quick, Jack jump over the candlestick." Jack, a type of the festive fool and of the sacrificial victim (as in jack-ass), must leap across flames, a common element of festive summer celebrations.

11. It is not beyond the realm of possibility that Cain arranges the sheaves in some garland or anthropomorphic pattern. Abel's scolding of Cain as he arranges the sheaves would have a double significance in this case. Indeed, the bickering and abuse between Cain and Abel as Cain prepares the fire is equally typical of the ritual abuse exchanged between a Lord of Misrule and any convenient kill-joys in a summer festival.

NOTES TO CHAPTER FOUR

1. We may note here the popularity of flood legends among cultures organized around the agricultural calendar.
2. Lollard testimony from the Norwich heresy trials will again be helpful here. Most Lollards thought the Church was a false church and that the ecclesiastical authorities had forfeited their spiritual authority by their corruption and sin. Hawise Moone, for example, confesses to believing that "the pope of Roome is fadir Antecrist, and fals in all hys werkyng, and hath no poar of god more than ony other lewed man but if he be more holy in lyvyng, ne the pope hath no poar to make bishops, prestes ne non other ordres, and he that the puple callen the pope of Roome is no pope but a fals extersioner and a deseyver of the puple" (Tanner 141).
3. Jeffrey Helterman, for example, hypothesizes that the duality originates from the combination of two plays. He writes, "During the course of the Wakefield Noah play, a viewer might be made uneasy by the contrast in style between the dignified opening of the play and the boisterous struggle between Noah and his wife. Had that person been to York to witness their cycle of plays, he would recall that a similar contrast of styles caused no such uneasiness. Further reflection would reveal the reason for his lack of discomfort at the York performance—at York there were two plays. . . . The point is that the Wakefield playwright, who had been to York (or at least had read the York plays) has made one play out of two. . . . The playwright has not, however, allowed the seams to disappear, as anyone listening to the varying cadences of the play would realize" (47–48).
4. Speirs, who interprets most of the imagery in the plays as pagan, writes, "The Play of Noah has a pattern of destruction and renewal for its theme, the destruction of what was created, because it has fallen or declined, and its subsequent renewal of re-creation. The play moves throughout with a sure rhythm to the completion of its ordered and unified structure" (321).
5. Other scholars who have studied the typology in the play include V. A. Kolve in *The Play Called Corpus Christi,* Thomas Raney Watson in "The Wakefield NOAH," Alan H. Nelson in "'Sacred and Secular' Currents in *The Towneley Play of Noah,*" and Clifford Davidson in "Jest and Earnest: Comedy in the Work of the Wakefield Master." For a look at typology in all the plays, see Walter E. Meyers' *A Figure Given: Typology in the Wakefield Plays.*
6. Gardner also notes this (46).
7. English quotations from the scripture come from the New American Standard Bible.
8. This and all other references to *The Plowman's Tale* are taken from the version printed in *Six Ecclesiastical Satires,* edited by James Dean.
9. This and all other references to Chaucer's *Canterbury Tales* are taken from *The Riverside Chaucer,* edited by Larry D. Benson

10. This and all other references to "The Simonie" are taken from the version printed in *Medieval English Political Writings,* edited by James Dean.

11. This and all other references to *Piers the Plowman's Creed* are taken from the version printed in *Six Ecclesiastical Satires,* edited by James Dean.

NOTES TO CHAPTER FIVE

1. An earlier version of this Chapter was published under the same title in *Medieval Perspectives* 15 (2000).

2. The titles *Prima Pastorum* and *Secunda Pastorum* are purely traditional and, unlike the titles of the other plays, do not reflect the the manuscript. At the beginning of this first Shepherds' play, the manuscript reads merely *Incipit Pagina pastorum,* and the second begins *Incipit Alia eorundem.* However, since the other titles of the plays are typically rendered in the Latin titles given them in the manuscript, scholars over the years have fallen into the habit of assigning similar Latin titles to these plays. As the manuscript is the only one of an alleged cycle that includes two Shepherds' plays, and as the two are clearly the work of the same author, there is no confusion as to what plays the titles refer to. While this is a less than satisfactory solution, I follow tradition here.

3. This and all other references to the York plays are taken from Richard Beadle's edition, *The York Plays.*

4. This and all other references to the N-Town dramas are taken from Steven Spector's edition, The N-Town Play.

5. Scriptural quotations here and elsewhere are given in the Vulgate as edited in *Biblia Vulgata,* ed. Alberto Colunga and Laurentio Turrado. Modern English translation is from the *New American Standard Version.*

6. Gardner gives the traditional interpretation that Gyb means here to "try his luck with dice" (78). Yet he also notes the problem with this interpretation that Gyb has nothing to gamble with: "The desperation of the plan is of course comically absurd. Since he is 'With purs penneles' (33) and thus has nothing to bet, he is laying everything on chance—Fortune. The first throw had better be a lucky one, or instead of buying himself sheep, as he says he will do, he will get himself a drubbing" (78). I find this interpretation unlikely. If, as it seems, Gyb's reference is to dicing, then, since he has no money, surely he means it metaphorically. When he says he will cast the "warld" in seven, he seems to be speaking largely and generally; he might just as well say, "life dealt me a bad hand," without meaning actual gambling. If this is the case, then he is casting himself upon the winds of fortune, a concept virtually identical to Ecclesiastes 11:1.

7. Gardner writes that the shepherds "are an early version of, say, the Marx brothers or the funnier of Beckett's tramps. They are, in effect, clowns (in the modern sense)" (78).

8. G. H. Cook explains the primary purpose of chantries: "In mediaeval England when a man died a mass was said for his soul by the parish priest and not infrequently provision was made in money or in kind for further masses to be recited periodically and on the anniversary of his death. Thus it came about that bequests were made to a church or to the priest solely for the purpose of securing prayers for the testator after death. This cult of masses for the dead was the motive underlying chantry endowments" (7).

9. Helterman notes this parallel with other references in the plays: "'The first shepherd addresses the bottle with words fit for Christ. . . . Noah, in the Processus, properly calls God, 'beytter of bayll.'" (84)

10. Although the Benedictines had existed since 529 and the Augustinians since the ninth century, the eleventh and twelfth centuries saw rapid multiplication of the monastic orders. The Cluniacs were founded in 927, the Caruthians in 1084, and the Cistercians in 1098. Reformed Benedictines also included the Camaldolians, founded in 1027, the Vallombrosians, founded in 1073, and the Grandmontines. Reformed Augustinians included the Premonstratensians, founded in 1134, the Gilbertines, founded in 1139, and the Bonhommes. To these may be added the many sister orders for nuns and the military monastic orders such as the Templars and Hospitalers. There were many orders of friars, although the four most prominent are the Franciscans, the Dominicans, the Carmelites, and the Augustines. All of these orders existed separately from the mainstream ecclesiastical body of the Church.

11. Eugene B. Cantelupe and Richard Griffith, for example, argue that these gifts represent God the father, God the son, and God the holy spirit (329). Helterman argues that the ball represents Christ's royalty, the coffer represents Christ's sacrifice, and the bottle represents Christ's wisdom (91–2).

NOTES TO CHAPTER SIX

1. A portion of this Chapter was previously published in English Language Notes 40 (2003)

2. See the first endnote to Chapter Five for a discussion of this title.

3. Gardner notes that "Daw berates masters in language which recalls Coll's complaint against 'gentlery-men' earlier" (88).

4. Stevens and Cawley gloss this as "foul weather, storms" (724).

5. The manuscript here says "weders" instead of "wyndys." Stevens and Cawley hypothesize that it is probably a scribal error (497).

6. There is no explicit textual evidence that "cok," denotes penis here, but such coarse meanings were rarely developed in text through explicit denotations. Where coarse meanings are intended, they are developed through innuendo, just as "cok" seems to be used here. The use of "cok" (rooster) as a pun for "cok" (penis) is at least common enough for the reader to enjoy the double meaning in the Middle English lyric "I hav a gentil cok."

7. While Daw's dream is of Mak covered in wolf-skin, Coll's reply places the dream of wolf-skin inside external garb, thus suggesting that both Mak and many others are wolves within, despite their external appearances.

8. Thematically, Mak's claim to aristocratic privilege and his tumultuous relationship with Gyll connect the opening monologues with the middle scene; his attempt at fraud in the middle scene creates the parody, which in turn connects this section with the final nativity. Mak is also the most interesting character, and the one that drives the action in the play.

9. T. M. Parrot points out that the Mak plot is not original or exclusive to this play (297). However, it is unique within a shepherds' play, and the Towneley Master changes the ending substantially.

10. Homer A Watt explicates a direct parodic connection between the nativity and the scene in which Mak and Gyll attempt to disguise a stolen sheep as a newborn son (271–82)· John Gardner points out that this scene "serves chiefly as a comic contrast to the shepherds' adoration of the Christ child" (91).

11. Stevens and Cawley note that such a cloak would be ideal for hiding stolen items: "If Mak's outer garment has sleeves big enough to conceal stolen things, this would explain why the Third Shepherd removes Mak's "chlamys" (as indicated by the Latin SD after 290). Later on , Mak says to the shepherds I pray you looke my slefe, That I steyll noght [ll.]571–2" (500).

12. "This and all other references to "Freers, Freers, Wo Ye Be" are taken from the version printed in *Medieval English Political Writings,* ed. by James Dean.

13. This and all other references to *Upland's Rejoinder* are taken from the version printed in *Six Ecclesiastical Satires,* ed. by James Dean.

14. This and all other references to *Jack Upland* are taken from the version printed in *Six Ecclesiastical Satires,* ed. by James Dean.

15. Diller notes this structural correlation between Christian and non-Christian elements, but he concludes that such a splicing is ordinary. He writes, " . . . we recognize that many of these correspondences which at first appear over-subtle, are in fact aesthetically effective because they belong to contrasting but comparable structures. The pagan rites, pushed aside into unofficial usage since the advent of Christianity, and the Christian liturgy, which had appropriated the forms and often the times and places of the former, were able to form an aesthetic unity because both, despite their development from totally conflicting social positions, went back to ritualistic origins" (242).

NOTES TO CHAPTER SEVEN

1. Act III, Scene 2

2. Parker argues that the ranting element of the Herod character builds gradually from medieval sermons, which were interested "in the dispensing of moral doctrine in palatable form" (63). However, his own evidence tends to supports a qualitative difference between the rage described in sermons and commentaries and the uncontrollable, grotesque wrath that Herod displays in many popular dramatic venues. Clearly, the tradition of Herod's ranting and raving derives almost exclusively from a performance medium, even in the liturgical plays, which suggests, again, the strong influence of indigenous, festive dramatic traditions.

3. Weimann also notes the festive nature of symbols often carried by Herod: "In Padua, Herod's boisterous antics were particularly revealing: an inflated balloon (*uesica inflata*) appeared in his train, and he held a staff or wooden spear in his hand (*cum hasta lignea in manu*) which he flung at the chorus in a state of extreme wrath at the beginning of his mock sermon (*et cum maximo furore prohicit eam uersus chorum*)" (66).

4. While the plays are represented as a cycle in the manuscript, it is speculative to assume that they were performed one after the other in a body, as were the plays at York. There is some evidence that suggests the manuscript may be a compilation of dramas drawn from different towns, and there is even more to suggest that many if not most towns presented only a small group of dramas at any one time. Therefore, we can not assume that Herod's unchecked arrogance is balanced by the other plays in the cycle. See Barbara Palmer, ("'Towneley Plays' or 'Towneley Cycle Revisited"),

318–48, and Martins Stevens, ("The Towneley Play Manuscripts: Compilatio and Ordinatio"), 157–73 for further discussion of this issue.

5. G. R. Owst notes of these soldiers that "when the summons to fight comes . . . , they are panic-stricken. As soon as they hear, however, that children are to be the target of their lances, courage returns. Yet even the blows of distaffs and the threats of broken-hearted mothers prove too much for their mettle at the Slaughter of the Innocents" (494–5).

6. Speirs sees this as a profoundly festive construct: "Though menacing and dangerous, the Herod of the Mystery Cycle is at the same time a kind of clown, a *sinister* clown" (349).

7. This pattern, while no longer particularly relevant in our culture, still finds expression in our art. At New Year celebrations, for instance, the old and the new year are represented by characters draped in a sashes which display their respective years (e.g. 1999 and 2000); the old year is portrayed as a stooped, white-haired old man leaning on a cane, whereas the new year is inevitably a young boy draped in diapers.

8. V. A. Kolve notes the union of nativity events with festive forms of overthrow and usurpation: "This notion of youth overcoming age, of the servant overcoming the master, must be referred to a theme pervasive in the religious life of the Middle Ages, deriving from the Magnificat spoken by the Virgin to Elizabeth at the Salutation. The verse that concerns us is from Luke 1:52 and had been used as the Canticle for Vespers throughout Roman Christendom since the sixth century: 'He hath put down the mighty from their seat, and hath exalted the humble.' It was used every day of the year, but the text came into special prominence . . . during the Christmas season at the feast of the Innocents, when the custom grew up of electing from the choir a Boy Bishop for the day and allowing the boys to sit in the seats of their elders and superiors and to conduct certain of the divine offices. . . . We see here wedded the two ideas: the humble overthrowing the mighty; the young overthrowing the old. It is a profound part of the meaning of the Nativity" (156–7).

9. Certain scriptural parallels suggest Micah might have been on the Wakefield Master's mind when he wrote the shepherd plays too. The prophetic passage referred to by the counselors in *Magnus Herodes,* for example, is followed in Micah 5: 4 by a reference to the messiah as a good shepherd: " And he will arise and shepherd His flock / In the strength of the Lord." This concept of Christian pastoral care, and particularly the corruption of that ideal by the contemporary priesthood is, as I have argued, at the root of the two plays.

NOTE TO CHAPTER EIGHT

1. John Gardner argues that "the five great black pageants dealing with Christ's capture, trial, and death" all reflect substantial revisions by the Wakefield Master (105).

2. In my opinion, the Wakefield Master avoids substantial festive revision of the crucifixion because the subject is too sacred and doctrinally static. The other Passion plays all show substantial revision from his hand, but the subject of the buffeting offers the best combination of violence, mockery, and abuse. Further, the subject had already been associated with festive games and traditions, and this association gave the perfect opportunity for turning Christ into a festive lord.

3. Kolve notes that the torturers "are shown killing Christ in outbursts of great energy, violence, laughter, and delight; they are shown turning the tasks assigned by their masters into a sequence of formal games, into a changing metamorphosis of play, and adding to them further games of their own devising" (180). Kolve acknowledges the importance of game here: "A new set of game words becomes important at this point—mainly the words 'jape,' 'jest,' 'bourde,' and 'layke,' all of which are used again and again to describe the actions by which Christ is captured, brought to trial, buffeted, scourged, and killed. . . . all indicate action in some sense arbitrary and formal. Once a game or play is begun, its inherent form governs the action; to begin it, game identities are superimposed upon real identities, and the object of the action is simply the game itself" (180–1).

4. The act of blindfolding a victim is closely tied to the act of sacrifice. The so-called "bog-men," pre-historic victims of ritual execution who have been discovered across Northern Europe, were invariably hooded. In medieval Europe, hanging victims were also usually hooded or blindfolded, and our culture continued until recently the practice of blindfolding those who were to be executed. While we tend to think of blindfolding as an act of mercy, it also has the effect of objectifying the victim, since he or she can be seen but cannot see his or her executioners.

5. Speirs argues, "This savage clowning becomes more understandable once we recognize some connexion between it and the ancient frenzied or orgiastic rites of mutilating or tearing to pieces the god, preparatory to his triumphant reappearance or resurrection in renewed power" (354).

6. Gardner notes the universal sense of disorder and reversal in the play. He writes, "The comedy in this system is typical Wakefield Master comedy, in which carnality parodies spirituality, earth's rules burlesque heaven's. One is the realm of illusion— in this case false religion, worship of the devil, 'God of the ground'—the other the realm of truth. The contrast of illusion and reality is supported by two main systems of imagery: animal imagery in which Christ is a workhorse and his tormentors are foxes or dogs and chickens; and game imagery, in which Christ (by implication) does real work and his enemies play games" (111).

7. Jeffrey Helterman writes, "In Caaphas's nearly inarticulate rage, The Wakefield Master again demonstrates his interest in characters like Herod and Cain, whose fear emerges as voluble madness" (149).

8. Rosemary Woolf argues that Cayphas and Annas are clearly "aristocratic villains . . . who retain a preposterous sense of rank" (245).

9. Woolf comments on the sharp difference between Cayphas and Anna: "But in the Wakefield Master's play of the *Buffeting* a sharp and effective distinction is made between the two: Caiaphas is raging and brutal, Annas quiet and fair-minded, though apparently only from a sense of public decorum. Caiaphas is violent both in intention and language. He would like to kill Christ with his own hands, to put out his eyes or to break his neck and, when restrained by Annas, urges on the torturers" (251).

10. Helterman argues that "The treatment of Annas is an innovation in dramatic technique. His 'fair play' and measured, whispered words place far greater strain on Jesus' composure than the bombast of Caiaphas. Several other versions of the play contrast the two judges, but they do not exploit the innuendo of the Pharisee's role" (150).

11. Gardner notes, "Christ is an enemy to the 'law'—religion—of the torturers, Cayphas, and Annas" (110).

NOTES TO CONCLUSION

1. A. C. Cawley writes, "The Wakefield playwright was no doubt a cleric or a man with clerical training, judging by his use of Latin and his biblical knowledge. We are at liberty to guess that he was a subdeacon or a chantry priest, but there is little or no evidence on which to base such guesses" ("*Wakefield Pageants*" xxx).

2. The Wakefield Master was likely not a Lollard, although he seems to share some of their beliefs. In *Iudicium,* he uses the term, "master Lollar" (l. 311) in reference to the devil Tutivillus (Cawley xxx). Heretofore, scholars have taken this statement as a denunciation of Lollardy; I suspect the issue will bear closer examination.

Bibliography

Primary Texts and Anthologies

Beadle, Richard, ed. *The York Plays*. London: Edward Arnold, 1982.

Benson, Larry D. *The Riverside Chaucer*. Boston: Houghton Mifflin, 1987.

Cawley, A. C., ed. *The Wakefield Pageants in the Towneley Cycle*. Manchester: Manchester UP, 1958.

Cawley, A. C. and Martin Stevens, eds. *The Towneley Cycle: A Facsimile of Huntington MS HM 1*. Leeds: University of Leeds, Department of English, 1976.

Chaucer, Geoffrey. *The Canterbury Tales*. Ed. by A. C. Cawley, New York: Knopf, 1958.

Cigman, Gloria. *Lollard Sermons*. Early English Text Society. Oxford: Oxford University Press, 1989.

Colunga, Alberto and Laurentio Turrado, eds. *Biblia Vulgata*. Madrid: B. A. C., 1965.

Dean, James, ed. *Medieval English Political Writings*. Kalamazoo: Medieval Institute Publications, 1991.

———, ed. *Six Ecclesiastical Satires*. Kalamazoo: Medieval Institute Publications, 1991.

England, George, and Alfred W. Pollard, eds. *Towneley Plays*. Early English Text Society. London: K. Paul, Trench, Trübner, 1897.

Gordon, James and Joseph Hunter, eds. *The Towneley Mysteries*. Surtees Society, 1836.

Hudson, Anne, ed. *Selections from English Wycliffite Writings*. Toronto: University of Toronto Press, 1997.

Matthew, F. D., ed. *The English Works of Wycliff*. Early English Text Society. London: Kegan Paul, Trench, Trubner & Co., 1902.

Spector, Steven. *The N-Town Play: Cotton MS Vespasian D.8*. Early English Text Society. Oxford: Oxford University Press, 1991.

Stevens, Martin, and A. C. Cawley, ed. *The Towneley Plays*. 2 vols. Early English Text Society. Oxford: Oxford University Press, 1994.

Tanner, Norman P., ed. *Heresy Trials in the Diocese of Norwich, 1428–31*. London: Butler and Tanner, 1977.

Historical and Critical Studies

Adams, Robert. "The Egregious Feasts of the Chester and Towneley Shepherds." The *Chaucer Review* 21 (1986): 96–107.

Agan, Cami D. "The Platea in the York and Wakefield Cycles: Avenues for Liminality and Salvation." *Studies in Philology* 94 (1997): 344–67.

Anderson, J. J. "The Towneley Shepherds and the York Primer." *Neophilologus* 75 (1991): 317–19.

Anttila, Raimo. "Loanwords as Statistical Measures of Style in the Towneley Plays." *Statistical Methods in Linguistics* 2 (1963): 73–93.

Ashley, Kathleen M. "An Anthropological Approach to the Cycle Dramas: The Shepherds as Sacred Clowns." *Fifteenth-Century Studies* 13 (1988): 123–35.

———. "The Guiler Beguiled: Christ and Satan as Theological Tricksters in Medieval Religious Literature." *Criticism* 24 (1982): 126–37.

Anderson, M. D. *Drama and Imagery in English Medieval Churches.* Cambridge: Cambridge UP, 1963.

Aston, Margaret. *Faith and Fire: Popular and Unpopular Religion, 1350–1600.* London: Hambledon, 1993.

Axton, Richard. "Popular Modes in the Earliest Plays." *Medieval Drama.* Stratford Upon Avon Studies 16. Ed. by Neville Denny. London: Arnold, 1973. 13–40.

Bakhtin, Mikhail. *The Dialogic Imagination.* Trans. by Caryl Emerson and Michael Holquist. Austin: U of Texas P, 1981.

———. *Rabelais and His World.* Trans. by Helene Iswolsky. Bloomington: Indiana U P, 1984.

Barber, C. L. *Shakespeare's Festive Comedy: A Study of Dramatic Form and Its Relation to Social Custom.* Princeton: Princeton UP, 1959.

Baskerville, C. R. "Dramatic Aspects of Mediaeval Folk Festivals in England." *Studies in Philology* 17 (1920): 19–87.

Beadle, Richard, and Pamela M. King. *York Mystery Plays.* Oxford: Clarendon, 1984.

Bernbrock, John E. "Notes on the Towneley Cycle Slaying of Abel." *Journal of English and Germanic Philology* 62 (1963): 317–22.

Blanch, Robert J. " The Gifts of the Shepherds in *Prima Pastorum:* A Symbolic Interpretation." *Cithara: Essays in the Judaeo-Christian Tradition* 13 (1974): 69–75.

Blum, Jerome, Rondo Cameron and Thomas G. Barnes. *The European World.* Boston: Little, Brown and Co., 1966.

Boone, Blair W. "The Skill of Cain in the English Mystery Cycles." *Comparative Drama* 16 (1982): 112–29.

Bradbury, Nancy. "Popular Festive Forms and Beliefs in Robert Mannyng's Handlyng Synne." *Bakhtin and Medieval Voices.* Ed. by Thomas J Farrell. Tallahassee: UP of Florida, 1995. 158–79.

Brawer, Robert A. "The Dramatic Function of the Ministry Group in the Towneley Mystery Plays." *Comparative Drama* 4 (1970): 166–76.

Briscoe, Marianne G. and John C. Coldewey, eds. *Contexts for Early English Drama.* Bloomington: Indiana University Press, 1989.

Brockman, Bennett A. "Comic and Tragic Counterpoint in the Medieval Drama: The Wakefield *Mactacio Abel.*" *Mediaeval Studies* 39 (1977): 331–49.

———. "The Law of Man and the Peace of God: Judicial Process as Satiric Theme in the Wakefield Mactacio Abel." *Speculum* 49 (1974): 699–707.

Campbell, Josie P. "Farce as Function in the Wakefield Shepherds' Plays." *Chaucer Review* 14 (1980): 336–43

———. "The Idea of Order in the Wakefield Noah." *Chaucer Review* 10 (1976): 76–86.

Campbell, Thomas P. "Why Do the Shepherds Prophesy?" *Comparative Drama* 12 (1978): 137–50.

Cantelupe, Eugene B. and Richard Griffith. "The Gifts of the Shepherds in the Wakefield 'Secunda Pastorum': An Iconographical Interpretation." *Medieval Studies* 28 (1966): 328–35.

Carpenter, N. C. "Music in the Secunda Pastorum" *Speculum* 26 (1951): 696–700.

Cawley, A. C. "The 'Grotesque' Feast in the Prima Pastorum." *Speculum* 30 (1955): 213–17.

Chambers, E. K. *The Mediaeval Stage.* 2 vols. London: Clarendon Press, 1903.

Chidamian, Claude. "Mak and the Tossing in the Blanket." *Speculum* 22 (1947): 186–90.

Clark, Cecily. "Another Late-Fourteenth-Century Case of Dialect-Awareness." *English Studies* 62 (1981): 504–5.

Clein, Wendy. "The Towneley *Magnus Herodes* and the Comedy of Redemption." *Renascence* 38 (1985) 54–63.

Cleland, John H. "*Second Shepherds'* and *Homecoming:* Two Dramatic Imitations of Life." *Faith and Reason* 3 (1977): 46–64.

Collins, Patrick J. "Narrative Bible Cycles in Medieval Art and Drama." *The Drama in the Middle Ages: Comparative and Critical Essays.* Ed. by Clifford Davidson, C. J. Gianakaris, and John H. Stroupe. New York: AMS, 1982. 118–39.

Cook, G. H. *Mediaeval Chantries and Chantry Chapels.* London: Phoenix House, 1963.

Cooper, Helen. "A Note on the Wakefield *Prima Pastorum.*" *Notes and Queries* 20 (1973): 326.

Craig, Hardin. *English Religious Drama of the Middle Ages.* Oxford: Clarendon, 1955.

Craik, T. W. "Violence in the English Miracle Plays." *Medieval Drama.* Ed. by Neville Denny. Stratford Upon Avon Studies 16. London: Arnold, 1973.

Crowther, J. D. W. "The Wakefield Cain and the 'Curs' of the Bad Tither." *Parergon* 24 (1979): 19–24.

Cutts, Edward L. *Scenes and Characters of the Middle Ages.* London: Simpkin, Marshall, Hamilton, Kent, and Co., 1925

Davidson, Charles. *Studies in the English Mystery Plays.* New York: Haskell House, 1965.

Davidson, Clifford. "Jest and Earnest: Comedy in the Work of the Wakefield Master." *Annuale Mediaevale* 22 (1982): 65–83.

De Vroom, Theresia. "In the Context of Rough Music: The Represntation of Unequal Couples in Some Medieval Plays." *European Medieval Drama 2.* Ed. by Sidney Higgins. Turnhout: Brepols, 1998. 237–60.

Diller, Hans-Jürgen. "Laughter in Medieval English Drama: A Critique of Modernizing and Historical Analyses." *Comparative Drama* 36 (2002): 1–19.

———. *The Middle English Mystery Play: A Study in Dramatic Speech and Form.* Trans. Frances Wessels. Cambridge: Cambridge UP, 1992.

Earl, James W. "The Shape of Old Testament History in the Towneley Plays." *Studies in Philology* 69 (1972): 434–52.

Edminster, Warren. "Foolish Shepherds and Priestly Folly: Festive Influence in the *Prima Pastorum.*" *Medieval Perspectives* 15 (2000): 57–73.

———. "Punning and Political Parody in *The Second Shepherds' Play.*" *English Language Notes* 40 (2003): 1–10.

Evans, Ruth. "Feminist Re-Enactments: Gender and the Towneley Vxor Noe." *A Wyf Ther Was: Essays in Honour of Paule Mertens-Fonck.* Ed. by Juliete Dor. Liège: English Department, University of Liège, 1992.

Findley, Robert R. "Confrontation in Waiting: Godot and the Wakefield Play" *Renascence* 21 (1969): 195–202.

Fionella, Mavis G. "The Conversion of the Sign in the Towneley Passion Plays." *New Approaches to Medieval Textuality.* Ed. by Dave Mikle. New York, Peter Lang, 1998. 105–16.

Frampton, Mendal G. "The Brewbarret Interpolation in the York Play, the 'Sacrificium Cayme and Abel.'" *PMLA* 52 (1937): 895–900.

———. "The Date of the 'Wakefield Master': Bibliographical Evidence." *PMLA* 53 (1938): 86–117.

Furnish, Shearle. "Play-within-the Play in the Dramas of the Wakefield Master." *Medieval Perspectives* 14 (1999): 61–69.

Gardner, John. *The Construction of the Wakefield Cycle.* Carbondale: Southern Illinois UP, 1974.

Gash, Anthony. "Carnival against Lent: The Ambivalence of Medieval Drama." *Medieval Literature: Criticism, Ideology, and History.* Ed. by David Aers. New York: St. Martins, 1986. 74–98.

Guilfoyle, Cherrell. "'The Riddle Song' and the Shepherds' Gifts in *Secunda Pastorum* with a Note on the 'Tre callyd Persidis.'" *Yearbook of English Studies* 8 (1978): 208–19.

Gurevich, Aron. *Medieval Popular Culture.* Trans. by Janos M. Bak and Paul A. Hollingsworth. Cambridge: Cambridge UP, 1988.

Gusick, Barbara I. "Ambrose's Idea of God's Superabundance and the Construction of Work in the Towneley Cycle." *Publications of the Medieval Association of the Midwest* 7 (2000): 1–36.

———. "Death and Resurrection in the Towneley *Lazarus.*" *Death and Dying in the Middle Ages.* Ed. by Edelgard E. DuBruck. New York: Peter Lang, 1999. 331–54.

Hanks, Dorrel T. "The Mactacio Abel and the Wakefield Cycle: A Study in Context." *The Southern Quarterly* 16 (1977): 47–57.

Happé, Peter. "The English Cycle Plays: Contexts and Development." *Early Drama, Art, and Music Review* 20 (1998): 71–87.

———. "Subversion in *The Towneley Cycle:* Strategies for Evil." *The Anatomy of Tudor Literature: Proceedings of the First International Conference of the Tudor Symposium.* Ed. by Mike Pincombe. Aldershot: Ashgate, 2001. 11–23.

Harris, John Wesley. *Medieval Theater in Context.* New York: Routledge, 1992.

Hartnett, Edith. "Cain in the Medieval Towneley Play." *Annuale Mediaevale* 12 (1971): 21–29.

Harvey, I. M. W., *Jack Cade's Rebellion of 1450.* Oxford: Clarendon, 1991.

Helterman, Jeffrey. *Symbolic Action in the Plays of the Wakefield Master.* Athens, GA: University of Georgia Press, 1981.

Hicks, James E. "Majesty and Comedy in the Towneley *Iudicium:* The Contribution of Property to Spectacle." *Rocky Mountain Review of Language and Literature* 44 (1990): 211–28.

Hilton, Rodney. *Bond Men Made Free.* London: Routledge, 2003.

Hirsh, John C. "Mak Tossed in a Blanket." *Notes and Queries* 28 (1981): 117–18.

Hodges, Laura. "'Noe's Wife' Type of Eve and Wakefield Spinner and 'Recalcitrant Wife' in the Ramsey Abbey Psalter." *Equally in God's Image: Women in the Middle Ages.* Ed. by Julia Bolton Holloway, Costance S. Wright, and Joan Bechtold. New York: Peter Lang, 1990. 30–45.

Holton, Frederick S. "The Wakefield Noah: Notes toward a Patristic Interpretation." *Fifteenth-Century Studies* 19 (1992): 55–72.

Holzknecht, Karl J. *The Backgrounds of Shakespeare's Plays.* New York: Routledge, 1950.

Jambeck, Thomas J. "The 'Ayll of Hely' Allusion in the *Prima Pastorum.*" *English Language Notes* 17 (1979): 1–7.

———. "The Canvas-Tossing Allusion in the *Secunda Pastorum*." *Modern Philology* 76 (1978): 49–54.

Jennings, Margaret. "Tutivillus: The Literary Career of the Recording Demon." *Studies in Philology* 74 (1977): 1–95.

Johnston, Alexandra F. "Evil in the Towneley Cycle." *Medieval English Theatre* 11 (1989): 94–103.

———. "What If No Texts Survived? External Evidence for Early English Drama." *Contexts for Early English Drama.* Ed. by Marianne G. Briscoe and John C. Coldewey. Bloomington: Indiana University Press, 1989. 1–19.

Johnson, Kenneth E. "The Rhetoric of Apocalypse in Van Eyck's 'Last Judgment' and the Wakefield *Secunda Pastorum*." *Legacy of Thepsis.* Ed. by Karelisa V. Hartigan. Lanham: University Press of America, 1984. 31–41.

Jungman, Robert E. "Mak and the Seven Names of God." *Lore and Language* 3 (1982): 24–8.

Kerby-Fulton, Kathryn. *Reformist Apocalypticism and Piers Plowman.* Cambridge: Cambridge UP, 1990.

Kinneavy, Gerald Byron. *A Concordance to The Towneley Plays.* New York: Garland, 1990.

Kolve, V. A. *The Play Called Corpus Christi.* Stanford: Stanford University Press, 1966.

Kroll, Norma. "The Towneley and Chester Plays of the Shepherds: The Dramatic Interweaving of Power, Conflict, and Destiny." *Studies in Philology* 100 (2003): 315–45.

Lepow, Lauren. *Enacting the Sacrament.* Rutherford: Fairleigh Dickinson UP, 1990.

———. "'What God Has Cleansed': The Shepherds' Feast in the *Prima Pastorum*." *Modern Philology* 80 (1983): 280–83.

Leshock, David. "The Representation of Islam in the Wakefield Corpus Christi Plays." *Medieval Perspectives* 11 (1996): 195–208.

Mack, Maynard Jr. "*The Second Shepherds' Play:* A Reconsideration." *PMLA* 93 (1978): 78–85.

Maltman, Nicholas. "Pilate—*Os Malleatoris*." *Speculum* 36 (1961): 308–11.

Manion, F. P., S. J. "A Reinterpretation of *The Second Shepherds' Play*." *American Benedictine Review* 30 (1979): 44–68.

Manly, W. M. "Shepherds and Prophets: Religious Unity in the Towneley Secunda Pastorum." *PMLA* 78 (1963): 151–55.

Marshall, Linda E. "'Sacral Parody' in the Secunda Pastorum." *Speculum* 47 (1972): 720–36.

Martin, Jeanne S. "History and Paradigm in the Towneley Cycle." *Mediaevalia et Humanistica* 8 (1977): 125–45.

Meyers, Walter E. *A Figure Given: Typology in the Wakefield Plays.* Pittsburgh: Duquesne University Press, 1970.

Miliaras, Barbara A. "The Politics of Religion and the Heretical Left in Northern England: Interaction between Theatre and Audience in the Towneley Cycle." *Fifteenth-Century Studies* 13 (1988): 435–445.

Mills, David. "'The Towneley Plays' or 'The Towneley Cycle.'" *Leeds Studies in English* 17 (1986): 95–104.

Morgan, Margery M. "'High Fraud': Paradox and Double Plot in the English Shepherds' Plays." *Speculum* 39 (1964): 676–89.

Munson, William F. "Audience and Meaning in Two Medieval Dramatic Realisms." *The Drama in the Middle Ages: Comparative and Critical Essays.* Ed. by Clifford Davidson, C. J. Gianakaris, and John H. Stroupe. New York: AMS, 1982. 118–39.

————. "Typology in the Towneley Isaac." *Research Opportunities in Renaissance Drama* 11 (1968): 129–39.

Nelson, Alan H. *The Medieval English Stage: Corpus Christi Pageants and Plays.* Chicago: University of Chicago Press, 1974.

————. "The Wakefield Corpus Christi Play: Pageant Procession and Dramatic Cycle." *Research Opportunities in Renaissance Drama* 13–14 (1970–71): 221–33.

————. "'Sacred and Secular' Currents in *The Towneley Play of Noah*." *Drama Survey* 3 (1964): 393–401.

Nitecki, Alicia K. "The Sacred Elements of the Secular Feast in *Prima Pastorum*." *Mediaevalia* 3 (1977): 229–37.

Oosterwijk, Sophie. "Of Mops and Puppets: The Ambiguous Use of the Word 'Mop' in the Towneley Shepherds' Plays." *Notes and Queries* 44 (1997): 169–71.

Owst, G. R. *Literature and Pulpit in Medieval England.* Oxford: Blackwell, 1966.

Palmer, Barbara D. "Corpus Christi 'Cycles' in Yorkshire: The Surviving Records." *Comparative Drama* 27 (1993): 218–31.

————. "Recycling 'The Wakefield Cycle': The Records." *Research Opportunities in Renaissance Drama* 41 (2002): 88–130.

————. "'Towneley Plays' or 'Wakefield Cycle' Revisited." *Comparative Drama* 21 (1987–88): 318–48.

Parker, Roscoe. "The Reputation of Herod in Early English Literature." *Speculum* 8 (1933): 59–67.

Parrot, T. M. "Mak and Archie Armstrang." *Modern Language Notes* 59 (1944): 297–304.

Paull, Michael. "The Figure of Mahomet in the Towneley Cycle." *Comparative Drama* 6 (1972): 187–204.

Paxson, James J. "A Theory of Biblical Typology in the Middle Ages." *Exemplaria* 3 (1991): 359–83.

Pietropoli, Cecilia. "The Characterisation of Evil in the Towneley Plays." *Medieval English Theatre* 11 (1989): 85–93.

Prosser, Eleanor. *Drama and Religion in the English Mystery Plays.* Stanford Studies in Language and Literature 23. Stanford: Stanford UP, 1961.

Purdon, Liam O. *The Wakefield Master's Dramatic Art: A Drama of Spiritual Understanding.* Gainesville: University Press of Florida, 2003.

Reiss, Edmund. "The Symbolic Plow and Plowman and the Wakefield *Mactacio Abel*." *Studies in Iconography* 5 (1979): 3–30.

Robertson, D. W. Jr. "The Question of 'Typology' and the Wakefield *Mactacio Abel*." *American Benedictine Review* 25 (1974): 157–73.

Robinson, J. W. "The Wakefield Master as a 'Master': Speculations on Influences and Imitations." *Acta* 12 (1988): 1–17.

————. "Form in the *Second Shepherds' Play*." *Proceedings of the PMR Conference* 8 (1983): 71–8.

Roney, Lois. "The Wakefield First and Second Shepherds Plays as Complements in Psychology and Parody." *Speculum* 58 (1983): 696–723.

Ross, Lawrence J., "Symbol and Structure in the Secunda Pastorum." *Medieval English Drama.* Ed. by Jerome Taylor and Alan H. Nelson. Chicago: University of Chicago Press, 1972. 198–216.

Rossiter, A. P. *English Drama from Early Times to the Elizabethans.* London: Hutchinson, 1950.

Roura, Sánchez and Maria Teresa. "Colloquial Language in the Wakefield Plays." *Revista Canaria de Estudios Ingleses.* 46 (2003): 183–98.

Slights, William W. E. "The Incarnations of Comedy." *University of Toronto Quarterly* 51 (1981): 13–27.

Speirs, John. *Medieval English Poetry: The Non-Chaucerian Tradition.* London: Faber and Faber, 1957.

Speyser, Suzanne. "Dramatic Illusion and Sacred Reality in the Towneley *Prima Pastorum.*" *Studies in Philology* 78 (1981): 1–19.

Stevens, Martin. "Did the Wakefield Master Write a Nine-Line Stanza?" *Comparative Drama* 15 (1981): 99–119.

———. "Herod as Carnival King in the Medieval Biblical Drama." *Mediaevalia* 18 (1995): 43–66.

———. "Language as Theme in the Wakefield Plays." *Speculum* 52 (1977): 100–17.

———. "The Manuscript of the Towneley Plays: Its History and Editions." *Papers of the Bibliographical Society of America* 67 (1973): 231–44.

———. "The Missing Parts of the Towneley Cycle." *Speculum* 45 (1970): 254–65.

———. "The Staging of the Wakefield Plays." *Research Opportunities in Renaissance Drama* 11 (1968): 115–28.

———. "The Towneley Play Manuscripts (HM 1): Compilatio and Ordinatio.: *Text: Transactions of the Society for Textual Scholarship* 5 (1991): 157–73.

Stevens, Martin and James Paxson. "The Fool in the Wakefield Plays." *Studies in Iconography* 13 (1989–90): 48–79.

Storm, Melvin. "Uxor and Alison: Noah's Wife in the Flood Plays and Chaucer's Wife of Bath." *Modern Language Quarterly* 48 (1987): 303–19.

Strauss, Jennifer. "Grace Enacted: The *Secunda Pastorum.*" *Parergon* 14 (1976): 63–8.

Sturges, Robert S. "Spectacle and Self-Knowledge: The Authority of the Audience in the Mystery Plays." *South Central Review* 9 (1992): 27–48.

Sutherland, Sarah. "'Not or I see more neede': The Wife of Noah in the Chester, York, and Towneley Cycles." *Shakespeare and Dramatic Tradition.* Ed. by W. R. Elton and William B. Long. Newark: University of Delaware Press, 1989. 181–93.

Taft, Edmund M. "Surprised by Love: The Dramatic Structure and Popular Appeal of the *Wakefield Second Shepherds' Pageant.*" *Journal of Popular Culture* 14 (1980): 131–40.

Tate, W. E. *The Enclosure Movement.* New York: Walker and Co., 1967.

Thompson, John A. F. *The Later Lollards: 1414–1520.* Oxford: Oxford UP, 1967.

Tiddy, R. J. E. *The Mummer's Play.* Oxford: Clarendon Press, 1923.

Tolmie, Jane. "Mrs. Noah and Didactic Abuses." *Early Theatre* 5 (2002): 11–35.

Vaughan, M. F. "Mak and the Proportions of *The Seconds Shepherd's Play.*" *Papers on Language and Literature* 18 (1982): 355–67.

Velz, John W. "Fox, Bull, and Lion in the Towneley Coliphizacio." *Early Drama, Art, and Music Review* 14 (1991): 1–10.

Watson, Thomas Ramey. "The Wakefield NOAH." *Explicator* 40 (1982): 5–7.

Watt, Homer. "The Dramatic Unity of the Secunda Pastorum." *Middle English Survey.* Ed. by Edward Vasta. South Bend: University of Notre Dame Press, 1965. 271–82.

Weimann, Robert. *Shakespeare and the Popular Tradition in the Theater.* Baltimore: Johns Hopkins UP, 1978.

Woolf, Rosemary. *The English Mystery Plays.* Berkeley: U. of California P., 1972.

Zimbardo, Rose A. "Comic Mockery of the Sacred: The Frogs and *The Second Shepherds' Play*." *Educational Theatre Journal* 30 (1978): 398–406.

———. "A Generic Approach to the First and Second Shepherds' Plays of the Wakefield Mystery Cycle." *Fifteenth Century Studies* 13 (1988): 79–89.

Index

A

Abel, 1, 21, 36, 39, 44, 45, 47, 49–51,
    53–60, 63–4, 66–9, 71, 180
  as priest, 36, 60, 110, 197
  as symbol of authority, 36–7
Abbot of Misrule, 33
  see also mock rulers
Abraham, 190
abuse, physical, 9, 11, 19, 25, 28, 29, 30,
    34, 36, 42, 44–5, 46, 53–4, 56,
    67, 73, 75–6, 80, 82, 95–7,
    145, 155–8, 160, 169, 171,
    173–4, 177, 179, 181–3,
    186–7, 192, 194–5, 197–8
abuse, verbal, 9, 11, 29, 42, 44, 45–7, 51,
    53–5, 56, 65, 66, 155, 157–8,
    180, 185, 198
abuse of power, 170–2, 189, 194
  see also aristocratic abuse and Church
      corruption
Adam, 78, 84
agents of landowners, 121–2, 126–7,
    129–30, 134, 146–7
allegory, 75
angels, 100, 116, 131–2, 145
anger / uncontrollable fury, 153–4, 161,
    179, 185–90
Annas / Anna, 1, 3, 4, 8, 35, 40, 174,
    176–7, 180, 182–8, 190–5
anthropomorphic figures, 60–1
Antichrist, 136, 138–40, 143
anti-clericalism, 1–4, 58–60, 65–7, 70–1,
    88, 90–4, 111, 132, 138–40,
    142–3, 147, 189
  see also clergy, perceptions of

anti-ecclesiasticism, 1–4, 21, 88–9, 92, 94,
    138, 167, 189, 200
  see also Church, perceptions of
apocalypse, the, 139
apocalypticism, 91–2, 95, 139
aristocratic / royal abuse, 103, 106–7, 121,
    126, 129–30, 167, 169–71,
    189, 195, 200
  see also landowners
ark, 28, 75, 79, 83, 85–7, 90
Arundel, Archbishop, 41
Ascencio Domini, 198
audience, *xi,* 29, 75, 105, 126, 130, 136,
    155, 162–3, 165, 171–2, 179,
    186, 188
Augustine, *City of God,* 50, 83
authority, 33, 78
  see also usurpation

B

Bakhtin, Mikhail, *xii,* 4, 9, 16, 18, 23–24,
    31, 33, 36, 37, 39, 43, 44,
    46–7, 55, 113, 175, 177
Ball, John, 92, 192
baptism, 74, 75
beguiling, 131–2, 140–4, 178
Bethlehem, 100, 144, 149, 168, 171
bias, in medieval records, 2
biblical history, 4, 7–8, 24
bigamy, 130
Bishops, 40, 188, 194–5
Black Plague, 95
blindness, 138
bonfires, *see* fire rituals
Boy Bishop, 14, 19, 33, 67

see also feast of Innocents and mock
        rulers
boy usurper / king, 153, 157, 160–2, 197
bribery, 188–9
bride of Christ, 83
Bridget of Sweden, 92
buffeting, 173–5, 179–81, 183, 186–7, 194
Buffeting, The, see Coliphizacio
buffoonery, 4, 24, 167
Bulgars, 95
burlesque, 4, 5, 7, 31, 38–41, 53, 68–9, 75,
        101, 129, 166
    see also parody

C

Caiaphas/ Cayphas, 1, 3, 4, 8, 35, 38, 40,
        44, 46, 47, 174–80, 182–95,
        198
Cain / Caym, 1, 19, 24–5, 30, 34–5, 36, 37,
        39, 44, 47, 49–71, 110, 153,
        180, 182, 185, 198
Candlemas, 10, 62
carnival, xii, 9, 13, 15, 18, 19, 29, 33, 35,
        145, 175
carnival lords, 29, 175–6, 187
    see also mock rulers
casting in canvas / tossing in blanket, 37, 38,
        131, 145, 198
casting lots, 85
Catharans / Albigensians, 17
Caym's Castel, 1, 49, 70, 71
chantries, 111
chaos, 25, 27, 28, 29, 35–6, 37, 38, 41, 45,
        50, 53, 54, 69, 73, 76, 78,
        80–1, 116, 175–6, 178–9,
        182–4
    see also patterns of order and disorder
Chaucer, Geoffrey, Canterbury Tales, 3, 47,
        65, 71, 82, 90, 94, 104–5, 111,
        141–2, 144
Chester cycle, 45, 75, 79, 105, 133, 152
childbirth, 129, 131, 140, 170
children, 128–9, 131, 134, 141, 146, 170
    likened to sheep, 124, 128–9, 131,
        146–7
chivalry, 166–7

Christ, 4, 22, 26, 35, 37, 38, 39, 40, 43, 44,
        45, 46, 47, 50, 57, 60, 74–6,
        83–4, 86–90, 94–6, 99–100,
        104–7, 115–18, 132–4, 136–7,
        139–40, 143, 145–6, 152–3,
        155–6, 162, 167, 169–70, 172,
        174–95, 198
Christian obligation, 1, 26, 36, 47, 57–8,
        60, 64, 67, 71
Christmas, 10, 21, 23, 33, 144
Christology, 83
    see also typology
Church, xi, 1, 3, 5, 18, 21, 36, 74, 83, 87,
        89, 133, 144–6, 170, 190, 197,
        199–200
    as corrupt, 1, 3, 49–50, 64, 88, 92–3,
        95, 97, 112, 136, 168, 170–2,
        187–8, 195, 200
    as official Christian culture, 17, 18, 21,
        22, 23, 31
    complicity in State abuse, 167–8, 172,
        187, 190–1, 193–5, 197
    doctrine, 17, 174
    ecclesiastical authority / hierarchy,
        16–17, 21, 23, 60, 67, 87–9,
        91, 93–5, 99, 114, 137, 170,
        189–90, 195
    ecclesiastical law / courts, 190–1, 193
    in rebellion, 76, 88–9, 90, 94, 96
    parody / satire of, 40, 96–7, 168, 188,
        200
    reformers, 14, 15, 91, 200
    wealth of, 111, 114, 147, 195
churchyard celebrations, 14, 21
class discontent, 2, 32
clergy, 18, 47, 199–200
    as corrupt, 1, 65–7, 70–1, 90–3, 111,
        113, 131, 139, 141, 146, 170,
        187–9
    as fools, 99–118
    as predators, 1, 26, 99, 131, 136–7, 143,
        146, 200
    parodies of, 40, 99
    see also shepherds and wolves
Clergy May Not Hold Property, The, 112
clerical poverty, 3, 17
clowns, 39, 158

see also fool

cock / rooster, 129, 146, 184

Coliphizacio, 8, 21, 26, 35, 37, 38, 40, 43, 44, 45, 46, 47, 51, 115, 172, 173–95, 198

Coll, 32, 39, 43, 46, 120–2, 124–6, 128–9, 134–5, 138, 143–44, 146

comic lords, 22
    see also mock rulers

comic Masses, *see* mock Masses

confession, 36, 57, 58–9, 60

congregations, 99, 104

Conspiracio, 22, 31, 173

Consultus, *see* counselors

Copyle, the hen, 122, 129, 146

Corpus Christi day, 6, 7, 23

Corpus Christi plays, 6–7, 16, 19, 20, 41

counselors, 153, 165, 167

covenant, new, 84, 86–7

creation, 77–8

critics, *see* Wakefield Master

cross, 85, 87

crucifixion, 84–6, 96

crucify, 96

crusades, 17

Cura Pastoralis, 104, 105

Cursor Mundi, 174

cyclical forms, 10, 28, 31, 36, 38, 44, 45, 73–4, 76–8, 81–2, 101–3, 121, 145, 160, 162, 172, 178–9, 182, 197
    see also seasonal regeneration

D

damnation, *see* divine judgment

Daw, 46, 120, 124, 131, 134, 138, 144

deception, 131, 139, 144

de Chanteloup, Walter, 15

degradation, 47, 55, 56, 116, 118, 180, 199
    see also abuse

De Officio Pastorali, 49–50, 66, 67, 115, 136

dethroning, *see* usurpation

Deus, 27, 28, 36, 37, 67, 78–9, 87

devil, or dwill, 29, 35, 38, 47, 51, 55, 56, 70, 138, 146, 149, 151, 153–4, 176

Diabolus, 151

dialogic, 23–4

disendowment, 3, 93, 112

disorder, *see* chaos

divine judgment / punishment, 74, 76, 78, 86–7, 92, 94, 96

divine will, 150–52, 167–8

doctors, in folk dramas, 12, 29

domestic violence, 45, 76, 80, 82, 87, 88, 95–6

doom, 74
    see also divine judgment

dramatic rituals, 11, 19
    see also Mummer's plays, morris dances, sword dances, processions, and Robin Hood plays

Dream of the Rood, 85

dunking, 73–4, 145

E

Easter, 10, 16, 23, 62

Ecclesiastes, 102–4, 107, 109, 114, 118

ecclesiastical authority, *see* Church and anti-ecclesiasticism

economic depression, 112

economic worth, 125

enclosure, 103, 111, 121, 125–6, 129–30, 170, 198

Epiphany, 62

Epiphany king, 33
    see also mock rulers

Eucharist, 58, 69, 89, 113–14, 140–1
    see also Mass

Eve, 84

Everyman, 17

examination, heretical, 190–1, 193

exegesis, 83, 105, 108, 149, 152

F

fabliaux, 24, 47

false miracles, 140–2

false priests, 139, 144

false shepherds, 119, 131–2, 137, 140, 144–5
    see also shepherds

farmers, 124, 126, 128–9, 131

feast of the Ass, 13, 21, 39

feast of Fools, 13, 14, 15, 19–20, 21, 34, 39, 41, 101, 149, 179
feast of Innocents / Boys, 13, 14, 19–20, 21, 39
see also Boy Bishop
feasting, 9, 10, 11, 15, 27, 31, 43, 69–70, 99, 100–1, 112–4, 116–7, 198
feasts, Christian, 9, 10, 13, 31, 56, 73–4
fertile / fertility, 18, 43, 46, 47, 55, 77
fertilization spirit, 73
festive culture, 9–16
  as pagan, 9–10, 13, 14, 16, 41, 73–4
  as unofficial counterculture, 18, 23, 24, 47, 48, 116
  seasonal nature, 10, 11, 12, 15
  suppression of, 14–15, 20
  suspension of order, morality, rank, 15
  see also dramatic rituals, Lords of Misrule, feast of Fools, feast of Innocents, and feast of the Ass
festive forms in plays, 5, 8–9, 18, 27–48
  abuse, physical 25, 44–5, 53–4, 56, 67, 75–6, 80, 82, 95–7, 145, 155–8, 160, 169, 171, 174, 177, 179, 181–3, 186–7, 192, 194–5, 197–8
  abuse, verbal, 28, 42, 45–7, 53–5, 56, 65, 66, 155, 157–8, 180, 185, 198
  burlesque, 4, 5, 7, 39, 51, 53, 68–9, 75, 129, 166
  chaos, 41, 45, 50, 53, 54, 69, 73, 76, 78, 80–1, 116, 175–6, 178–9, 182–4
  cyclical forms, 73–4, 76–8, 81–2, 101–3, 121, 145, 160, 162, 172, 178–9, 182, 197
  feast / feasting, 43, 69–70, 99, 100–1, 112–4, 116–7, 198
  folly, 99, 100–3, 106–12, 114–16, 118, 130, 182, 184, 195, 198
  fools, 42–3, 51–3, 56, 99, 109–10, 115, 152, 179, 181–2, 184, 187–8, 198
  grotesque, 4, 7, 123, 143–4, 152–3, 156, 163
invocation 25, 27, 28, 29–33, 51, 53, 156–8, 160, 163–4, 198
inversion, 35, 53, 56, 134–5, 138–40, 142–3, 156
license, 4, 76, 123, 177, 187
material body, 26, 113
mock Masses, 55, 69–71, 99, 112–4, 116, 140–1
mock rulers, 34–5, 37, 61, 67, 155–7, 171, 174–6, 179–80, 186–7
overthrowal, 45, 102–3, 122, 145, 162, 175, 186–7, 197–9
parody, *xi,* 5, 7, 9, 24, 38–41, 42, 46, 53, 66, 69, 71, 99, 112, 114, 116, 119, 124, 129–31, 140–1, 144–7, 159–60, 163–5, 168, 170, 187, 195, 198–200
profanity, *see* abuse, verbal
regeneration, 73–4, 76–8, 81–2, 96–7, 116–17, 123, 172, 178–9, 182, 186, 197
renewal, 76, 78–9, 81–2, 96–7, 116, 118, 145, 162, 172, 197
reversals, 4, 19, 28, 37–8, 52–4, 56, 68–71, 78, 79–80, 82, 107, 109, 123–4, 159–60, 163, 175, 177–9, 182, 195
usurpation of authority, 19, 25, 28, 35, 36–7, 56, 60, 65, 67–8, 70–1, 76, 78, 79, 80, 81, 90, 107, 109, 129, 160–2, 167, 175–7, 179–80, 187, 193, 195, 197, 199
festive lord / king, 9, 162, 171, 174–6, 179
  see also mock rulers
festum fatuorum or *festive stultorum, see* feast of Fools
feudal structure / liege law, 2, 22, 39, 163, 167, 189, 193, 195
fire rituals, 62–3, 197
First Shepherds' Play, see Prima Pastorum
Flagellacio, 173, 199
folk culture / festivals, 9, 80
folly / foolishness, 38, 39, 42, 99, 101–2, 100–3, 106–12, 114–16, 118, 130, 149, 151–2, 182, 184, 195, 198

fools, 31, 39, 41–3, 51–3, 56, 99, 101, 109–10, 115, 137, 152, 179, 181–2, 184, 187–8, 198
  dress / costume, 41, 42, 52
fools of Gotham, 42, 101, 103, 109
foundling, 176, 185, 188
  see also boy usurper
fraud, 132–3, 141, 144, 146, 198
"Freers, Freers, Wo Ye Be," 138
Froward, 51, 115, 179, 182, 184, 198
fury, *see* anger

G

gambling, 103
games, 12, 27, 35, 36, 37, 145, 174–5, 180–1, 187
gender conflict, 82, 88–9
Genesis, 63, 74, 80
Gethsemane, 84
Gloria in excelsis, 100, 132, 135
God's will, *see* divine will
Gower, John, *Vox Clamantis,* 3, 90, 105
grace, 86
Great Schism, 89, 167
Gregory the Great, 104
Grosseteste, Robert, 15, 41, 91
grotesque forms, 7, 9, 43, 47, 123, 143–4, 152–3, 156, 163
Guy Fawkes, 62
Gyb, in *Prima Pastorum,* 31, 38, 40, 42, 101–5, 107–11, 114–15, 117–18, 119, 132
Gyb, in *Secunda Pastorum,* 32, 46, 120, 122–5, 127–30, 134, 138, 144–7
Gyll, 124, 129, 131, 135, 140, 143–4, 146–7, 171, 198

H

Halloween, 10
harvest feasts, 10
Harvest-home, 10
harvest-lord, 33
  see also mock rulers
harvest-May, 61, 73
heat charm, 62–3
Hell Mouth, 63

henpecked husbands, 122, 127, 129–30
heresy, 3–4, 6, 17, 60, 191–4, 198
  see also examination
  nature of heretical movements, 2–3, 17
hero-combat, 29
Herod, 30, 34, 35, 37, 44, 45, 149–72, 173, 185, 198
  raging, 1, 19, 31, 34, 149, 152–5, 161–2, 165, 169–70, 186, 197
Herod's court, 4, 40, 163–5, 171
  as metaphor for contemporary abuse, 1, 3–4, 165–6, 170–1, 175
heteroglossia, 24
Hildegard of Bingen, 92, 137
hobby-horse, 145
Hocktide, 10
holy wells, 74
homiletic commentaries, 150, 152
hot cockles, 4, 181
husbands, 40, 123, 124, 125–31
  as shepherds, 129
  oppressed husbands, 126–7, 129 *see also* henpecked husbands
husbandry, 126
Hussites, 17

I

Iak Cope, 110
Iak Garcio, 31, 42, 51, 101, 109, 115, 184, 198
incarnation, 83, 85, 100, 116, 141, 146, 153, 195
infanticide, 165
  see also slaughter of the innocents
invocation, 27, 28, 29–33, 42, 51, 53, 156–8, 160, 163–4, 198
inversion, 9, 35, 37, 38, 41, 42, 47, 53, 56, 134–5, 138–40, 142–3, 156
Iohn Horne, 31, 40, 42, 103, 105–9, 111–15, 117, 119, 121, 132
Iudicium, 5, 8, 48, 199

J

Jack, the name, 42, 110
Jack Cade's Rebellion, 2, 93
Jack Finney, 51
jack of the harvest, 61

Jack Upland, 139
John, Gospel of, 104, 115, 133–7
Joseph, 100, 150

K

kern-baby, 61
kill-joys, 11, 46, 67
King Copyn, 35, 175, 179–80
king of fools, 149–50, 157, 179–80, 182,
    186, 195
    see also mock rulers
king of the bean, 33
    see also mock rulers
knights, 37, 40, 153–5, 158–62, 164,
    166–7, 180, 189, 191, 193–5,
    198

L

lamb of God, 39, 57, 118, 140, 145
landed classes, 166–7, 200
    see also landowners
land management practices, 124
land rents, 189
landowners, 103–4, 121, 126, 129, 146–7,
    172
    see also agents and seignurial system
Langland, *Piers Plowman,* 3, 90, 141
language / linguistic forms, 24, 27–8, 47,
    51, 96, 103, 120, 142–3, 165,
    169, 180, 182, 190, 199
Lanterne of Light, The, 136
Last Will and Testament, 36, 39, 162–3
Latin, in plays, 39, 105, 132, 192
laughter, 16, 17–18, 19, 23, 97, 188
legal injustice, 190, 195
legal procedure, 185–6, 189–92
legal system, 2, 22, 176–7, 187, 190, 192
    as corrupt, 175, 190, 192–4
Lent, 23
license, 4, 76, 123, 177, 187
liege law, see feudal structure
linguistic forms, see language
liturgical drama, 7, 174
Lollards / Lollardy, 3, 17, 58–9, 60, 92–3,
    110, 112, 114, 136–7, 141–2,
    189, 200
    persecution of, 6, 194

Lord of Misrule, 11, 12, 21, 22, 30, 31, 33,
    34, 35, 36, 44, 49, 54, 56, 61,
    62, 65, 67, 71, 149–50, 153,
    155, 157–8, 162–3, 165, 172,
    175, 185–8, 198
    see also mock rulers
lower bodily stratum, 46, 55, 180, 198
Lucifer, 78
ludi, festive, 15, 16, 21
Luke, Gospel of, 132

M

Mactacio Abel, xi, 1, 8, 21, 22, 24–5, 26, 29,
    34–5, 36–7, 38, 39, 42, 44, 45,
    47, 48, 49–71, 74, 75, 99, 100,
    110–11, 115, 156, 180, 198–9
magi, 149–50, 153–6, 159, 164
Magnus Herodes, 3, 4, 26, 28, 30, 37, 38,
    40, 44, 45, 149–72, 185, 189,
    198–9
Mahowne, 22, 30, 157, 164, 168
Mak, 26, 32, 37, 38, 39, 43, 45, 46, 47,
    119, 124, 127, 128, 131–40,
    143, 144–7
manger, 38, 39, 113
manorial system, 2
Margery Kempe, 175, 194
marriage, 122–3, 127–8
marriage feasts, 10
married men, 127–8
    see also husbands
Mary, 46, 83, 100, 140
Mass, 39, 40, 57, 84, 89, 113, 140, 187,
    198
    see also mock Masses
master / masters, 29, 30, 32, 34, 79, 130,
    153, 157, 184
mastery / *maistrye,* 79, 89, 130, 152, 161,
    184
material body, 26, 43, 44, 47, 113
Matthew, Gospel of, 149
May Day, 10, 11, 12, 62
May games, 15, 21, 42, 74
May King, 11, 12, 33
    see also mock rulers
May pole, 73
mendicant orders, 3, 91

mercenary clergy / shepherds, 105, 115, 132, 137, 144, 168
   see also clergy, anti-clericalism, and shepherds
Micah, 168–71
Midsummer Eve, 10, 62
Miles, 37
   see also knights
miracle plays, 15
misrule, 149, 155, 182, 184
   see also chaos
mock authority, 12–14, 22, 36
mock ceremonies, 12
mock/ comic Masses, 13–14, 18, 20, 21, 37, 39, 40, 55, 69–71, 99, 112–4, 116, 140–1
mock court, 34
   see also Herod's court
mockery, 18
mock-mayor, 33
mock rulers, 11, 15, 33–35, 37, 38, 39, 41, 46, 61, 67, 175–6, 179–80, 186–7
mock sermons, 40, 99, 105–9, 110
mock sacrifice, 12
Moll / Mowll, 108
monks / monastic orders, 111
morris dances, 12, 21
Mors, 151
Moses, 190
Mummer's plays, 12, 42, 51, 155
music, religious, *xi,* 40, 105, 197
Muslims, 95
mutability, 102, 120, 200
mystery plays, 7

N

nativity, 4, 9, 19, 45, 99–100, 102, 109, 116, 118, 119, 124, 131–3, 135, 141, 143, 170
   parody of, 9, 19, 21, 39, 129, 131–2, 135, 140–1, 143–4
nether kiss, 55, 56
new covenant, 84, 190
New Year, 43, 118, 197
Noah, play of, see *Processus Noe*

Noah/ Noe, 19, 21, 24, 26, 27–8, 37, 44, 73–90, 93–97
   as type of Christ, 74–6, 83–90, 93–6, 123
Noah's flood, 1, 27–8, 73–78, 80–82, 86, 88, 95–7, 123
Noah's wife, 6, 19, 24, 28, 37, 38, 44, 74–76, 79–84, 86–90, 93–7
   as type for Church, 75, 96
nonsense, 38, 41, 52, 99, 109
Northern Passion, 174
Norwich, 33
Norwich heresy trials, 92, 114, 142, 191, 194–5
N-Town cycle, 100, 150, 153, 198
Nuncius, 30, 34, 35, 156–8, 163–5, 198

O

Oblacio Magorum, 164
Of Clerks Possessioners, 66, 91, 113
Office of Curates, 59
official culture, 18, 21, 23, 24, 31, 38, 40, 47, 48, 55
   see also Church
Of Prelates, 66, 91, 189
Order of Priesthood, The, 66
orthodoxy / orthodox doctrine, 1, 6, 8, 16–17, 18, 24, 64, 74–5, 83, 87, 99–100, 114, 116, 150–3, 174–5, 187, 195, 198, 200
overthrowal, 45, 102–3, 122, 145, 162, 175, 186–7, 197–9
   see also usurpation
Oxford University, 15, 36

P

pagan forms, see festive culture
pageants, 12
papacy, 21, 94–5, 167–8, 200
   see also Pope
parody, *xi,* 9, 38–41, 42, 45, 46, 53, 66, 69, 71, 99, 112, 114, 116, 119, 124, 129–31, 140–1, 144–7, 159–60, 163–5, 168, 170, 174–5, 187, 195, 198–200
paschal rire, 23
Passion of Christ, 85, 173–5, 186–7, 195

pastor, spiritual, 99, 104, 110, 136, 144
  see also shepherds, as priests
pastor bonus / good shepherd, 99, 104, 115,
      117–18, 132, 142, 144
pastoral metaphor, 3, 104–5, 110, 131,
      135–6, 144
  see also shepherds, as priests
pastores play, see shepherds' play
patterns of order and disorder, 28, 71, 73,
      77–8, 79, 81, 82
Pearl Poet, 83
peasant agitation, 2
Peasant's Revolt of 1381, 2, 22, 92, 167, 192
penis, 129
Peter, 87, 94, 135–6
Piers the Plowman's Creed, 3, 94, 137, 138,
      143
Pikeharnes, Garcio, 24–5, 29, 34, 37, 39,
      42, 44, 47, 50–3, 55–6, 64,
      68–9, 71, 115, 156, 184, 198
Pilate, 22, 31, 39, 173, 188, 194
planets, in or out of order, 38, 79, 81, 100
play-within-the-play, 175
Plough Monday drama, 54, 62
plow animals, 38, 52, 53, 62, 182
plowmen, 125–6
plows / plowing, 121, 129, 147
Plowman's Tale, The, 3, 89, 90, 94, 96,
      135–6, 138–9, 143
Pope, 3–4, 17, 168
  as Antichrist, 3
poverty, 94
preaching fox, 1, 26, 65–6
predator shepherds / clergy, 132, 134–6,
      144–6, 172, 200
  see also wolves
prelates, 40, 187–9, 193, 197
Preste, Ne Monke, Ne Yit Chanoun, 143
priests, see clergy
Prima Pastorum, 4, 7, 26, 31, 32, 38, 39–40,
      42, 43, 51, 99–118, 119–21,
      125, 132, 134, 144–5, 170–1,
      182, 198–200
privy counsel, 165
processions, 9, 12, 14, 16, 18, 27, 42, 73,
      74
Processus Crucis, 31, 173

Processus Noe, 8, 9, 24, 26, 27–28, 37, 44,
      45, 62, 71, 73–97, 99, 100,
      124, 198
Processus Talorum, 31, 173
profanity, see abuse, verbal
prophecies, 100, 105, 116, 132, 153, 155,
      160–1, 167–9
Proverbs, 107
punishment, 79
puns, 40, 42, 89, 94, 119, 124–9, 145–7

R

rage, see anger and Herod, raging
rainbow, 74, 82
regeneration, festive / seasonal, 12, 18, 24,
      27, 36, 73–4, 76–8, 81–2,
      96–7, 102, 116–17, 121, 123,
      172–3, 178–9, 182, 186, 197
religious discontent, 3, 103
  see also anti-clericalism and anti-ecclesias-
      ticism
religious obligation, see Christian obligation
renewal, 76, 78–9, 81–2, 92, 96–7, 116,
      118, 145, 162, 172, 197
  see also regeneration, seasonal
reversal, 9, 36, 37–8, 42, 44, 52–3, 56,
      68–71, 78, 79–80, 82, 101–2,
      107, 109, 123–4, 159–60, 163,
      175, 177–9, 182, 195
revolt of 1431, 93
rex stultorum, see king of fools
Richard Rolle, 83
ritual violence, see abuse, physical
Robert of Uzès, 92
Robin Hood plays, 11, 12, 42
Roman de la Rose, 141
royal letters, 165
royal pardon, 37, 39, 68
royal prerogative, 163
rushbearings, 74

S

Sabbath, 177
sacrifice
  Cain and Abel's, 50, 54, 57, 60, 63, 65,
      69

rituals of, 10, 28, 41, 43, 44, 49, 54, 62–3, 162, 173, 180–1, 197
saints, 17
Salisbury, 93
salvation, 84–6, 100, 116, 123, 132
satire, 5, 114, 163, 166–8, 187, 200
saturnalia, 35
scripture, infallibility of, 17
seasonal forms, 9–10, 41
Second Shepherds' Play, see *Secunda Pastorum*
Secunda Pastorum 6, 7, 9, 21, 22, 26, 31, 32, 37, 38, 39, 40, 43, 45, 46, 47, 82, 99, 103, 115, 116, 119–47, 170–1, 198
seignurial system, 22, 122
serfdom, 2
sermons, 99, 105–9, 110, 137, 174, 189
sexual will, 129
sheep, 39, 40, 55, 100–1, 103, 107, 109, 112, 114–15, 125–6, 129–30, 132, 134, 139, 171
  as children, 38, 124, 128–30, 146–7
  as congregation, 66, 104–5, 114–15, 136
  diseased, 66–7, 110–11
shepherds, 4, 21, 26, 31, 32, 38, 42, 43, 45, 46, 55, 99–100, 103–6, 109–118, 119–47, 170, 172, 184, 197, 198
  as types of clergy, 4, 26, 39–40, 60, 63, 66, 71, 99, 104–6, 109–11, 115, 131–2
  see also pastoral metaphor, false shepherds, and mercenary clergy
shepherds' plays, 20, 99, 101, 104, 132, 172, 199
shrewish wives / women, 79, 81, 96, 123, 129–31, 134, 146, 171
Shrove Tuesday, 10, 36, 62, 184
silence, calls for, 29, 51, 156
"Simonie, The," 91, 95
sin, 84, 87, 96, 107, 110
singing, 116, 134, 140, 141
slaughter of the innocents, 4, 38, 149–53, 156, 160–1, 162, 166–7, 171
Slawpase, 38, 40, 42, 105, 107–9, 111, 113–14, 116–17, 119, 132
social discontent, 2, 103–4, 121, 129–30

Société Joyeuse, 41, 101
sorcery, 131–2, 138–9
spinning, 87, 94
spirit of the corn, 60, 62
sports, festive 12, 15
spring, 44, 116, 121, 162, 172
sprinkling, 73–4
stage directions, *xi,* 42
stanzaic evidence, *xi,* 173, 198–9
stars, ordered and disordered, 28
St. Francis, 91
St. George and the dragon, 12
stock elements, 82, 127, 129–31
straw man, 64
subversion, popular, 1–3
  within festive expression, 4, 22, 24, 48, 67
Sudbury, Archbishop of Canterbury, 2, 93, 167
summer festival, 61
summer lords, 12, 21, 33, 34, 36, 39, 62, 149, 155, 157, 162–3, 198
  see also mock rulers
sword dances, 12, 42

T

Tacitus, 73
tax collectors, 22
taxes, 32, 121
Tenby, 33
tennis, 144
theft, 133
thirteener stanza, *xi,* 173, 198
tilling, see plowing
tithe, 1, 3, 17, 36, 50, 58, 59–60, 64, 65, 66–9, 71, 92, 111, 188
topsy-turvy, 31, 34, 37, 38, 41, 42, 96, 100, 101, 109, 120, 124, 149, 156–7, 160, 177, 182, 195
torturers, 35, 40, 43, 44, 46, 175–83, 187, 189, 195, 198
Towneley Cycle / Plays
  as biblical history, 6
  as defense of orthodoxy, 6
  Christian interpretation of, 5, 19–20, 50, 74–5

festive influence, 27–48, *see also* Wakefield Master
subversive nature of, 25–26, 58
Tractabus de Regibus, 83
transubstantiation, doctrine of, 3, 114
Tutivillius, 5, 42
Twelfth Night, 10
Tyler, Wat, 92, 193
typology, 49, 50, 60, 63, 66, 74–6, 83–90, 93–6, 109–10, 123, 132

U

uncrowning, 65, 71, 80, 107
    see also reversal and usurpation
unofficial culture, see festive culture
Upland's Rejoinder, 138
usurpation, 27, 28, 29, 33, 35–37, 44, 46, 49, 56, 60, 65, 68, 70–1, 76, 78–81, 90, 107, 109, 129, 160–2, 167, 175–7, 179–80, 187, 193, 195, 197, 199
Uxor, see Noah's wife

V

variability, see mutability
Vatican hill, 87, 95
villains, 2
violence, see abuse, physical
Vulgate, 81

W

Wakefield, *xi-xii,* 41, 180
Wakefield Master, *xi-xii,* 197–200
    as dramatist, 1, 4, 5, 7, 18, 75, 76–82, 87–8, 97, 99–101, 114, 119, 133, 164, 168, 170–2, 188, 195

choice of play topics, 49, 73, 99, 119, 149, 173, 197
critics of, *xi-xii,* 5, 7–9, 18–20, 21, 65, 75, 82–3, 113–14, 117, 119, 159, 171, 175, 187
influenced by festive forms, 8–9, 18, 23–6, 31, 48
wakes, 10, 74
Waldensians, 17, 194
wassailings, 12
water charms, 62, 73–4
weather / weders, 120, 123, 124–6, 128, 145–6
wethers /weders, 40, 124–6, 128, 146
well-dressings, 74
wheat sacrifice, 61–2
Whitsuntide, 10
winter, 31, 32, 36, 44, 116, 121–2, 125, 145, 162, 172, 197
winter game, 32
wisdom, 101–2, 108–9, 114
wolves, 115, 134, 136
    as predatory clergy, 131–3, 136–7, 144
wolf skin, 131, 134
worship, 56, 60, 64
Wycliffe, John, 3, 60, 92

Y

York, 41, 179
York cycle, 16, 45, 75, 79, 100, 152–3, 156, 167
    Memorandum Book, 16, 21
Yorkshire shepherds, 171
Yule, 16, 33, 35, 41, 43, 99, 114, 116, 118, 121, 124, 175, 179, 180, 197

Margins . in Nat. or
Cruit. phys

Center

lots of explication

Festive =
ritual yun regueroni
dopeony — vregueroni
[what is festive worldview?
P. 198

For
whiting F 605
farlunnes at 15 of Mul 184
I ak   I ade plants
Each loose L. 17   P. 84

gyb   woll will skup to int

I was tool?

words/friends ←
137